Microsoft Dynamics GP 2016 Cookbook

Over 100 powerful and effective recipes to help you solve real-world Dynamics GP problems

Ian Grieve

Mark Polino

[PACKT] enterprise

PUBLISHING   professional expertise distilled

BIRMINGHAM - MUMBAI

Microsoft Dynamics GP 2016 Cookbook

First published: August 2016

Production reference: 1160816

Published by Packt Publishing Ltd.
Livery Place
35 Livery Street
Birmingham B3 2PB, UK.

ISBN 978-1-78646-340-1

www.packtpub.com

Credits

Authors

Ian Grieve

Mark Polino

Reviewers

Jivtesh Singh

Leslie Vail

Commissioning Editor

Kunal Parikh

Acquisition Editor

Nitin Dasan

Content Development Editor

Priyanka Mehta

Technical Editors

Dhiraj Chandanshive

Ravikiran Pise

Copy Editor

Safis Editing

Project Coordinator

Izzat Contractor

Proofreader

Safis Editing

Indexer

Rekha Nair

Production Coordinator

Aparna Bhagat

Cover Work

Aparna Bhagat

About the Authors

Ian Grieve is a Microsoft Most Valuable Professional for Microsoft Dynamics GP. He is also a certified Dynamics CRM consultant, specializing in the delivery of Microsoft Dynamics GP. He is the ERP Practice Manager at Perfect Image Ltd., a Microsoft partner, and VAR in the North-East of England, where he is responsible for the delivery, by his team, of all Dynamics GP projects.

Ian has worked with Microsoft Dynamics GP since 2003, and over the years, he has dealt with all aspects of the product's life cycle, ranging from presales, implementation, technical, and functional training post go-live support to subsequent upgrades and process reviews.

Ian is the author of *Microsoft Dynamics GP 2013 Financial Management* by Packt Publisihing and *Microsoft Dynamics GP Workflow 2.0* and *Implementing the Microsoft Dynamics GP Web Client* by azurecurve Publishing. He is also the co-author of *Microsoft Dynamics GP 2013 Cookbook* by Packt Publisihing. Additionally, he has produced the *Microsoft Dynamics GP Techniques* online learning course and was the technical reviewer for several books on Microsoft Dynamics CRM published by Packt Publishing, including *Microsoft Dynamics CRM 2011 Cookbook*.

In his spare time, Ian runs the *azurecurve* blog, *Ramblings of a Dynamics GP Consultant* (`http://www.azurecurve.co.uk`), which is dedicated to Microsoft Dynamics GP and related products.

The most recent offshoot of running his blog is that Ian has started writing plugins to extend the functionality of the blogging platform, WordPress. A new site, azurecurve Development (`http://development.azurecurve.co.uk`), contains information about his plugins.

Thanks to my parents for their support through the years and to my employer, Perfect Image Ltd., for giving me the opportunity to work with clients in many different fields and, not least, for being open to me taking on outside projects such as this book and its predecessors.

I also owe thanks to all the clients I have worked with over the years, whose needs and questions have prompted me to learn ever more about Microsoft Dynamics GP, thereby putting me in a position to write this book.

Thanks to the technical reviewers, Leslie Vail and Jivtesh Singh, and fellow Microsoft Most Valuable Professionals, for their valuable feedback, which helped make this book better.

And finally, thanks to Mark Polino, my co-author on this book and the author of the first edition. It was a pleasure working with him on this book.

Mark Polino is a Microsoft MVP for Business Solutions, a certified public accountant, and a Dynamics Credentials professional for Dynamics GP. He runs the premier Dynamics GP-related blog, *DynamicAccounting.net*. Mark has worked with Dynamics GP and its predecessor, Great Plains, for more than 15 years. He has worked as an author and co-author on five Dynamics GP-related books. He works as the Director of client services for Fastpath.

About the Reviewers

Jivtesh Singh is a Microsoft Dynamics Certified Technology Specialist for Dynamics GP, based in Sydney, Australia. He has been awarded as the Microsoft MVP for Dynamics by Microsoft for 6 years in a row (2011-2016). Through his blog, which is widely read in the Dynamics GP and CRM community, he covers tips and tricks and news on Dynamics GP.

Over the last 15 years, Jivtesh has lead and managed successful product development and Dynamics implementations for multiple clients, including some of the Fortune 500 companies. He is a Dynamics consultant and systems implementer, and he has been associated with the Microsoft technologies since the launch of the Microsoft .NET framework. He has over 10 years of experience in development and maintenance of enterprise software using coding best practices, refactoring and usage of design patterns, and test-driven development.

Jivtesh recently built a Kinect interface to control the Microsoft Dynamics GP Business Analyzer with gestures. Later, he built a part of the GP future demo for Convergence GP Keynote.

He has set up a custom search engine directory for the Dynamics GP blog (www.gpwindow.com) to help with easier access of Dynamics GP resources for the GP community. With MVP Mark Polino, he has also set up a Dynamics GP product directory (www.dynamicsgpproducts.com).

Jivtesh's blog on Dynamics GP is available at www.jivtesh.com.

You can visit his custom search engine for GP blogs at www.gpwindow.com.

You can reach him on LinkedIn at http://www.linkedin.com/in/jivtesh or contact him on his e-mail id jivtesh@gmail.com.

Leslie Vail is a CPA and is working as a Microsoft Dynamics GP consultant for nearly 20 years. She started off working on version 1.0 in 1993. During this period, she completed numerous implementations, conversions, and custom development projects. She is a session leader at many partner and customer technical conferences and conducts training classes throughout North and Central America.

Leslie has been a Microsoft Dynamics GP MVP since 2007. She is recognized throughout the industry for her product expertise and contributions to the Dynamics community. She is the principal of ASCI, Inc., a consulting firm located in Dallas, TX.

As a Microsoft Certified Trainer (MCT), she serves as a subject matter expert (SME) for the Microsoft Assessments and Certification Exams (ACE) team. She is a member of the US MCT Advisory Council and has been listed as one of the Microsoft Dynamics Top 100 Most Influential People by DynamicsWorld. She is one of the top contributors to the Microsoft Dynamics GP Newsgroup and Dynamics Community forum. Leslie maintains the popular *Dynamics Confessions Blogspot* (http://dynamicsconfessions.blogspot.com/) site.

She has reviewed and developed Microsoft Courseware, co-authored the book *Confessions of a Dynamics GP Consultant, Accolade Publications*, and is the Technical Editor of several books dedicated to Microsoft Dynamics GP.

Leslie provides implementation and consulting services for companies ranging from a family office to a multinational manufacturing firm. She is a Microsoft Certified IT Professional in Microsoft Dynamics GP Applications and Microsoft Dynamics GP Installation & Configuration as well as a Microsoft Certified DBA (Database Administrator).

She holds a Microsoft Certified Technology Specialist certification in Dexterity, Modifier with VBA, Integration Manager, Report Writer, HR/Payroll, Financials, Inventory and Order Processing, FRx Report Designer, SQL Server 2000, SQL Server 2008, and Microsoft XP Professional.

A skilled developer, Leslie uses Dexterity, Modifier with VBA, Integration Manager, and eConnect to provide custom solutions to her clients. She is a Certified Integration Developer (CID), a Dexterity CID, a Dynamics Tools CID, and a Dexterity Certified Systems Engineer.

Her training proficiency spans the entire Microsoft Dynamics GP product line. She is an experienced trainer and teaches classes for Dexterity, Financials, Inventory and Order Processing, HR/Payroll, Integration Manager, Modifier with VBA, FRx Report Designer, SQL Server Reporting Services, Report Writer, Crystal Reports, SmartList Builder, Excel Report Builder, Integrated Excel Reports, Extender, and System Manager.

Prior to working with Microsoft Dynamics GP, Leslie was the tax director for a large financial institution, before which she worked for one of the original Big Eight accounting firms as a senior tax accountant.

www.PacktPub.com

eBooks, discount offers, and more

Did you know that Packt offers eBook versions of every book published, with PDF and ePub files available? You can upgrade to the eBook version at www.PacktPub.com and as a print book customer, you are entitled to a discount on the eBook copy. Get in touch with us at customercare@packtpub.com for more details.

At www.PacktPub.com, you can also read a collection of free technical articles, sign up for a range of free newsletters and receive exclusive discounts and offers on Packt books and eBooks.

https://www2.packtpub.com/books/subscription/packtlib

Do you need instant solutions to your IT questions? PacktLib is Packt's online digital book library. Here, you can search, access, and read Packt's entire library of books.

Why subscribe?

- Fully searchable across every book published by Packt
- Copy and paste, print, and bookmark content
- On demand and accessible via a web browser

Instant updates on new Packt books

Get notified! Find out when new books are published by following @PacktEnterprise on Twitter or the *Packt Enterprise* Facebook page.

Table of Contents

Preface

Tens of thousands of Microsoft Dynamics GP users keep the accounting functions of their rms running day in and day out. They ensure that vendors get paid, customer payments are tracked, and the financial statements balance at the end of the month. In short, they provide the information critical to corporate decision making.

Of the many tens of thousands of people using Dynamics GP, the majority of them only ever use a small subset of the available functionality. They may get basic training when Dynamics GP is implemented or when they join the company; they learn enough to do their job but never look beyond this set of skills for ways to improve processes and become more efficient.

On top of this, many users start working with a particular version of Dynamics GP and continue to use the system in the same way as the years pass and upgrades are installed with many new features available.

The work gets done but good employees are left with a nagging feeling, an itch, that there must be a better way. This book is designed for those people who want to scratch the itch and learn how to get more out of Dynamics GP.

Many of the ways to get more from Dynamics GP do not require extensive knowledge of the system, merely a desire to learn and to make Dynamics GP easier, faster, and simpler. These features, tips, and techniques have been compiled into a set of recipes designed to let Dynamics GP users cook up solutions to their problems.

Like any good cookbook, the recipes are laid out into simple steps optimized for quick application and are easy to follow and get right in the first attempt. This easy gratification is designed to draw users deeper into the recipes with the goal of improving efficiency, allowing the time saved to be put back into other finance activities, or the simple pleasure of wrapping up the day and going home early.

What this book covers

Chapter 1, Personalizing Dynamics GP, contains recipes designed to enhance the usefulness of Dynamics GP by personalizing the look and feel of the application.

Chapter 2, Organizing Dynamics GP, contains recipes that are designed to help administrators get more out of Dynamics GP for their users by changing the way Dynamics GP is organized.

Chapter 3, Automating Dynamics GP, contains recipes that focus on efficiency and automation and are designed to be time savers across the system.

Chapter4, Leveraging New and Updated Features in Dynamics GP, contains recipes demonstrating some of the key new and updated features in Dynamics GP 2016 from the Financial and Distribution series.

Chapter 5, Exposing Hidden Features in Dynamics GP, contains recipes on techniques that are often well known to consultants but missed by users. It contains hidden settings that can help save a lot of time.

Chapter 6, Improving Dynamics GP with Hacks, contains recipes that are used to hack existing features in Dynamics GP so as to improve efficiency.

Chapter 7, Preventing Errors in Dynamics GP, contains recipes for administrators and users to help prevent errors in Dynamics GP. It also includes ways to fix erroneous transactions that managed to make it to the general ledger.

Chapter 8, Harnessing the Power of SmartLists, contains recipes to harness the power of Dynamics GP's ad hoc reporting tool and ways to leverage the reporting power of SmartLists.

Chapter 9, Extending SmartLists with SmartList Designer, contains recipes to extend SmartLists by building your own objects from tables or SQL Views using SmartList Designer.

Chapter 10, Connecting Dynamics GP to Microsoft Office, contains recipes that help connect Dynamics GP with Microsoft Office 2013 and discusses the ways in which Office can be used to improve processes in Dynamics GP.

Chapter 11, Maintaining Dynamics GP, contains recipes for an administrator or power user to help maintain Dynamics GP.

Chapter 12, Extending Dynamics GP with Professional Services Tools Library, contains recipes which use the Professional Services Tools Library (PSTL) to ease company and data setup and to modify data in an existing Dynamics GP implementation.

Chapter 13, Modern Business Intelligence for Dynamics GP, contains recipes based on Microsoft's new BI tools, OData and PowerBI.

What you need for this book

The following software is required for this book:

- Microsoft Dynamics GP 2016 with the Fabrikam, Inc. sample company deployed and a second company without any configuration created
- Microsoft SQL Server 2012 or later
- Microsoft Office 2016 or later
- Windows Server 2012 or later with a domain controller available
- An Internet browser compatible with Power BI

Who this book is for

This book is for Dynamics GP users and Dynamics GP partners and is primarily focused on delivering time-proven application modifications. This book assumes that you have a basic understanding of business management systems and basic knowledge of Dynamics GP. All of these recipes are real-world tested and designed to be used immediately.

Sections

In this book, you will find several headings that appear frequently (Getting ready, How to do it, How it works, There's more, and See also).

To give clear instructions on how to complete a recipe, we use these sections as follows:

Getting ready

This section tells you what to expect in the recipe, and describes how to set up any software or any preliminary settings required for the recipe.

How to do it...

This section contains the steps required to follow the recipe.

How it works...

This section usually consists of a detailed explanation of what happened in the previous section.

There's more...

This section consists of additional information about the recipe in order to make the reader more knowledgeable about the recipe.

See also

This section provides helpful links to other useful information for the recipe.

Conventions

In this book, you will find a number of text styles that distinguish between different kinds of information. Here are some examples of these styles and an explanation of their meaning.

Code words in text, database table names, folder names, filenames, file extensions, pathnames, dummy URLs, user input, and Twitter handles are shown as follows: "Save the sheet to the desktop as `Segment3Import`."

A block of code is set as follows:

```
Delete fromSY01401
wherecoDefaultType = 13
```

New terms and **important words** are shown in bold. Words that you see on the screen, for example, in menus or dialog boxes, appear in the text like this: "In the **Class ID** field perform a lookup and select **COMP**."

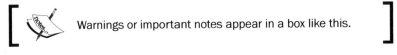
Warnings or important notes appear in a box like this.

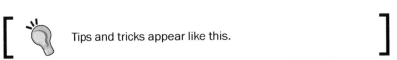
Tips and tricks appear like this.

Reader feedback

Feedback from our readers is always welcome. Let us know what you think about this book—what you liked or disliked. Reader feedback is important for us as it helps us develop titles that you will really get the most out of.

To send us general feedback, simply e-mail `feedback@packtpub.com`, and mention the book's title in the subject of your message.

If there is a topic that you have expertise in and you are interested in either writing or contributing to a book, see our author guide at `www.packtpub.com/authors`.

Customer support

Now that you are the proud owner of a Packt book, we have a number of things to help you to get the most from your purchase.

Downloading the color images of this book

We also provide you with a PDF file that has color images of the screenshots/diagrams used in this book. The color images will help you better understand the changes in the output. You can download this file from `http://www.packtpub.com/sites/default/files/downloads/MicrosoftDynamicsGP2016Cookbook_ColorImages.pdf`.

Errata

Although we have taken every care to ensure the accuracy of our content, mistakes do happen. If you find a mistake in one of our books—maybe a mistake in the text or the code—we would be grateful if you could report this to us. By doing so, you can save other readers from frustration and help us improve subsequent versions of this book. If you find any errata, please report them by visiting `http://www.packtpub.com/submit-errata`, selecting your book, clicking on the **Errata Submission Form** link, and entering the details of your errata. Once your errata are verified, your submission will be accepted and the errata will be uploaded to our website or added to any list of existing errata under the Errata section of that title.

To view the previously submitted errata, go to `https://www.packtpub.com/books/content/support` and enter the name of the book in the search field. The required information will appear under the **Errata** section.

Piracy

Piracy of copyrighted material on the Internet is an ongoing problem across all media. At Packt, we take the protection of our copyright and licenses very seriously. If you come across any illegal copies of our works in any form on the Internet, please provide us with the location address or website name immediately so that we can pursue a remedy.

Please contact us at `copyright@packtpub.com` with a link to the suspected pirated material.

We appreciate your help in protecting our authors and our ability to bring you valuable content.

Questions

If you have a problem with any aspect of this book, you can contact us at `questions@packtpub.com`, and we will do our best to address the problem.

1
Personalizing Dynamics GP

In this chapter we are going to cover the following topics:

- ▶ Personalizing the home page by selecting the right role
- ▶ Improving visibility by setting required fields to bold and red
- ▶ Further personalizing the home page by customizing the layout
- ▶ Speeding access to data with Quick Links
- ▶ Rearranging navigation to make it easier
- ▶ Managing personal reports with My Reports
- ▶ Viewing open items with Task List
- ▶ Accessing accounts faster with Favorites in lookups
- ▶ Cleaning up the mess by fixing Auto Complete errors

Introduction

This chapter explores recipes designed to enhance the usefulness of Microsoft Dynamics GP by personalizing the look and feel of the application. These recipes provide the first few steps in harnessing the full power of Dynamics GP. They are designed to improve productivity now, so don't wait to put them to use.

In almost all cases, the recipes in this chapter do not require an administrator and are available to the average user. The ability of each user to tailor these items to their own needs is what makes them so powerful.

By personalizing Dynamics GP, users get the opportunity to fine-tune the system to the way that they work. There is something incredibly satisfying about tailoring a system to make it more efficient, and we'll cover some of these personalizing options here.

While the nature of these recipes makes them useful right away, it is strongly recommended that these items be attempted in a test environment first.

Personalizing the home page by selecting the right role

Since version 2010 of Dynamics GP, Microsoft has placed a strong emphasis on user roles in both the organization and the software. Selecting the right role in the system presents many of the best **Home Page** options by default.

A role is usually selected by default when a user is created, and it's often wrong because at setup the focus is placed on job titles and not on the tasks the user performs. Additionally, user's roles evolve and change over time. Fortunately, changing a user's role is easy, so we'll look at how to do it in this recipe.

How to do it...

To change a user's **Home Page** role, complete the following steps:

1. In **Home Page**, click on the **Customize this Page** link in the upper-right corner.

2. Click on the **Change Role** button in the bottom-right corner.

   Changing the role resets any customizations that a user has made to their **Quick Links** or **Business Analyzer** settings in the home page; the user is prompted with a warning that their customizations will be lost and is given the choice of cancelling the change of role.

3. Click on **OK** to indicate an understanding of the consequences of changing a role.

4. Select **Your Industry** at the top. Changing an industry simply adds or removes the available role options immediately below. Selecting **Other** as the industry provides all of the role options.

5. On the left-hand side, select the role that's closest to a user's responsibilities. As a role is highlighted, a description of that role's tasks is included on the right-hand side. Click on **OK** to accept the role:

See also

▸ *Managing personal reports with My Reports*

▸ *Further personalizing the home page by customizing the layout*

▸ The *Speeding up Navigation lists by disabling Business Analyzer* recipe in *Chapter 11, Maintaining Dynamics GP*

Improving visibility by setting required fields to bold and red

Microsoft Dynamics GP provides an option for each user to identify the required fields on any form. By activating this setting, users can get a definitive visual cue indicating the minimum required fields on any form. This recipe shows you how to turn Required Fields bold red and what the end result looks like in both the desktop and in the web client (which was introduced in Microsoft Dynamics GP 2013 R2).

Getting ready

Prior to changing the appearance of required fields, the **Show Required Fields** feature needs to be turned on—first in the desktop client and then in the web client as well. To activate this feature in either the desktop client or the web client, perform the following steps:

1. Select **Help** (the white question mark on a blue background in the upper-right corner) from the main home page of Dynamics GP.

2. Ensure that **Show Required Fields** has a check mark next to it. If it does not, click on the **Show Required Fields** item to turn this option on.

How to do it...

To improve the visibility of the required fields, follow these steps:

1. The shortcut bar is the vertical bar on the top-left side of the screen when the **Home** button is selected on the left-hand side. From the shortcut bar, click on **User Preferences**, and then click on the **Display** button to open the **User Display Preferences** window; if you don't have **User Preferences** in the shortcut bar, click on the **Microsoft Dynamics GP** menu and then click on **User Preferences**.

2. In the bottom-right corner, under the **Required Fields** heading, set **Font Color** equal to **Red** and **Font Style** equal to **Bold**:

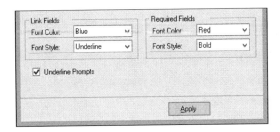

3. Click on **Apply** to accept the changes and close the window, and then click on **OK** to close **User Preferences**. Now, any windows that allow data entry will show their required fields in the desktop client in bold red, as shown in the following screenshot:

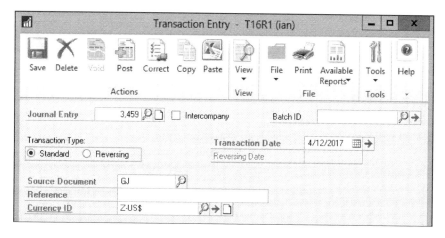

How it works...

Dynamics GP contains identifiers behind the scenes to mark fields as required. Dynamics GP uses these identifiers to change the color of the field name. Highlighting the required fields provides a quick visual cue in order to ensure that at least the minimum amount of data is entered prior to saving a form. This will save hours of time by preventing annoying messages indicating that the required fields have not been completed, especially since there is no indicator as to what field is missing.

There's more...

By default, activating **Show Required Fields** simply sets the required fields to black and regular. That is, it doesn't distinguish them at all. This is important because if **Show Required Fields** is off completely, Dynamics GP will prompt users to turn it on but that won't appear to have any effect.

There are some areas in Dynamics GP where required fields are not marked in red and bold despite this feature being properly applied. In almost all cases, these required fields occur in the grid section of a transaction entry form. This area of a form has a heading at the top and a grid that allows multiple entries under one heading. The nature of the programming behind the grid format prevents Dynamics GP from properly highlighting these fields, and unfortunately, there is no way to force a field inside the grid to reflect the **Show Required Fields** setting.

When a user receives a warning that a required field is missing but all the required fields appear to be correctly filled in, they should examine the fields in the grid for missing information. The most common culprits are the **Unit of Measure** and **Site ID** fields.

Modifier with VBA

With the available Modifier with VBA utility for Dynamics GP, an administrator or developer can make additional fields required, and in most cases, Dynamics GP will properly apply the red and bold formatting automatically. More information on Modifier with VBA is available from the manuals in Dynamics GP or from an authorized Microsoft Dynamics partner.

Further personalizing the home page by customizing the layout

The customization possible on the home page has been enhanced further in Microsoft Dynamics GP from the options that were available in Microsoft Dynamics GP 2010.

A default two-column layout will be loaded when the **Home Page** role is selected, but it can be customized by the user:

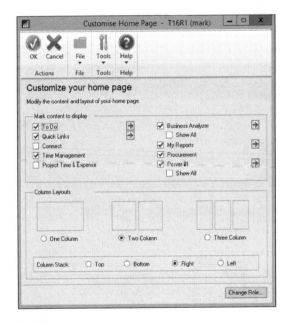

How to do it...

To change a user's **Home Page** role, complete the following steps:

1. On the home page, click on the **Customize this Page** link in the upper-right corner.

2. The content being displayed can be amended in the top **Mark content to display** section. To disable a piece of content, such as **Connect**, unmark the checkbox and click on **OK**, and this section will be removed from the home page.

3. The expansion buttons, represented by a horizontal blue arrow, allow additional criteria to be defined.

4. **Business Analyzer** has an additional option, **Show All**, which will show all of the selected **Business Analyzer** reports on the home page.

5. **Power BI** also has an additional option, **Show All**, which will show all of the selected **Power BI** reports on the home page.

6. The three available **Column Layout** fields can be selected by marking the required radio button.

7. The final customization option available is the **Column Stack** option, which controls the display of home page sections when one is maximized by moving the remaining small windows to the top, bottom, right, or left.

8. A section is maximized by clicking on the **Maximize/Multicolumn Mode** button (a square containing four arrows pointing outward from the center):

9. Once the desired customization options have been selected, click on the **OK** button.

There's more...

In Microsoft Dynamics GP 2010, sections on the home page were reorganized within the **Customize this page...** window. In both Microsoft Dynamics GP Desktop Client and Web Client, reorganization is accomplished on the home page itself using the mouse to drag and drop the section in the same way as you would drag and drop a window.

The home page will automatically shuffle the other sections around as the selected one is being moved. When placed in the required position, release the mouse button and the section will drop into place:

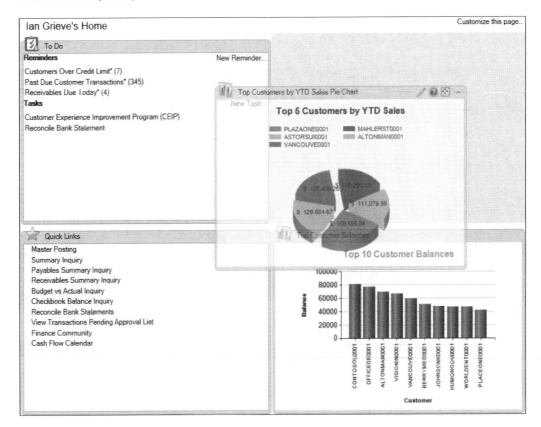

See also

▸ *Managing personal reports with My Reports*

▸ The *Speeding up Navigation lists by disabling Business Analyzer* recipe in Chapter 11, *Maintaining Dynamics GP*

Speeding up access to data with Quick Links

Like the shortcut bar, Quick Links provides fast access to data both inside and outside Dynamics GP. Although there is some overlap with shortcuts, Quick Links provide some unique features. For starters, related Quick Links are provided based on the user's home page role. Additionally, Quick Links also provide fast access to navigation lists, something that shortcuts can't do. In this recipe, we'll select an included navigation list and then add it as a Quick Link.

Getting ready

Navigation lists provide another way to work with data in Dynamics GP, and they can't be added to Shortcut bar. For our Quick Links example, we will look at adding a navigation list as a Quick Link.

How to do it...

To add a navigation list as a Quick Link, perform the following steps:

1. Click on the **Home** button on the navigation bar to the left. On the main home screen, find the section labeled **Quick Links**.

2. Place the cursor in the **Quick Links** box and a pencil will appear in the upper-right corner. Click on the small pencil icon and go to **Add | Dynamics GP Navigation List**:

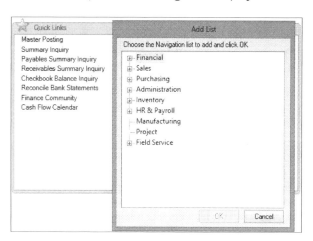

3. Click on the plus (**+**) sign next to **Sales** to expand these lists.

4. Click on the plus (**+**) sign next to **Accounts** and select **Customers**. Click on **OK** to finish.

5. In the open **Quick Links Details** box, find and select the **Customers** link. Click on the **Move Up** button repeatedly until **Customers** is at the top of the list and then click on **OK**:

How it works...

This process put the **Customers** Quick Link at the top of the **Quick Links** area. Now, clicking on the **Customers** Quick Link will immediately open that navigation list. Without this Quick Link, a user would need to select **Sales** from the home page and find the **Customer** link every time they need to add a customer. Simply selecting a Quick Link is a much faster way to get deep into Dynamics GP.

See also

▶ *Personalizing the home page by selecting the right role*

Rearranging navigation to make it easier

The Navigation pane on the left-hand side of Dynamics GP is full of useful functions. Sometimes, it is too full! For many users, it's beneficial to rearrange items on the Navigation pane to better suit their role. We'll look at how to do that in this recipe.

Getting ready

Most users quickly discover that left-clicking and dragging the separator above the **Home** button on the left-hand side allows them to shrink and expand the space available for Navigation pane buttons. This expands the room for lists and shortcuts above the separator bar, by transforming the large buttons into smaller, less intuitive icons. However, there is so much more that can be done to personalize Navigation pane.

How to do it...

Cleaning up the Navigation pane can provide faster and simpler navigation options. Let's see how by completing the following steps:

1. In the Navigation pane, select the bottom-right corner of the pane and click on **Navigation Pane Options**.

2. From here, select **Purchasing** and move it to the top using the **Move Up** and **Move Down** buttons on the right-hand side.

3. Then, select the **Sales** module and uncheck the **Sales** selection. Click on **OK**:

Now, the **Purchasing** choice has been moved to the top, where a user can have easy access to it, and the **Sales** option not (required for this user) has been removed.

How it works...

In our example, a heavy user of the **Purchasing** module now has the Navigation pane button immediately below the **Home** button and easily accessible. The **Sales** button, which wouldn't be used by a typical **Purchasing** employee, has been removed in order to clean up the interface.

Managing personal reports with My Reports

My Reports is a section of the Dynamics GP home page designed to provide fast access to reporting options in Dynamics GP. Similar to the Quick Links functionality, My Reports provides single-click access to reports, replacing multiple clicks and drill-downs with a direct connection.

In Dynamics GP, every prebuilt report (also known as a Report Writer report) requires an option. An option is simply a named group of settings for a particular report. For example, a user may have a Receivables Aged Trial Balance report with date and selection criteria designed for month-end reporting. The report name is always Receivables Aged Trial Balance, but the option name to describe these particular month-end settings might be Month End.

The **My Reports** feature provides one-click access to reports with saved options. In this recipe, we'll look at how to add a report to **My Reports**.

How to do it...

To add a report to **My Reports**, we will need to complete the following steps:

1. Select the **Sales** button from the Navigation pane on the left-hand side. In the list on the left-hand side, select **Report List**.

2. In the center section, scroll down to the report named `Aged Trial Balance` with the **Option** demo and check the box to the left.

3. Demo is a prebuilt, saved report option. **Report** options are saved report settings for items such as dates and restrictions.

4. Click on the **Add** to button to add this to the **My Reports** section of the home page. Accept the default name for the report by clicking on **OK**:

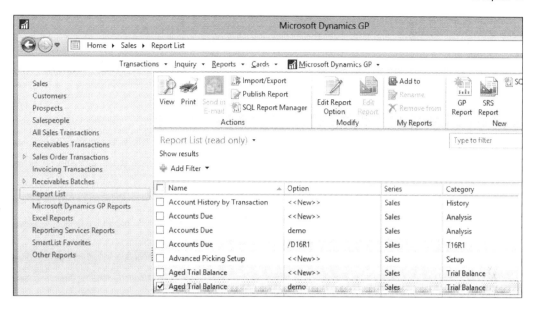

5. Click on the **Home** button in Navigation pane to return to the home page. The Aged Trial Balance-demo report now appears on the home page under **My Reports**:

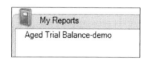

6. Clicking on the Aged Trial Balance-demo link under **My Reports** now runs the report automatically.

There's more...

Other features and options are available in order to assist with managing reporting in Dynamics GP.

Reports without options

Reports without options cannot be added to the **My Reports** section of the home page. Consequently, users need to create and save report options to make them available to the home page.

Better dates in report options

A technique to set up report dates for automatic reporting is covered in detail in the the *Controlling reporting dates with beginning and ending periods* recipe in *Chapter 3, Automating Dynamics GP.*

See also

- ▶ *Personalizing the home page by selecting the right role*
- ▶ *Speeding access to data with Quick Links*
- ▶ *Viewing open items with Task List*
- ▶ The *Controlling reporting dates with beginning and ending periods* recipe in *Chapter 3, Automating Dynamics GP*

Viewing open items with Task List

Dynamics GP provides a **Task List** feature to manage items to be accomplished within the system. While not quite as powerful as, say, Outlook's tasks, **Task List** in Dynamics GP can provide direct links to the appropriate window, web page, or external file required to accomplish the task. Even Outlook can't provide a direct link to the right window in Dynamics GP. In addition, tasks can be assigned to other users in the system in order to better delegate the workload. Let's take a look at how to use **Task List** in Dynamics GP in this recipe.

Getting ready

Open tasks are displayed on the home page in Dynamics GP under the **To Do** heading.

To get started, select **New Task** from the home page to view the complete task list. Yes, it's not particularly intuitive, but that is how it works:

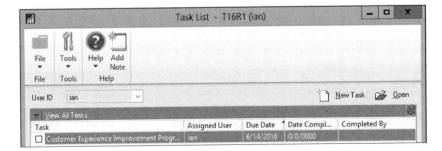

How to do it...

As an example, we'll look at how to add a month-end bank reconciliation task by completing the following steps:

1. To create a new task, select **New Task** from the home page in the **To Do** section to open the complete task list.

2. Select **New Task** in the **Task List** window. In the **Task** section, enter `Reconcile Bank Statement`. Set the due date to 5th of the next month, and set the status to **Pending**:

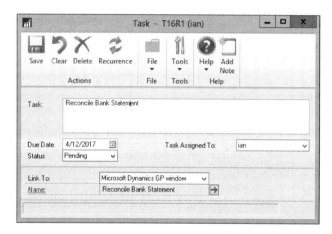

3. In the **Task Assigned To:** box, select a user to assign this task to. In the **Link To:** box, select **Microsoft Dynamics GP window**.

4. To attach the **Reconcile Bank Statement** window, click on the blue arrow next to **Name:**.

5. In the new **Add Command** box that opens, select **Transactions** on the left-hand side and then click on the plus (**+**) sign next to **Financial** on the right-hand side.

6. In the right-hand side pane, select **Reconcile Bank Statement** and click on **OK**:

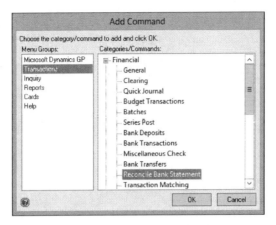

7. Click on **Save** to save the task. If the task was assigned to another user, it will now appear in their task list.

How it works...

The new task now appears in the **Tasks** area on the home page. Checking the box next to a task marks it as complete and sets the user who completed the task as well as the date on which it was completed:

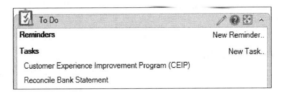

There's more...

Tasks can be repeated, which means that they work great for regular processes, such as month-end or quarter-end tasks.

Recurring tasks

To set a task as recurring, perform the following steps:

1. Select the **Recurrence** button during the task creation or double-click on an existing task and select **Recurrence**.

2. From the previous example, select the **Reconcile Bank Statement** task and double-click on that line.

3. Click on the **Recurrence** button. Set **Recurrence Pattern** to **Monthly** on the First Thursday of every 1 month.

   This means the task will recur on the first Thursday of each month.

4. Leave **Range of Recurrence** set to **No End Date** and click on **OK**.

5. Now, this task will repeat each month on the first Thursday of the month. If a company's bank changes the statement cut-off date to some other time during the month, these settings can be changed easily:

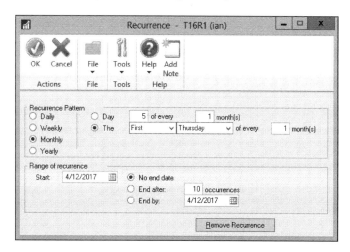

▸ The *Using Reminders to remember important events* recipe in *Chapter 3, Automating Dynamics GP*

Accessing accounts faster with Favorites in lookups

In larger organizations, it is common for users to only work with a subset of the chart of accounts. Often, these accounts are limited to a certain division or department. To find a set of accounts quickly, Dynamics GP provides a mechanism to look up a more limited set of accounts and save them as Favorites. This provides faster access when selecting accounts in transactions. In this recipe, we'll look at using Favorites in Lookups. Favorites are actually part of SmartLists, which are covered in detail in *Chapter 4, Leveraging New and Updated Features in Dynamics GP*.

This recipe showcases the power of integrating SmartLists into the application interface. It provides an unlimited number of ways to target account selection, including selections based on the department, company, account type, financial statement type, and more—all with just a few clicks.

Getting ready

To begin this recipe, we are required to set up a simple Account SmartList in order to set up the account limits:

1. Select the **Microsoft Dynamics GP** menu and click on **SmartList** in order to open SmartLists.

2. Click on the plus sign (**+**) next to **Financial** and select **Accounts**:

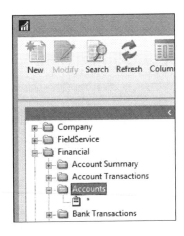

3. Now, select the **Search** button. Click on the lookup icon (it looks like a magnifying glass) and select **Account Number**. Click on **OK**.

4. Set the **Filter** set to **begins with** and enter 000. Click on **OK** to confirm:

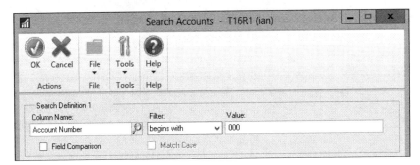

5. Select the **Favorites** button. In the **Name** box, enter Segment 000, click on **Add**, and add favorite:

This process creates a specialized list based on a segment in the chart of accounts and then saves it in order to make it available for account selection.

How to do it...

The favorites list only needs to be built once. After that, the real fun starts:

1. First, select **Financial** from the Navigation pane on the left-hand side and select **General** from the **Financial Area** page.

2. Click on the **Account** field in the middle and select the lookup button. Click on the arrow next to view and hover over **Favorites**.

3. Select Segment 000, in the Account **Favorites** created earlier:

This presents a specialized list to users, giving them a more targeted list of accounts to select from when creating a transaction.

There's more...

There are more options than just this recipe in order to limit the selections from the chart of accounts.

Set as default view

Improved in Dynamics GP is the ability for a user to save a Favorite as the default view. Once a Favorite has been selected in the view, simply click on **Set as Default View** from the **View** menu. Default views are per-user and only available for the master record lookup and not transactions.

Restricted list

If users only need to restrict the available accounts occasionally, there is a temporary option. After selecting the lookup button and clicking on the arrow next to **View**, users can select **Restricted List** instead of **Favorites**. The **Restricted List** option provides a functionality similar to **Favorites**, but the search is not saved and **Restricted Lists** cannot be set as the default view.

Resetting

Selecting **All Accounts** resets the list, removing all restrictions.

Account security

Account security is a feature in Dynamics GP that limits a user's access to certain accounts in the chart. A user cannot even see an account that they don't have access to. This is another option to limit the selection of accounts available to a user, but it requires an administrator and a lot of thought to set up correctly. Setting up account security is less like a recipe and more like a seven-course meal, so it's not covered here.

Activating account security without proper setup makes it appear as if the chart of accounts has been deleted. Deactivating account security returns users' access to the chart but not before triggering a gut-wrenching fear that it's time to find a new job.

See also

  ▶ *Chapter 8, Harnessing the Power of SmartLists*

Cleaning up the mess by fixing AutoComplete errors

Dynamics GP includes a fantastic feature known as AutoComplete, which remembers what a user has typed in a field and later makes data entry suggestions based on that information. This can significantly reduce repetitive data entry. However, if a user makes an error during data entry, such as a misspelled or incorrect word, that error will continue to be suggested over and over again.

There is a simple way to remove erroneous entries, and we'll look at how to do this in this recipe.

Getting ready

To demonstrate this feature, we first need to intentionally create an AutoComplete error.

1. Select **Sales** from Navigation pane on the left-hand side.

2. On the **Area** page for **Sales**, select **Customer** under **Cards** on the right-hand side to open up the **Customer Maintenance** window.

3. Select **Sales** from the Navigation pane on the left-hand side.

4. On the **Area** page for **Sales**, select **Customer** under **Cards** on the right-hand side in order to open up the **Customer Maintenance** window:

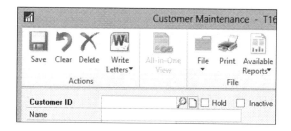

5. With the **Customer Maintenance** window open, type MISPELL in the **Customer ID** field and click on *Tab*. Press the **Clear** button to remove this customer entry.

How to do it...

Now that we have an error, let's look at how to fix it:

1. Back in the **Customer ID** field, type MIS. Dynamics GP will suggest MISPELL. Right-click on the suggested word, MISPELL, and select **Remove From List**:

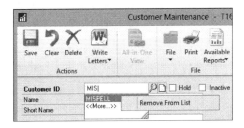

2. Now, typing MIS in the **Customer ID** field doesn't provide the MISPELL suggestion.

How it works...

AutoComplete is controlled in User Preferences, which is accessed via shortcut bar. The AutoComplete settings are defined for each user. This means that each user has a different set of AutoComplete entries, so removing an errant entry doesn't affect other users.

There's more...

To better manage AutoComplete, there are some other settings that can be adjusted on a per-user basis.

Removed unused entries

The AutoComplete cache of entries can grow quite large and unwieldy, leading to a significant number of entries to sort through and reducing the effectiveness of this feature. A consistent way to manage the size of the AutoComplete list is by letting AutoComplete remove unused entries automatically. To set this up, perform the following steps:

1. Select **User Preferences** from shortcut bar and click on **AutoComplete**.

2. In the **Remove Unused Entries After** field, enter 90 and click on **OK**.

3. This means that any AutoComplete entries will be removed after 90 days without any use.

Reducing the number of AutoComplete entries

Another option to manage the size of the AutoComplete cache is to limit the maximum number of AutoComplete entries. To accomplish this, perform the following steps:

1. Select **User Preferences** from shortcut bar and click on **AutoComplete**.

2. For the **Max. Number of Entries to Store per Field** entry, the default is 10,000, which is a huge limit.

3. This can safely be lowered to 1,000 by changing the number in the **Max. Number of Entries to Store per Field** box and entering 1,000.

Resetting AutoComplete

If significant changes are made to a system, users can get a fresh start by completely resetting their AutoComplete entries. This is accomplished via the **Remove Entries** button available by clicking on **User Preference** and then clicking on the **AutoComplete** button.

2
Organizing Dynamics GP

In this chapter, we will look at:

- ▸ Speeding up account entry with account aliases
- ▸ Cleaning account lookups by removing accounts from lookups
- ▸ Gaining visibility with horizontal scroll arrows
- ▸ Streamlining payables processing by prioritizing vendors
- ▸ Getting clarity with user-defined fields
- ▸ Developing connections with Internet User Defined fields
- ▸ Controlling reporting with account rollups
- ▸ Remembering processes with an ad hoc workflow
- ▸ Improving financial reporting clarity by splitting purchasing accounts
- ▸ Speeding up lookups with advanced lookups
- ▸ Going straight to the site with web links

Introduction

Dynamics GP provides a number of features to better organize the overall system and improve its usefulness for all users; these recipes are designed for the use of administrators rather than typical users. This chapter is designed to demonstrate how to implement and fine-tune these features to provide the most benefit.

Speeding up account entry with Account Alias

As organizations grow up, the chart of accounts tends to grow larger and more complex as well. Companies want to segment their business by departments, locations, or divisions; all of this means that more and more accounts get added to the chart and, as the chart of accounts grows, it gets more difficult to select the right account. Dynamics GP provides the Account Alias feature as a way to quickly select the right account. Account aliases provide a way to create shortcuts to specific accounts, which can dramatically speed up the process of selecting the correct account. We'll look at how that works in this recipe.

Getting ready

Setting up account aliases requires a user with access to the **Account Maintenance** window.

To get to this window perform the following steps:

1. Select **Financial** from the Navigation pane on the left. Click **Accounts** on the **Financial** area page under **Cards**. This will open the **Account Maintenance** window.

2. Click the lookup button (the glass) next to the account number or use the keyboard shortcut *Ctrl + Q*.

3. Find and select account **000-2100-00**.

4. In the middle of the **Account Maintenance** window is the **Account Alias** field. Enter AP in the **Alias** field.

This associates the letters AP with the accounts payable account selected. This means that the user now only has to enter AP instead of the full account number to use the accounts payable account:

How to do it...

Once aliases have been set up, let's see how the user can quickly select an account using the alias:

1. To demonstrate how this works, click **Financial** on the Navigation pane on the left. Select **General** from the **Financial** area page under **Transactions**.

2. On the **Transaction Entry** window, select the top line in the grid area on the lower half of the window.

3. Click the expansion button (represented by a blue arrow) next to the **Account** heading to open the **Account Entry** window.

4. In the **Alias** field type AP and press *Enter*:

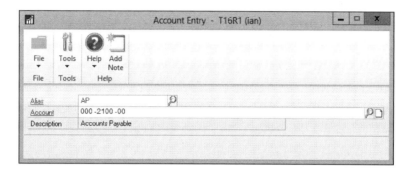

5. The **Account Alias** window will close and the account represented by the alias will appear in the **Transaction Entry** window:

How it works...

Account aliases provide quick shortcuts for account entry. Keeping them short and obvious makes them easy to use. Aliases are less useful if users have to think about them. Limiting them to the most commonly used accounts makes them more useful. Most users don't mind occasionally looking up the odd account but they shouldn't have to memorize long account strings for regularly used account numbers.

It's counter-productive to put an alias on every account since that would make finding the right alias as difficult as finding the right account number. The setup process should be performed on the most commonly used accounts to provide easy access.

See also

▶ *Gaining visibility with horizontal scroll arrows*

Cleaning account lookups by removing accounts from lookups

A consequence of company growth is that the chart of accounts grows and account lookups can get clogged up by the number of accounts on the system. While the general ledger will stop showing an account in a lookup when the account is made inactive, other modules will continue to show these inactive codes.

However, Dynamics GP does contain a feature which can be used to remove inactive account from lookups; this same feature can also be used to remove accounts from lookups in series where the account should not be used, such as a sales account in the purchasing or inventory series.

How to do it...

Here we will see how to remove inactive accounts from lookups.

1. Open **Financial** from the Navigation pane on the left. In the main area page, under **Cards**, select **Account**.

2. Enter, or do a lookup for, the account to be made inactive and removed from the lookups:

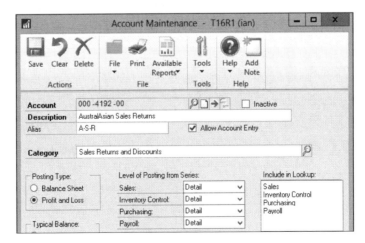

3. Check the **Inactive** checkbox.

4. Press and hold the *Ctrl* key and click on each of the lines in the **Include in Lookup** list.

5. Click **Save** to commit the changes.

Next time a lookup is done in any of the now deselected modules, the account will not be included in the list.

If the account is to be included in lookups in some modules but not others, simply leave selected the modules in which the account should be included:

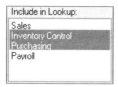

How it works...

Accounts will only show in lookups when the series is selected in the **Include in Lookup** list. For series other than General Ledger, simply marking an account as **Inactive** is not enough to remove it from the lookup although the code can't be used when the account is inactive.

Gaining visibility with horizontal scroll arrows

A consequence of company growth is that not only does the chart of accounts grow larger and less intuitive, but the actual length of account numbers tends to grow longer as well. Companies want to be able to report by account, department, location, and so on, which results in a proliferation of segments added to the main account number and can create very long accounts. Dynamics GP can accommodate an account number as long as 66 characters. The longest I've seen used in practice was 27 characters and even that was unwieldy. Most users only need a portion of that length for their day-to-day work.

This presents a problem because very long account numbers won't fit into the account number field on most screens. For this recipe, we'll look at how Dynamics GP provides a solution to this in the **User Preferences** area.

How to do it...

Here we'll see how to increase the visibility of long account numbers:

1. On the Navigation pane on the left, select **Home**.

2. Click on **User Preferences** on the shortcut bar.

3. Check the **Horizontal Scroll Arrows** box:

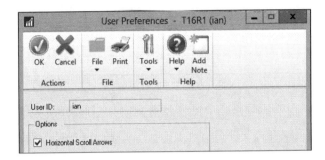

4. This allows users to scroll horizontally within the **Account** field, allowing them to see the full account number:

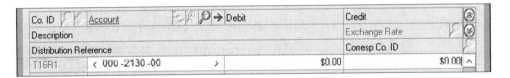

How it works...

Once **Horizontal Scroll Arrows** are activated, small arrows appear at the left and right side of the **Account** field, letting users scroll right and left to see the full account number.

There's more...

Horizontal scroll arrows are implemented on a per-user basis, meaning each user has to turn this on individually. Administrators can make this active for all users with a SQL script.

Additionally, for companies using alphanumeric characters in their chart of accounts, wide letters such as M or W are often difficult to see. There is also an option to increase the visible width of a particular segment.

Activating Horizontal Scroll Arrows for all users

Horizontal Scroll Arrows are activated by the user. However, an administrator can turn this feature on for all users in all companies by running the following SQL script against the Dynamics database:

```
Update
SY01400
Set
HSCRLARW=1
```

Widening segments for better visibility

When companies use alphanumeric characters in their chart of accounts, wide letters, such as M or W, are often cut off. Horizontal scroll arrows don't help because the problem is that the segment field is too narrow, not the entire account field. To resolve this problem, Dynamics GP provides an option to widen the segment fields as well.

On the Navigation pane, click **Administration** and select **Account Format**. For each segment that needs to be wider, select the **Display Width** column and change it from **Standard** to **Expansion**, 1, 2 or 3, to widen the field; **Expansion 3** represents the widest option.

Companies using only numbers in their chart of accounts won't need to widen the segment field but firms that include letters as part of their chart will need to increase the width. The following is a list of the expansion options and the letters they are designed to accommodate:

- ▸ **Expansion 1**: A,B,E,K,P,S,V,X,Y
- ▸ **Expansion 2**: C,D,G,H,M,N,O,Q,R,U
- ▸ **Expansion 3**: W

Streamlining payables processing by prioritizing vendors

Management of vendor payments is a critical activity for any firm; it's even more critical in difficult economic times. Companies need to understand and control payments and a key component of this is prioritizing vendors. Every firm has both critical and expendable vendors. Paying critical vendors on time is a key business driver.

For example, a newspaper that doesn't pay their newsprint supplier won't be in business long. However, they can safely delay payments to their janitorial vendor without worrying about going under.

Dynamics GP provides a mechanism to prioritize vendors and apply those priorities when selecting which checks to print. That is the focus of this recipe.

Getting ready

Setting this up first requires that the company figure out who the priority vendors are. That part is beyond the scope of this book. The **Vendor Priority** field in Dynamics GP is a three-character field, but users shouldn't be seduced by the possibilities of three characters. A best practice is to keep the priorities simple by using 1, 2, 3 or A, B, C. Anything more complicated than that tends to confuse users and actually makes it harder to prioritize vendors.

Once the vendor priorities have been determined, the priority needs to be set in Dynamics GP. Attaching a priority to a vendor is the first step. To do that follow these steps:

1. Select **Purchasing** from the Navigation pane. In the **Purchasing** area page under **Cards**, click **Vendor Maintenance**.

2. Once the **Vendor Maintenance** window opens, select the lookup button (magnifying glass) next to **Vendor ID**.

3. Select a vendor and click **OK**.

4. Once the vendor information is populated, click the **Options** button. This opens the **Vendor Maintenance Options** screen.

5. In the center left is the **Payment Priority** field. Enter 1 in **Payment Priority** and click **OK** on the **Vendor Maintenance** window:

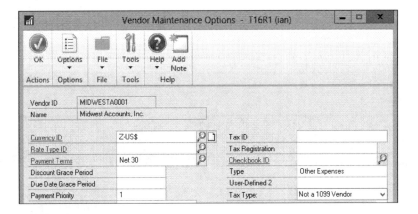

How to do it...

Now that a vendor has been set up with a priority, let's see how to apply that information when selecting checks to print:

1. To use vendor priorities to select invoices for payment, click **Select Checks** from the **Transactions** on the **Purchasing** area page.

2. In the **Select Payables Checks** window enter CHECKS to name the check batch. Press *Tab* to move away from the **Batch ID** field and click **Add** to add the batch.

3. Pick a checkbook ID and click **Save** to save the batch.

4. In the **Select** field, click the drop-down box and select **Payment Priority**. Enter 1 in both the **From** and **To** boxes.

5. Click the **Insert >>** button to lock in **Payment Priority** as an option:

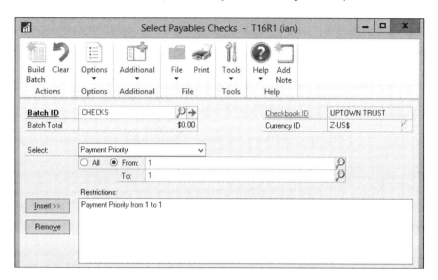

6. Click **Build Batch** at the top. If there are any transactions where the vendor is set to a priority of 1 this will populate a batch of checks based on the vendor priority:

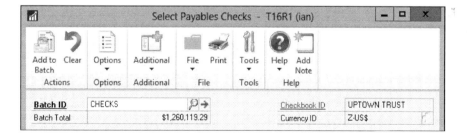

How it works...

Since priority is one of the built-in options for selecting checks, it's easy to ensure that high-priority vendors get selected to be paid first. All of this is easily accomplished with basic Dynamics GP functionality that most people miss.

Getting clarity with user-defined fields

Throughout Dynamics GP, maintenance cards typically include at least two user-defined fields. User-defined fields can be renamed in the setup screen for the related module. This provides a great mechanism to add in special information. We'll take a look at a typical use of a user defined field in this recipe.

How to do it...

For our example, we'll look at using a user-defined field to rename the **User-Defined1** field to `Region` in **Customer Master:**. To do so use the following steps:

1. From the Navigation pane select **Sales**. In the **Sales** area page under **Setup** click **Receivables** and then, finally, the **Options** button.

2. In the **User-Defined 1** field type `Region` and click **OK** to close each window:

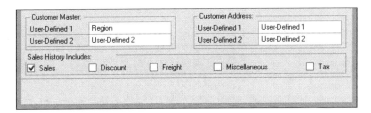

3. Back on the **Sales** area page, click **Customer** under the **Cards** area. On the bottom left above **User-Defined 2** is the newly named **Region** field, ready to be filled in:

How it works...

Changing the field name only changes the display field; it doesn't change the underlying field name in the database. SmartLists are smart enough to show the new name. In our example, the description **Region** will appear in a SmartList, not **User-Defined 1**.

User-defined fields like this are present for customers, vendors, accounts, sales orders, fixed assets, inventory items, and purchase receipts among others. They can each be renamed in their respective setup screens.

There's more...

All user defined fields are not the same; some have special features.

Special User-Defined 1 features

User-Defined 1 has special features inside Dynamics GP. Most of the built-in reports inside of Dynamics GP allow sorting and selection with the **User-Defined 1** field. These options aren't provided for **User-Defined 2**. Consequently, administrators should carefully consider what information belongs in **User-Defined 1** before changing its name since the effects of this selection will be felt throughout the system.

Company Setup user-defined fields

On the **Company Setup** window there are two user-defined fields at the top right and there is no option in Dynamics GP to rename these fields. The **Company Setup** window is accessed by clicking **Administration** on the Navigation pane, then clicking on **Company** under **Setup and Company headers**.

Expanded user-defined fields

Certain areas such as **Fixed Assets**, **Inventory Items**, and **Purchase Receipts** have more complex types of user-defined field that can include dates, list selections, and currency.

See also

- ▶ The *Renaming the SmartLists fields for Clarity recipe in Chapter 8, Harnessing the Power of SmartLists*
- ▶ *Developing connections with Internet User Defined fields*
- ▶ *Going straight to the site with web links*

Developing connections with Internet User Defined fields

Dynamics GP provides a built-in set of Internet fields for users to enter information such as web pages, e-mail addresses, and FTP sites. What many people don't know is that these are actually user-defined fields and can be changed by an administrator, which allows a firm to add a second email address or remove the FTP link if they want to. In this recipe, we'll look at how to customize these fields.

It is important to keep in mind, when setting up Internet User Defined fields, that these settings affect all the Internet User Defined field names attached to address IDs assigned to a company, customers, employees, items, salespeople, and vendors.

How to do it...

Customizing Internet User Defined fields is easy, so let's take a look at how to do it. For our example, we'll add the social networking service Twitter as a new label:

1. Select **Administration** from the Navigation pane. Under the **Setup** option and **Company** headers in the **Administration Area** page, pick **Company**.

2. Click the **Internet User Defined** button and change the image description next to **Label 4** to Twitter. Click **OK**:

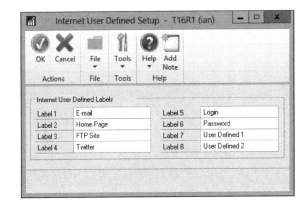

3. Back on the **Company Setup** screen, click the globe icon to the right of the Address ID to open the **Internet Information** window. In the **Twitter** field type http://www.twitter.com/azurecurve.

4. Click the link associated with the **Twitter** field on the left. This opens a web browser and navigates to my Twitter account so that you can follow me. Click **Save** to update the record:

How it works...

The secret to Internet User Defined fields is how the data is entered. Internet items use a prefix in the field to identify the type of internet transaction to be used with the link. http:// is used for web pages, Mailto:// for e-mail, and ftp:// for FTP sites. These prefixes tell Dynamics GP what to do when a link is clicked; if no prefix is entered, it will try to figure out what to do and may or may not succeed.

If `http://www.microsoft.com` is entered in a field, the link to the left will start the default browser and open the Microsoft web page. If `http://` is not included, but www is, GP figures out that it should open a web page. Just putting in Microsoft.com isn't enough for GP to understand that the link corresponds to a web page. Similarly, if a user enters `mailto://` `mpolino@gmail.com` and clicks the link, the default email client opens up ready to send an email to me. If no prefix is used on an email address, GP will respond with a **File Not Found** error when the link is clicked. It's not smart enough to know that the @ symbol means that this is an e-mail account.

Using a prefix in Internet User Defined fields explicitly defines how this link should work and provides the most consistency to users.

There's more...

Some Internet User Defined fields look special but aren't and some really are special.

Login and password

By default, the Internet User Defined field **Label 5** is named `Login` and **Label 6** is named `Password`. These fields are supposed to represent the login and password for one of the associated web pages or FTP sites. However, these fields are not encrypted and there is limited security control, so it may be not be appropriate to leave these fields named `Login` and `Password` if a company doesn't want users entering that information here.

Labels 7 and 8

Labels 7 and 8 are Internet User Defined special fields that allow a user to look up and attach links to files located on the computer or the network. Clicking the label name on the left opens the associated file. Other fields can accept files and these fields can still accept a prefix and link or freeform text, but their special ability to lookup file names means that administrators should consider reserving them for file attachments.

See also

- ▸ *Chapter 8, Harnessing the Power of SmartLists*
- ▸ *Going straight to the site with web links*
- ▸ *Getting clarity with user-defined fields*

Controlling reporting with account rollups

Microsoft Dynamics GP provides great functionality for analyzing and reviewing individual accounts and sequential groups of accounts. Many users don't know that it also provides impressive functionality for analyzing non-sequential groups of accounts via a feature known as Account Rollup.

Account Rollups are enquiries built to allow users to see different GL accounts rolled up together and to provide drill-back capability to the details. Additionally, these queries can include calculations for things such as budget versus actual comparisons and calculations.

Management Reporter provides similar functionality and Account Rollup allows users to access this functionality without the wait time in starting up Management Reporter. Let's see how to mix up some account rollups in this recipe.

Getting ready

Before using Account Rollups, it's important to understand how to set them up:

1. To set up Account Rollup, select **Financial** from the Navigation pane then select **Account Rollup** in the **Inquiry** section to open the **Account Rollup Inquiry Options** window.

2. In the **Option ID** field enter the name `Actual vs. Budget` and hit *Tab*. Select **Yes** to add the option. On the right, set the number of columns to **3**.

3. In the first row, type `Actual` in the column heading and set the type to **Actuals**.

4. In the second row, type `Budget` in the column heading and set the type to **Budget**. In the **Selection** column select the lookup button (magnifying glass) and select **Budget 4**.

5. In the third row, type `Variance` in the column heading. Set the type to **Calculated**. Click the blue arrow next to **Selection** to set up the calculation.

6. In the **Column** field, select **Actual** and click the double arrow (**>>**). Click the minus (-) button. Back in the **Column** field select **Budget** and click the double arrow (**>>**). Click **OK**.

7. Back in the **Account Rollup Inquiry Options** window select the **Segment** field and select **Account**. Use the lookup buttons (magnifying glass) in **From** and **To** to add account `4130` and click **Insert**. Repeat this process inserting `4120` and then `4100` into the **Restrictions** box below. Click **Save** and close the window:

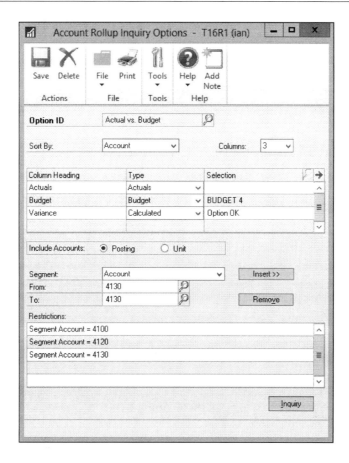

Notice when looking up these accounts for selection that these numbers are not sequential; there are a number of accounts in between.

How to do it...

Now that we've built an account rollup, let's see how to make it work:

1. Select **Account Rollup** under **Inquiry** on the **Financial** area page.

2. In the **Option ID** field, lookup `Actual vs. Budget` with the lookup button (magnifying glass).

3. The screen will show **Actual**, **Budget**, and **Variance** for each period in this year.

The year can be changed at the top and the display can be changed to show either **Net Change** or **Period Balance** for each period in the year, along with a total at the bottom, using the controls next to the year. The **Difference** field is the **Actuals** minus **Budget** calculation that we created when setting up the rollup:

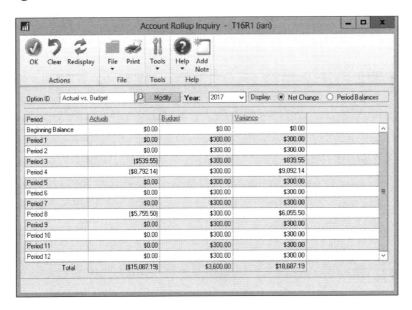

4. Click on a period with an amount in the **Actuals** column and select the **Actuals** link at the top. A new window will open with the included accounts and the actual amounts for each account.

5. When drilling down to the **Account Rollup Detail Inquiry Zoom** window, Dynamics GP provides a checkbox option to show accounts even if they have a zero balance.

6. Additionally, an option at the top controls the printing of **Account Rollup** information. The rollup can be printed in **Summary** or in **Detail**:

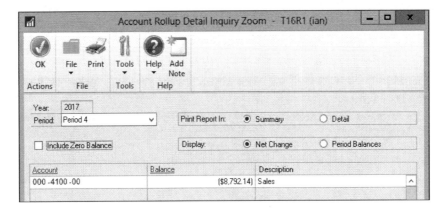

7. Selecting a line and clicking **Balance** from Account Rollup Detail Inquiry Zoom drills back to the detail transactions behind the balance:

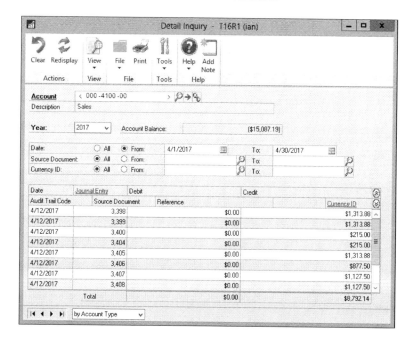

How it works...

Account Rollups combine account totals from disparate accounts for reporting. This is great for tying back multiple accounts that rollup to a single line on financial statements. Account Rollups also work well for analyzing a single segment, such as a department, across multiple accounts. In the past I've used this for easy comparisons of Fixed Asset general ledger accounts to the subledger and for rolling up full time equivalent unit accounts to get the number of employees across the company, with drill-back to the employees in each department.

See also

Additional options for reporting and analysis via SmartLists are covered extensively in *Chapter 5, Exposing Hidden Features in Dynamics GP*.

Remembering processes with an ad hoc workflow

Microsoft Dynamics GP offers a flexible built-in approval workflow engine, but this is sometimes more complicated, or specialized, that users require and is limited to approvals. For users who only need a simple workflow to ensure that they remember the steps for a particular task, a basic workflow can be built using shortcuts and folders.

This process works well for irregular tasks such as month-end or quarter-end processes where tasks are performed infrequently enough to make it easy to forget the steps. For this recipe, we'll look at setting up a basic month-end workflow.

Getting ready

The basic steps of this task are to create a folder to hold the workflow and then add the steps in order to that folder. For our example, we will assume that a month-end financial closing workflow includes posting a quick journal, processing a clearing entry, and closing the month.

How to do it...

Here are the steps to create a basic, ad hoc workflow:

1. Select the **Home** button from the Navigation pane on the left. This makes the shortcut bar available on the top left.

2. Right-click on the shortcut bar and select **Add | Folder** to add a folder to the shortcut bar that can be used to organize entries.

3. Right-click on the new folder and select **Rename**. Name the folder Month End and press *Enter*. Now there is a folder to hold month-end entries.

4. The next step is to add our three sample entries. Select the **Month End** folder on the shortcut bar. Right-click on the folder and select **Add | Add Window**:

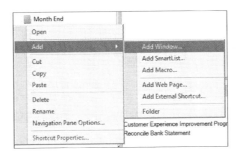

5. Click the plus sign (**+**) next to **Microsoft Dynamics GP**. Click the plus (**+**) next to **Financial** and select the window named `Quick Journal Entry`. Change the name at the top to `1) Quick Journal Entry`. Click **Add**:

 Putting a number in front prevents this shortcut from interfering if the same shortcut appears somewhere else on the shortcut bar.

6. Next, select **Clearing Entry** also under **Microsoft Dynamics GP** and **Financial**. Rename it **2) Clearing Entry in the Name box** and click **Add**.

7. Finally, select the plus (**+**) next to **Company** under **Microsoft Dynamics GP** and select **Fiscal Periods Setup**. Rename this `3) Close Fiscal Period` and click **Add**. Select **Done** to finish.

8. The items will appear on the shortcut bar on the left under the **Month End** folder. Selecting an item with the left mouse button will allow moving items around to adjust the order if necessary:

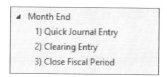

How it works...

Ad hoc workflows provide an option to group a set of steps together and make them all available in one place. Clicking the arrow to the left of the folder closes it up and keeps the steps out of the way until they are needed. Clicking the arrow again reopens the folder to run the steps. Some common uses include creating a basic set of steps for new users, month-end and quarter-end processes, and any other process where it is important to ensure that all the steps are followed.

See also...

> * The *Speeding up access to data with Quick Links* recipe in *Chapter 1, Personalizing Dynamics GP*

Improving financial reporting clarity by splitting purchasing accounts

By default, in Dynamics GP, when a payables invoice is fully or partially paid via the Payables Transaction Entry window, the payment portion of the transaction doesn't flow through the payables account. Typically, this occurs when payment is recorded at the same time as the invoice is entered into Dynamics GP. It can make it more difficult to trace a transaction since the transaction could skip the payables account alltogether by crediting cash and debiting an expense.

GP provides an optional setting to force transactions to flow through the payables account and that's what we'll look at in this recipe.

How to do it...

Setting up GP to pass voucher payments through payables is as easy as following these steps:

1. Select the **Administration** button from the Navigation pane on the left. In the **Administration Area** page, under **Setup**, click **Company** in the **Company** section.

2. Click the **Options** button. Scroll down to the setting marked **Separate Payment Distributions** and check the box next to it:

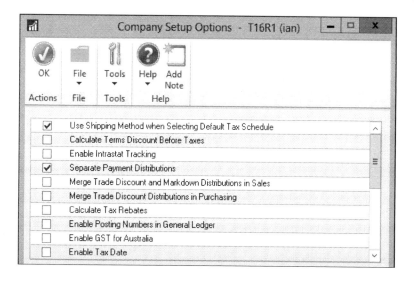

3. Click **OK** to close the window and accept the changes.

How it works...

Let's assume a $100 purchase transaction where $20 is paid in cash and the remaining $80 will go to accounts payable. By default, GP will create a transaction distribution that looks like this:

Account	Debit	Credit
Account A (Purch)	$100.00	
Account B (Cash)		$20.00
Account C (Payable)		$80.00

After the **Separate Payment Distribution** box is checked, GP will create a transaction that looks like this:

Account	Debit	Credit
Account A (Purch)	$100.00	
Account B (Cash)		$20.00
Account C (Payable)		$80.00
Account D (Payable)	$20.00	

Notice that the full $100 is credited to payables and then the $20 payment is debited to reduce accounts payable to the amount due.

Speeding up lookups with advanced lookups

Dynamics GP provides very robust functionality in lookup windows for finding data like accounts, vendors, customers, items and more. Various fields can be used for sorting or searching and some additional fields are always provided by default. However, if all of that is not enough, Dynamics GP provides an option for administrators to add additional fields to lookups. This recipe demonstrates how to accomplish that.

Getting ready

Before using Advanced Lookups, they need to be set up. Up to four custom lookups can be created for each type in the system. We will do this now:

1. Select **Administration** on the Navigation pane under **Setup** and **Company** heading and select **Advanced Lookups**.

2. On the **Advanced Lookups** window, use the lookup button (magnifying glass) to select **Lookup Name**.

3. For our example, select **Customers**. In the first **Sort By** field, scroll down and select **Zip**.

4. Change the **Description** to Zip Code.

5. Click **Save** to save the lookup and close the window.

These setup steps added a lookup based on zip code to any place where customers are selected in the system:

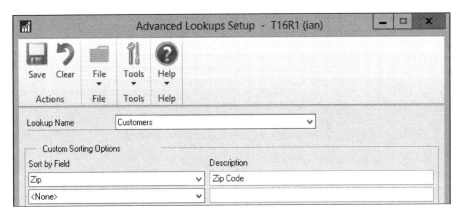

How to do it...

Once an Advanced Lookup has been set up, let's look at how to use it by completing the following steps:

1. Select **Sales** from the Navigation pane on the left. Select **Customer** under **Cards** on the **Sales** area page.

2. In the **Customer ID** field select the lookup button (magnifying glass) and click the arrow next to **Additional Sorts**. A predefined set of lookups is shown at the top of the drop-down box and customer lookups are at the bottom. In the middle is the **Zip Code** lookup created above.

3. Click on **Zip Code** and the zip codes will appear on the right side of the window. The search box at the top also changes to allow searching by selected lookup, in this case, zip code:

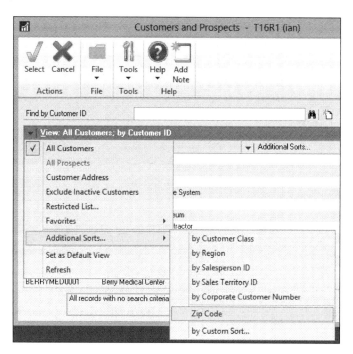

How it works...

Administrators get the chance to set up four extra lookups for each of the lookup options. Lookup options include:

- Accounts
- AddressesCustomersEmployeesItemsOpen
- DocumentsOpen
- Payables
- DocumentsProspectsPurchase
- OrdersSales
- Document
- NumbersSales
- DocumentsVendor
- AddressesVendorsVouchers

This allows users even more opportunities to ensure that they are selecting the right information with a minimum amount of work.

See also

- *Speeding up account entry with Account Alias*
- The *Accessing accounts faster with Favorites in lookups* recipe in *Chapter 1, Personalizing Dynamics GP*

Going straight to the site with web links

Dynamics GP provides a great feature to tie web page links to specific values in Dynamics GP. For example, when a bank account is selected, a link is made available to that bank's website. The link is contextual, meaning that it is tied to the value in the field. In this recipe, we'll look at setting up and using the Custom Link feature.

Getting ready

Before users can benefit from this recipe, an administrator needs to set up the custom links. To set up the links:

1. Select **Administration** from the Navigation pane on the left, then click **Custom Link** under the **Company** heading in the **Setup** pane:

2. Click **New** on the action pane.

3. In the **Prompt** box, select **Checkbook**. In the **Custom Link Label** field, type `Website`.

4. In the **Field Value** box click the lookup button (magnifying glass) and select the **FIRST BANK** checkbook.

5. Type `www.firstbank.com` into the **Internet Address** box as the bank's website then click **Save** to save the record.

Congratulations, that's all there is to setting up a custom link.

How to do it...

Now we'll see how to use Custom Link by completing the following steps:

1. To demonstrate how Custom Link works for users, click **Financial** on the Navigation pane. Select **Bank Deposits** from the **Financial** area page under **Transactions**.

2. In the **Checkbook ID** field, use the lookup button (magnifying glass) to select the checkbook used in the above setup. Once the checkbook shows in the **Checkbook ID** field, click on the **Checkbook ID** label.

3. A field will drop down with two options. One, **Checkbook Maintenance**, leads back to the **Checkbook Maintenance** window. This is the typical behavior if Custom Links have not been set up:

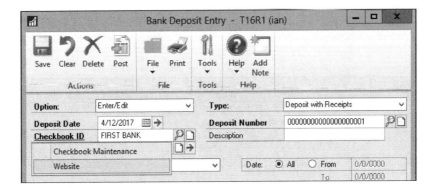

4. Select the second link, **Website**, to open a web browser and go to the website set up in the link.

How it works...

This process associates website links with values in specific fields. This allows contextual drill-through to web pages for more information. Custom Links can be created for checkbooks, credit cards, currency, customers, employees, exchange rates, items, salespeople, tracking numbers, and vendors, providing plenty of options to link to more information on the Internet.

There's more...

A single site can be made available for all of the choices or multiple choices can be applied to a single value.

The All Field Values box

Checking the **All Field Values** box means that the website entered will be used for all values in this field. For example, if a single currency website is used for all currencies, checking the **All Field Values** box points all currency values to that one website. This option is available for prompts named:

- ▸ Checkbook
- ▸ Credit card
- ▸ Currency
- ▸ Exchange rate
- ▸ Tracking number

Multiple values

For Custom Links, the **Prompt** box is the key identifier. There can be multiple prompts for a single value by creating more than one link for a value. For example, a bank might have a website used to check balances and a completely different one for processing ACH transactions. By creating two links, one named `Balances` and one named `ACH`, both links can be available for a single checkbook.

See also

▸ *Developing connections with Internet User Defined fields*

▸ The *Speeding up access to data with Quick Links* recipe in *Chapter 1, Personalizing Dynamics GP*

3

Automating Dynamics GP

In this chapter, we will look at ways to automate Dynamics GP including:

- ▸ Copying security from an existing user
- ▸ Using Reminders to remember important events
- ▸ Controlling reporting dates with beginning and ending periods
- ▸ Speeding up entry by copying an inventory item
- ▸ Automating processes with macros
- ▸ Getting early warnings with business alerts
- ▸ Splitting AP across departments automatically with Control Account Management
- ▸ Speeding up document delivery with e-mail
- ▸ Relating or linking items for suggested sales
- ▸ Automatically posting cash receipt deposits
- ▸ Simplifying statement delivery with print remaining documents

Introduction

Up to this point we've looked at recipes for personalizing Microsoft Dynamics GP for users and ways that administrators can organize GP for smoother operation. In this chapter, we'll take these themes even further and look at recipes to improve efficiency by automating Dynamics GP. Automating and improving the efficiency of tasks allows users and administrators to focus on value-adding items instead of getting bogged down in repetitive processes.

Copying security from an existing user

Creating users and granting them all of the necessary access can be a fairly time-consuming affair, especially if there are a lot of companies. One of the relatively new features in Dynamics GP is the ability to copy security from one user to another which can be massively time saving.

To copy security access from one user to another, perform the following steps:

1. Select **User** from the **System | Setup** section of the **Administration** area page.

2. Select an existing user or create a new one and click the **Copy Settings** button on the action pane; if you are creating a new user, click **Yes** when asked **Do you want to save changes to this user ID?** to open the **Copy User Settings** window:

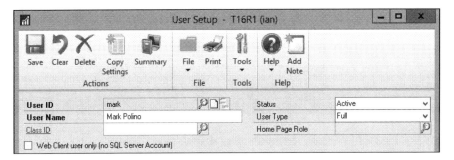

3. In the **Security Access** section, set the **User ID** field to the user from which the security access should be copied from:

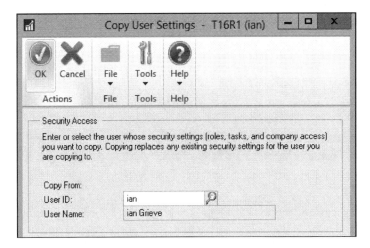

4. The **Home Page** and **Area Pages** configuration can also be copied to the new user from an existing one, which does not need to be the same one as the **Security Access** section is being copied from. To do so, mark the relevant checkbox and enter a user ID in the **Copy From** box:

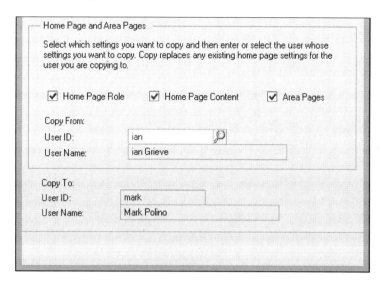

5. Click the **OK** button on the action pane to copy the security access and page configuration. This will also automatically close the **Copy User Settings** window.

Using Reminders to remember important events

It's always nice to be reminded when you're about to forget something important and it's even better to get an automatic reminder triggered by certain events. Well, Microsoft Dynamics GP has prebuilt functionality to remind users when certain thresholds are approaching or met. For example, GP can provide a reminder when invoices are overdue or payables are due.

In this recipe we'll look at how to set up the built-in Reminders.

How to do it...

To set up a reminder follow these steps:

1. Click **Home** on the Navigation pane on the left to open the home page. In the **To Do** section, click **New Reminder**.

2. The **Predefined Reminders** section is at the top and contains a set of commonly used reminders and the ability to set the number of days around which a reminder is given.

3. For our example, check the **Remind Me** box next to **Overdue Invoices** and **Payables Due**. In the **Remind Me** days box, enter 5 next to days after the due date on the **Overdue Invoices** line.

4. Check the **Display as a Cue** box for each of the options selected:

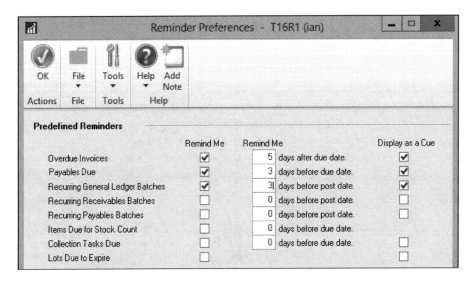

5. On the **Payables Due** line, key in 3 next to days before due date and click **OK**.

6. Reminders are refreshed when the home page is refreshed. Click the two swirling arrows on the top right next to the breadcrumbs to refresh the page.

How it works...

After the prebuilt reminders are set up, a reminder will appear in the **Reminders** section of the home page when an invoice is five days past the due date; this is great for following up after a five day payment grace period.

Similarly, the **Payables Due** option from our example would provide a reminder three days before payment is due.

Prebuilt reminders are available for **Overdue Invoices**, **Payables Due**, **Recurring General Ledger Batches**, **Recurring Receivables Batches**, **Recurring Payables Batches**, **Items Due for Stock Count**, **Collection Tasks Due**, and **Lots due to Expire**.

There's more...

Just getting a reminder is nice, being able to drill down into the reminder is even better.

Drilling down into reminders

Clicking on a reminder opens a window that lists each individual reminder. For the prebuilt reminders, each item gets a line of its own. Therefore, each overdue invoice and each upcoming payable in our example gets its own line and clicking on a line drills back into the actual transaction. The reminder details can be sorted and the **Open** button on the right provides additional drill back options beyond the default drill back from clicking on a line.

For example, for an overdue payable transaction, such as the one for Business Equipment Center, the **Open** button includes a link to select checks where this voucher can be added to a check batch for payment:

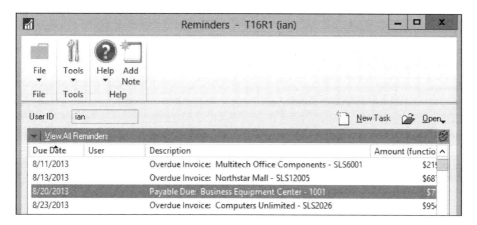

See also

▸ The *Getting warnings with SmartList alerts* recipe in *Chapter 8, Harnessing the Power of SmartLists*

▸ *Getting early warnings with Business Alerts*

Controlling reporting dates with beginning and ending periods

Dynamics GP provides a number of features to improve and simplify reporting. One of the most overlooked features is the ability to automatically control dates when running reports. That functionality is the juicy goodness covered in this recipe.

Dynamics GP contains a large number of built-in reports which were created with the included Report Writer tool. They are often referred to as Report Writer reports to distinguish them from other report types such as SmartLists or SQL Server Reporting Services reports.

Report Writer reports have several common elements, one of which is an option name. A report option is simply a named collection of settings for a particular report. For example, `Historical Aged Trial Balance` is the name of a report. Prior to running it, a user might name an option for that report `072016 North` to indicate that the report settings have been limited to information from July 2016 and the North region.

Since many reports are run at regular intervals, the same option can be reused to avoid recreating the report settings each time. This works fine except for dates as most users set the dates in a report option to a fixed period such as from 1/1/2016 to 1/31/2016. This works until it's necessary to report on February; then users have to manually change the date again. Dynamics GP provides beginning and ending date controls for both fiscal periods and calendar months to eliminate manual adjustment of dates. Let's see how it works.

Getting ready

Beginning and ending date options can greatly simplify reporting. To set up a report option using the beginning and end of previous periods:

1. Select **Sales** from the Navigation pane on the left.
2. Pick **Posting Journals** under the **Reports** section and select **New**.
3. In the **Option** box type `Last Period`.
4. In **Ranges**, select **Posting Date** from the drop-down box.
5. In the **From** date box, use the drop-down selection to pick **Beginning of Previous Period**. Repeat this with the **To** date box and select **End of Previous Period** as shown in the following screenshot:

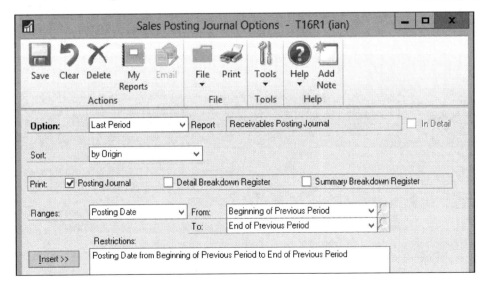

6. Click **Insert** to update the **Range** and pick **Save** at the top to save this report option.

How to do it...

Once these report options are set up, running a report is incredibly simple:

1. Pick **Posting Journals** from the **Report** section of the **Sales** area page.
2. Select the **Last Period** option and click the **Insert** button in the center.
3. Click **Print**:

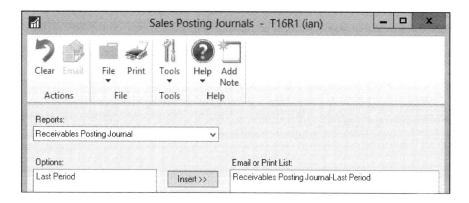

How it works...

Using the beginning and end of previous periods for report dates makes use of the Fiscal Period Setup in Dynamics GP to control report dates. Since much of accounting is backward looking, this provides a fast way to print reports for the last fiscal month right after month-end. Dynamics GP also provides an option to use the beginning and ending dates of the current period for in-period reporting.

There's more...

In addition to Periods, Dynamics GP provides an option to use beginning and end dates for the previous and current month. Since month can mean something different than period, this is often confusing to users.

Fiscal period versus month

In Dynamics GP, a period is a Fiscal period as defined in the Fiscal Period Setup. A month is a calendar month. For companies reporting on a calendar basis, the two are interchangeable. For most companies, using period is the better option because it ties reporting to the company's fiscal period in GP. Even for calendar-based firms, using periods instead of months provides some insurance in case the firm decides to change to a different fiscal calendar later.

Using the beginning and end of previous months are often useful for tax-based reporting. Certain taxes, including sales tax, use tax, and payroll taxes are typically calendar-based. They require calendar year reporting even if a firm reports financial results based on a fiscal year.

Beyond the period

The focus of this recipe has been on using the beginning and ending period or months to simplify repetitive reporting. In addition to period and month reporting, Dynamics GP offers beginning and ending fiscal year and calendar year choices as well.

Not all reports provide the option of beginning and ending dates but whenever these two options can be combined, they create a powerful way to reduce the time and effort spent generating reports.

Speeding up entry by copying an inventory item

When entering master records, it's always a challenge to ensure that records are entered consistently. This is especially true for inventory items since there are a large number of potential settings. Using inventory classes can provide some help but even classes have their limits.

It's also common for a new inventory item to be very similar to an existing inventory item. Vendors often make small but key changes resulting in the need for a new item to allow proper tracking.

Dynamics GP provides a great feature that allows copying an inventory item when creating a new item. That's the focus of this recipe so let's take a look at how to use it.

How to do it...

To copy an inventory item to a new item number, follow these steps:

1. From the Navigation pane select **Inventory**. On the **Inventory** area page click **Item** under **Cards**.

2. The new item number goes in the **Item Number** field. Enter 1-A3261B for our example and click the **Copy** button above.

3. Use the lookup button (magnifying glass) to pick an item to copy from. Select item 1-A3261A if using the Fabrikam sample company. Otherwise any item will do.

4. Notice that there are a number of attributes available to copy to the new item. We'll leave them all checked and click **Copy** to create the new item:

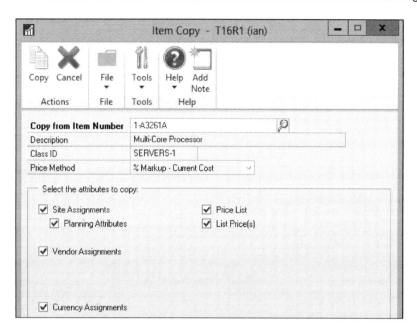

5. When done, there is a new item with the new item number. Changes can still be made. To illustrate this, change **Description** to **New Copied Item** and click **Save**.

How it works...

By using an existing inventory item as a base, Dynamics GP provides a mechanism to copy an inventory item to a new item number. The process is extremely flexible, allowing fine-grained control over which settings are copied and changes after the copy is created.

Users need to remember that they can choose not to copy all of the information from one item to another. For example, users might not want to copy vendor assignment if a different vendor will be used for the copied item. Additionally, users may never want to copy price list information from an original item to a copy. The key is to use the copy feature to get only what is required in the new item.

Automating processes with macros

Macros provide a way to automate processes within Dynamics GP. They are actually very easy to create and use. Macros are perfect for moderately complex but repetitive processes. For example, a cash transfer between bank accounts is a common repetitive task but there is some complexity to it because the amount is usually different. This example provides a great, practical lesson in macros, so we'll look at it in this recipe.

How to do it...

To create a macro for a bank transfer, follow these steps:

1. From the **Microsoft Dynamics GP** menu, select **Tools | Macro | Record...**:

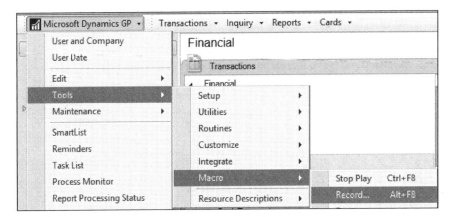

2. Note where the macro is being saved and name the macro Bank Xfer.

3. Select **Financial** on the Navigation pane and pick **Bank Transfers** from the **Financial** area page under **Transactions**. Click **Save**.

4. Tab to the **Description** field and type Bank Transfer.

5. Enter UPTOWN TRUST in the **Checkbook ID** field to transfer from. Leave the amount set to zero (**0**).

6. Enter FIRST BANK in the **CheckBook ID** field to be transferred to:

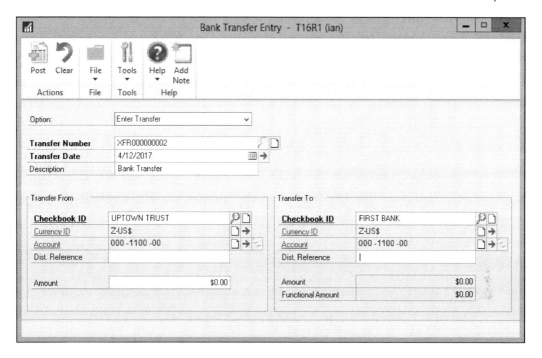

7. From the **Tools** menu select **Macro | Stop Record**. Click **Clear** and close the **Bank Transfer Entry** window.

8. Now, select the **Microsoft Dynamics GP** menu item then pick **Tools | Macro | Play**.

9. Find and select the `Bank Xfer` macro saved earlier and click **Open**.

10. The macro will run. As the macro runs, the **Bank Transfer Entry** window will open and the description, to and from accounts will fill in automatically. The window will then be left open for a user to add the transfer amount. Click **Post** when finished, to complete the transfer.

How it works...

Recording a macro is easy. Macros can be recorded by any user with proper security and because they are stored as a file, they can be shared among users. There are an infinite number of uses for macros. They can be reused or built only for a specific scenario. Learning to create and run macros provides a terrific opportunity to automate any number of functions in Dynamics GP.

There's more...

Macros can be attached to the shortcut bar and run from there. They can also be run with a keystroke combination. Finally, users can insert pauses in macros or string them together into a set of steps.

Macros can be made faster

Macros are very useful, but if you are using them to do a bulk update then they can take a while to run. Fortunately, there is a switch which can be added to the `Dex.ini` file (located by default in `%ProgramFiles(x86)%\Microsoft Dynamics\GP2016\Data`). To add the switch, open the `Dex.ini` file and, under the **[General]** title add the following and save the file:

```
ShowAdvancedMacroMenu=TRUE
```

Once the switch has been added, a new **Advanced** menu is added to the **Macro** menu. To use the additional functionality now available, follow these steps:

1. On the **Microsoft Dynamics GP** menu, click **Tools | Macro | Advanced | Status**.

2. Click the ellipsis button (**...**) and select the required macro.

3. Click the **No User Interface Flash** checkbox:

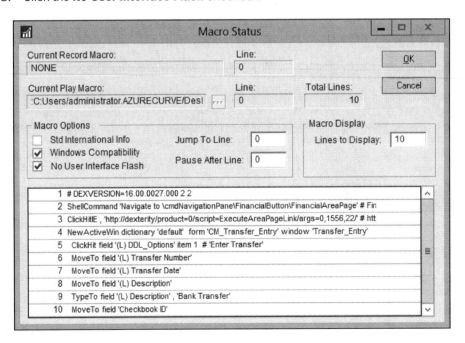

4. Click the **OK** button to run the macro.

You should notice that the macro runs at least twice as fast as the original; if you are using macros to integrate large amounts of data, the performance of the macro should be even better.

Macros and the shortcut bar

Macros can be added to the shortcut bar, making them easy to run with a single click.

Macros can be run with a keystroke combination

Once a macro has been added to the shortcut bar, a keystroke combination can be added, allowing it to be run from the keyboard.

Macro pauses

Pauses can be inserted into macros to allow for data entry in the middle of a macro. To insert a pause, click **Tools | Macro | Insert Pause** while recording a macro. A box will open, allowing the creation of instructions for the user. The problem with pausing macros is that the process to restart a macro is not intuitive. When a user executes a macro, the macro pauses at the selected point and waits for user input. After user input, the user must select **Tools | Macro | Continue** to resume the macro.

That set of steps is not obvious to a user. Also, there is not enough room to reasonably enter instructions and restart steps in the instruction box. Nor is there a keystroke combination to resume a macro after a pause.

Sequential macros

An alternative to pausing macros is to create more than one macro. Create the first macro up to the point where a pause would be inserted. Then create a second macro for the next portion of the process. Add the macros to the shortcut bar in a folder in the order they should be executed. After the first macro finishes, the user simply needs to insert any data required and click the second macro to continue the process.

See also...

> ▶ The *Remembering processes with an ad hoc workflow* recipe in *Chapter 2, Organizing Dynamics GP*

Getting early warnings with Business Alerts

It's always nice to find out about problems early because early notification usually means that there is still time to fix the issue. Dynamics GP provides a great mechanism for early warnings in the form of Business Alerts. Business Alerts allow companies to build criteria for notification and then to get notified via e-mail or within the application. Additionally, a report of information related to the alert can be sent as a part of an e-mail. A wizard-like interface is used to set up alerts but they can get very complex.

For this recipe we'll build a basic business alert with all of the foundational pieces for a more complicated alert. For our sample business alert, we'll assume that a company would like to be notified when their bank balance falls below $10,000 to allow them to transfer cash from another account.

Getting ready

Users must be logged in as sa (the SQL Server system administrator, otherwise known as the head chef) to create business alerts. Log in as sa prior starting this recipe.

How to do it...

Let's look at how to build a business alert:

1. On the Navigation pane, select **Administration**. Pick **Business Alerts** under **Setup** and **System**. If the **System Password** box opens, enter the system password and click **OK**.

2. Leave **Create a New Alert** marked and click **Next** to start an alert.

3. Select a company database. The company database for the sample company in this example is T16R1.

4. Name this alert BANK BAL <10k in the **Business Alert ID** box.

5. In the **Description** field type Bank Bal <10k. Click **Next** to move on.

6. In **Series**, select **Financial**. Find the **CM Checkbook Master** table in the middle window. Highlight it and click **Insert** to add this table. Then click **Next >>** to continue:

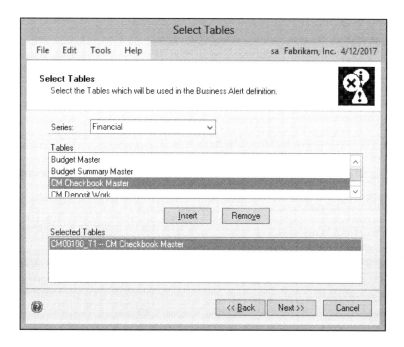

7. After selecting the appropriate tables, it's time to define the alert formula. In the **Define Alert Formula** window, select **CM00100_T1 - CM Checkbook Master** under **Table**. Pick **Current Balance** in the **Column Name** box and click **Add Column**:

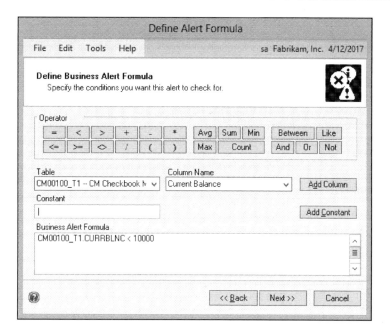

8. Click the less than (**<**) button. Type `10000` in the **Constant** field and click **Add Constant**. Click **Next**.

9. After the alert criteria have been established, it's time to set up the alerts. Click the email selection next to **Send To**. Pick **Message and Report** in the **Send** selection. Enter your email address and click **Insert**. In the **Message Text** area, type `Bank Account Balance is below $10,000` and click **Next**:

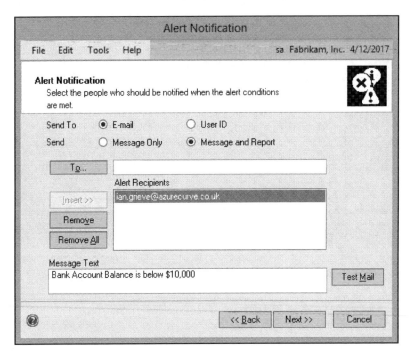

10. Finally, we'll lay out the report to accompany the alert. Select the `CM00100_T1 - CM Checkbook Master` table in **Table**. Scroll down to **Checkbook ID** in **Columns**. Select it and click **Insert**. Scroll down to **Current Balance**. Select it and click **Insert**. Click **Next** to move on:

11. Click **Next** past the **Sorting** options.

12. The **Schedule Alert** window can be used to adjust the timing of alert deliveries. We'll leave the defaults and pick **Finish** to wrap up.

How it works...

This process creates a business alert that checks the bank balance in Dynamics GP every night at midnight and e-mails an alert and detailed report if the balance drops below $10,000. A manager might then get this alert via email on their phone and be prepared to move cash even before they leave for the office in the morning. Business alerts are extremely useful for checking items against a threshold. This includes scenarios such as accounts over budget, checkbook balances below a limit, customers over their credit limit, inventory items at their reorder point, purchase orders awaiting approval, and payments past due. This is just a sample of the scenarios that can be created.

There's more...

A great place to start working with business alerts is with the included prebuilt alerts.

Prebuilt alerts

Microsoft Dynamics GP comes with a prebuilt set of common business alerts, including alerts for many of the scenarios described above and more. Modifying an existing business alert is a great way to learn about the process and move into creating more complex alerts. When creating a business alert, simply select **Modify Existing Alert** instead of **Create New Alert** and walk through the wizard.

There is a *Microsoft Knowledge Base* article which explains how to configure Microsoft SQL Server for use with business alerts which can be found at `http://support.microsoft.com/kb/915097`.

See also

▸ The *Getting warnings with SmartList alerts* recipe in *Chapter 8, Harnessing the Power of SmartLists*

▸ *Using Reminders to remember important events*

Splitting AP across departments automatically with Control Account Management

Control Account Management in Dynamics GP provides a mechanism to report consolidated payables to divisional expenses for divisional reporting.

Often companies say that they want to see each division reported as if it was a standalone business. Though all divisions may be part of a single legal entity, companies frequently need to evaluate divisional performance by treating each division as a separate business. Frequently, balance sheet accounts such as fixed assets and accounts payable are included to provide a measure of the capital required to run each division.

Control Account Management is designed to deliver the cost and management efficiency of centralized payables, while providing payables reporting at a divisional level.

In Control Account Management, payables are processed centrally. At month-end, a routine is run to allocate open payables from the payables GL account to divisional payable accounts. The allocation is based on a segment of the chart of accounts that corresponds to the company's divisions. An automatically created reversing entry is processed to repopulate central accounts payable and allow the normal payables process to continue. In this recipe, we'll see how to make it all work seamlessly.

Getting ready

Before using Control Account Management, the divisional payable accounts need to be associated with the appropriate general ledger segment. For our example, we'll be using the sample company:

1. Select **Financial** on the Navigation pane. Under the **Setup** heading pick **Control Account Management**.

2. In **Account Segment**, select **Segment 3** to represent the departments. Check the **Activate Control Account Management** at the top. Click **Account Types** to continue.

3. Set **Account Type** to **Payables**. Set the **Batch ID** option to AP CONTROL, and set both **Batch Comment** and **Reference** to Control Account.

4. Next to each **Segment ID**, lookup or enter the corresponding divisional payable account and click **Save** when finished. For the sample company, use the control accounts shown in the screenshot. Click **Save** when done:

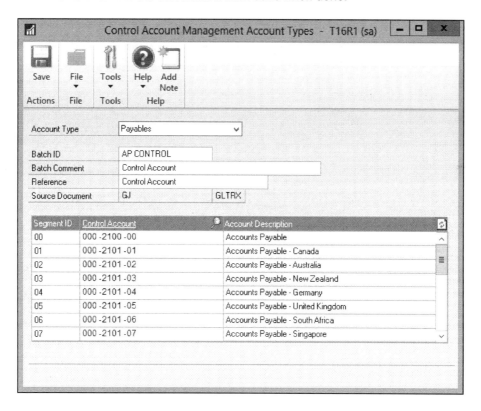

How to do it...

Once the divisional AP accounts have been mapped, it's time to see how this process works each month:

1. Select **Financial** from the Navigation pane on the left. Pick **Control Account Management** under **Transactions**.

2. Click **Report** to load the payables distribution data. Review the payables distributions at the bottom of the window:

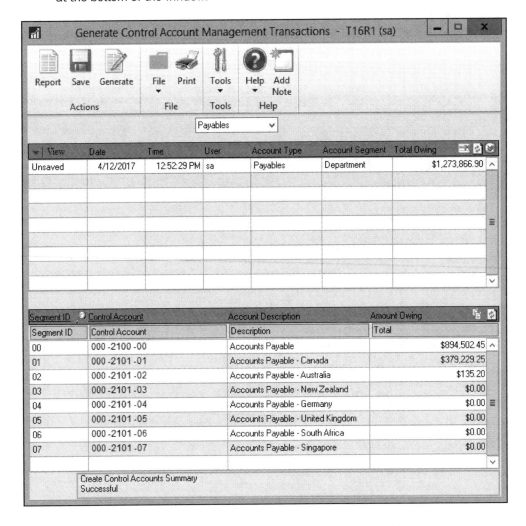

3. Select the double arrow in the top right of the first scrolling window to see more information.

4. From this screen, the batch and date information can be changed. Click the **Doc Info** and **Dist Info** tabs to see more information about how the payables will be distributed:

5. Click **Generate** to create the unposted GL transaction and associated reversing transaction.

How it works...

The month-end routine examines open accounts payable transactions and sums the open amounts by the divisional segment of the purchase. GP then uses this information to calculate the outstanding percentage for each division. From there, a reversing transaction is created to move the accounts payable balance out to the divisional payable accounts.

By providing a GL segment to identify the division and then mapping it to a corresponding payables account, GP provides a best of both worlds solution. This allows centralized AP management with decentralized reporting at month, quarter, and year-end.

The fact that the process resets automatically at the start of the next month makes this a first class solution to an otherwise difficult process.

There's more...

This process is so exciting that many people want to see if it will meet similar needs for multi-company scenarios.

Multi-company

When people see this process for the first time, it often registers as a potential solution to related multi-company issues. This process will work for splitting centralized AP across multiple companies, if the companies are all stored in a single GP company with an identifying GL segment. If the companies are split across multiple GP databases, this process will not work because it can't post across company databases.

See also

▶ The *Improving financial reporting clarity by splitting purchasing accounts* recipe in Chapter 2, *Organizing Dynamics GP*

Speeding document delivery with e-mail

Dynamics GP 2010 added the ability to directly e-mail documents either individually or in bulk with the feature being improved further with almost every version. This feature provides a number of options for e-mailing:

▶ Sales Quotes, Orders, Fulfillment Orders, Invoices, Returns, Back Orders, and Packing Slips

▶ Receivables Invoices, Returns, Debit Memos, Credit Memos, Finance Charges, Warranties, Service/Repair documents, and Customer Statements

▶ Standard Purchase Order, Blanket Purchase Order, Drop Ship Purchase Orders, and Drop Ship Blanket Purchase Orders

▶ Vendor Remittances

Documents can be emailed in HTML, DOCX, XPS, or PDF formats (Adobe Acrobat is not required). E-mailing HTML and DOCX formatted attachments does NOT require that Word 2012 or higher be installed on the client computer. Emailing documents in XPS and PDF formats does require Word 2013 or higher on the client but Adobe Acrobat is not necessary.

By default, Dynamics GP is configured to integrate with Microsoft Exchange (the user needs to log onto Exchange each time an e-mail action is performed), but this can be toggled back to MAPI for integration with a 32-bit Microsoft Outlook client.

Only DOCX and HTML document formats are supported in the Dynamics GP web client.

In this recipe, we will look at e-mailing documents individually or in bulk along with some set up items using the sample company.

Getting ready

Before we start, we need to add an e-mail address to a few customers to demonstrate how this feature works.

To add e-mail addresses, follow these steps:

1. Select **Sales** from the Navigation pane. On the **Sales Area** page, click **Customer** under **Cards**.

2. Use the lookup button (magnifying glass) to select customer CENTRALC0001. Click the globe icon next to the **Address ID** field.

3. Enter your e-mail address in the **To** field and click **Save**. Close the window:

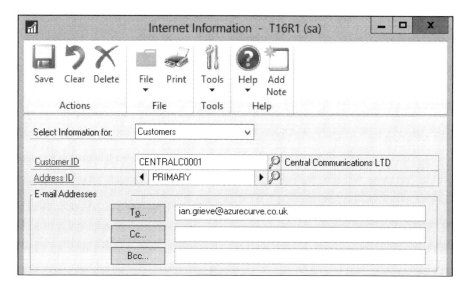

4. In the **Customer Maintenance** window, click **Save** and close the window.

5. Repeat this process with customers AARONFIT0001 and ASTORSUI001.

How to do it...

Now that some customers have email addresses, we will look at how to e-mail invoices to them. To e-mail individual invoices, follow these steps:

1. Select **Sales** from the Navigation pane. Click on **Sales Transaction Entry** under **Transactions** on the **Sales** area page.

2. Set the **Type** to **Invoice**. Use the lookup button (magnifying glass) to select invoice STDINV2262.

3. Click the e-mail icon in the upper-right under the company name. Dynamics GP will indicate that an e-mail has been sent:

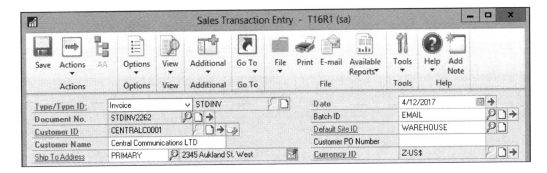

To e-mail multiple invoices at once, follow these steps:

1. Select **Sales** from the Navigation pane. Click on the **Sales Transaction Entry Navigation** list at the top of the Navigation pane.

2. In the Navigation list, click the **Document Number** header twice to sort by document number in descending order.

3. Check the boxes next to invoices **STDINV2259**, **STDINV2260**, **STDINV2261**, and **STDINV2262**:

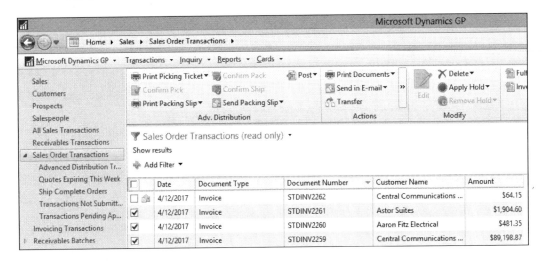

4. Click **Send** in E-mail on the Navigation menu and then click **Send**.

5. Dynamics GP will e-mail the selected invoices.

How it works...

Emailing documents is a fantastic way to speed up communication with customers and vendors. Dynamics GP 2010 provides fast, easy, and flexible ways to e-mail documents.

There's more...

Dynamics GP provides a number of setup options to control the e-mailing of documents.

Customer and vendor setup

When we configured the e-mail account on the customer record earlier, it defined a single address for all document types. Dynamics GP allows for different document types to be e-mailed to different e-mail addresses:

1. Select **Sales** from the Navigation pane. On the **Sales** area page, click **Customer** under **Cards**.

2. Use the lookup button (magnifying glass) to select customer CENTRALC0001.

3. Click the blue **Bill To** hyperlink to open the **Customer Address Maintenance** window for the bill to address and then click the globe icon next to the **Address ID** field.

4. Enter your e-mail address in the **To** field and click **Save**. Close the window.

5. Click the **Email** button in the bottom right corner of the window (or the **Email** tab at the top of the window if you're using the web client).

6. In the e-mail address based on **Doc Type**, click on the **Enable** radio button and then on the ellipsis (**...**) button next to **Sales Invoice**:

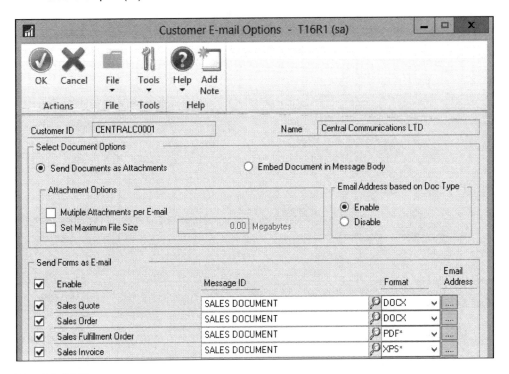

7. Mark the checkbox next to the **Billing Address** code; as we want to send returns and statement documents to the same e-mail as the invoice, mark the **Sales Return** and **Customer Statement** checkboxes at the bottom of the window:

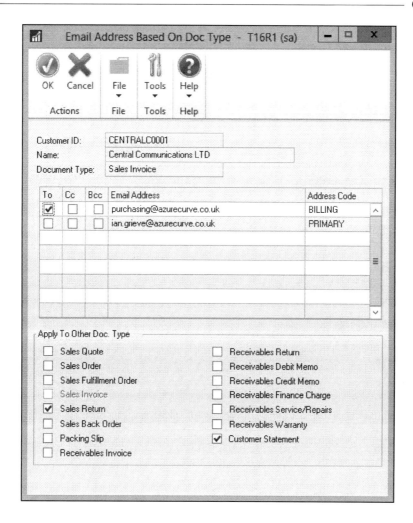

8. Repeat Step 6 and Step 7 for the other document types which are to be e-mailed and then click **OK** and close the e-mail window.

Company setup

1. The setup of e-mails is controlled primarily by the **Company E-Mail Setup** window. It is reached by selecting **Administration** from the Navigation pane and then clicking on **E-mail Setup** under **Setup and Company**.

2. The **Company E-Mail Setup** window controls whether or not documents are embedded in the e-mail body and then formats the attachments:

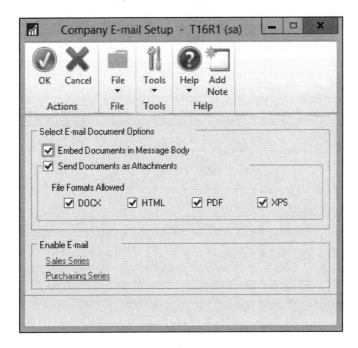

3. Selecting either **Sales Series** or **Purchasing Series** under **Enable E-Mail** opens the related **E-Mail Setup** window allowing a user to set the **Message ID** field which controls the message included in the e-mail. This window also allows a company to set a central return address for these e-mails:

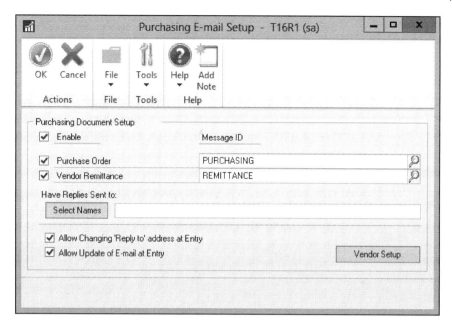

4. Finally, the content in a **Message ID** field is set up by selecting **Administration** from the Navigation pane and then clicking on **E-mail Setup** under **Setup and Company**.

Relating or linking items for suggested sales

Dynamics GP 2013 brought the ability to relate, or link, items together in order to allow for up- or cross-selling within Sales Order Processing. This functionality can also be of benefit for linking together items which are required for the initially entered item to work.

Getting ready

1. In Dynamics GP, select **Inventory** from the Navigation pane. On the **Inventory** area page select **Item** in the **Cards** area. This will open **Item Maintenance**.

2. Enter, or use a lookup and select **Item Number 2-A3284A** to enter the suggested items.

3. Click the **Suggest Items** button to open the **Suggest Sales Item Maintenance** window.

4. Mark the checkboxes in the **Document Type** section to enable the suggested items for **Quotes**, **Orders**, **Invoices**, and **Fulfillment Orders** as required.

5. In the scrolling window, enter **Item Number** and **Suggested Quantity** for each item which is to be suggested when **Sales Transaction** is entered.

6. You can also enter an optional **Sales Script** as a prompt for the user when they are talking to the customer.

7. In this example, three items have been entered, each with **Suggested Quantity** of 1 and **Description** as 256 SDRAM, 24X IDE, and 4-A3539A:

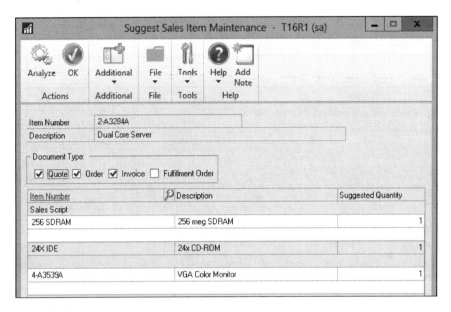

How to do it...

Let's now look at how the related or linked items are used on **Sales Transactions** for suggesting items for sale:

1. Open the **Sales Transaction Entry** window in Dynamics GP by selecting **Sales** from the Navigation pane and clicking on **Sales Transaction Entry** in the **Transactions** section.

2. Select **Type/Type ID** of **Order** and **STDORD**.

3. Enter **Customer ID** AARONFIT0001.

4. Click on the **Currency ID** field to default in Z-US$.

5. In the scrolling window, enter **Item Number** 2-A3284A.

6. Enter 1 in the **Quantity Ordered** field.

7. Select **Override Shortage** and click **OK**.

8. Enter **Serial Number** 000052 in **Sales Serial Number Entry** when it pops up.

9. Click **OK** to close **Sales Serial Number Entry**.

10. Tab through the remaining fields and enter the credit limit override password and click **OK**.

11. Suggest **Sales Item Entry** will pop up showing the available suggested items.

12. Check the box next to `256 SDRAM` and `24X IDE` and accept **Suggested Quantity** of `1`:

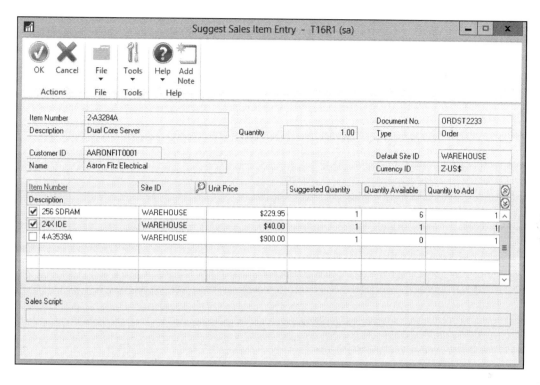

13. Click **OK** to accept these suggested items.

14. The selected **Suggested Items** will be added to **Sales Transaction** for processing as standard transaction lines.

See also

▶ The *Tracking serial and lot numbers on drop ship POs* recipe in *Chapter 4, Leveraging New and Updated Features in Dynamics GP*

▶ The *Gaining flexibility with Inventory Tolerance Handling* in *Chapter 5, Exposing Hidden Features in Dynamics GP*

▶ The *Preventing sales of discontinued inventory* recipe in *Chapter 7, Preventing Errors in Dynamics GP*

▶ The *Select multiple serial or lot numbers* recipe in *Chapter 4, Leveraging New and Updated Features in Dynamics GP*

Automatically post cash receipt deposits

This is a feature which was introduced in Dynamics GP 2015 R2 and can greatly improve the speed of processing cash receipts. For users of Analytical Accounting, this feature may sound familiar as it used to be part of this module, but was made available in the core dictionary, expanding the option to companies not using Analytical Accounting.

To select the option, mark the **Automatically post cash receipt deposits** checkbox in the **Company Setup Options** window found via **Administration | Setup | Company | Options**:

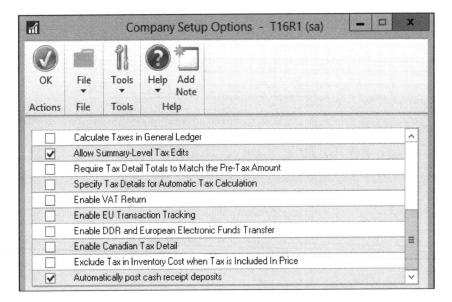

When this option is marked, cash receipts entered in **Cash Receipt Entry**, **Receivables Transaction Entry**, **Sales Transaction Entry**, and **Invoice Entry** will be deposited automatically in the checkbook, updating the checkbook balance.

Simplifying statement delivery with print remaining documents

In past versions of GP, users could either print or email statements requiring users to run the statement generation process separately for each type. Even worse, printing statements to paper wouldn't automatically exclude statements that had already been e-mailed.

The new **Print Remaining Documents – Statements** feature was added to allow a user to e-mail and print customer statements at the same time without duplication:

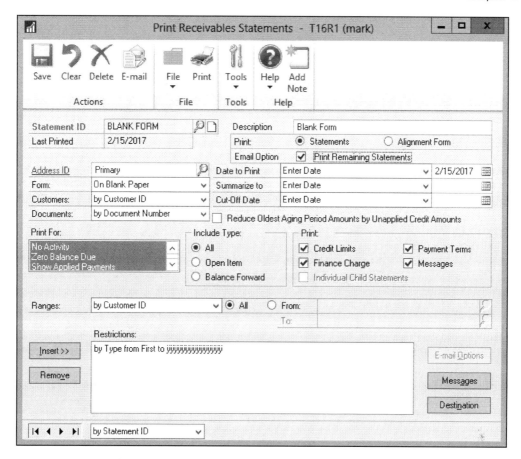

How to do it...

To set up **Print Remaining Statements** follow these steps:

1. Ensure that statements can already be printed and emailed in GP. Refer to GP help for statement and e-mail setup if necessary.

2. In Dynamics GP select **Sales | Routines | Statements**.

3. Lookup the **Statement ID** field and select a statement form.

4. In the **Form** field, select **On Blank Paper**. This is required and will activate the **Email Option: Print Remaining Statements** field.

5. Check the box marked **Print Remaining Statements** next to the **Email** field.

6. Finish any statement setting changes or restrictions for this statement run.

7. Select **Print**.

8. Statements will be e-mailed to companies that have been set up for e-mail statements and the remaining statements will print.

How it works...

Statement printing and delivery had been stuck without much in the way of updates for the last several versions. Statements are an important part of cash collection. This new functionality removes inefficiencies in the old process, helps eliminate duplicate paper and e-mail statements, and makes emailing statements more consistent.

4
Leveraging New and Updated Features in Dynamics GP

In this chaper, we take a look at leveraging some of the new and updated features in Dynamics GP. We will look at how to do the following:

- ▶ Taking the company offline for maintenance
- ▶ Copying and pasting journals from Excel
- ▶ Budget Import Exception Reporting
- ▶ Enhanced GL Year-End Closing
- ▶ Fixing cross-company mistakes by voiding intercompany transactions
- ▶ Improving cross-company visibility with Intercompany Journal Inquiry
- ▶ EFT Format Enhancements
- ▶ Expanding payment options with credit card payment runs
- ▶ Merging records with Customer Combiner and Modifier
- ▶ Modifying sales order ship to address
- ▶ Getting a complete view with the All-In-One Document View
- ▶ Tracking serial and lot numbers on Drop Ship POs
- ▶ Selecting multiple serial or lot numbers
- ▶ Transferring intercompany assets

- ▸ Historical depreciation report
- ▸ Fixed Asset Batches
- ▸ Improving year-end with the Fixed Asset Year End Closing Report
- ▸ Purchase requisitions
- ▸ Gaining efficiency by printing or e-mailing any report with Word templates
- ▸ Attaching documents to records

Introduction

This chapter explores recipes covering the new functionality introduced in Microsoft Dynamics GP 2013 and later versions, and assumes some familiarity with the base functionality where it has been extended.

In almost all cases, the recipes and new features in this chapter do not require an administrator and are available to the average user.

Take the company offline for maintenance

As of Dynamics GP 2013 R2, it is possible to easily take a company offline for maintenance; this will prevent users from logging in and potentially interfering with a maintenance task. A message can be configured to be for sent to users if they try to access the offline company.

How to do it...

To disable a database, follow these steps:

1. Open **Take Company Offline for Maintenance** under **Utilities** on the **Administration** area page.
2. Select the company to be taken offline in the **Online Companies** list and click the **Insert** button.

3. To set a custom message, click the **Custom** radio button and enter the message in the text field below:

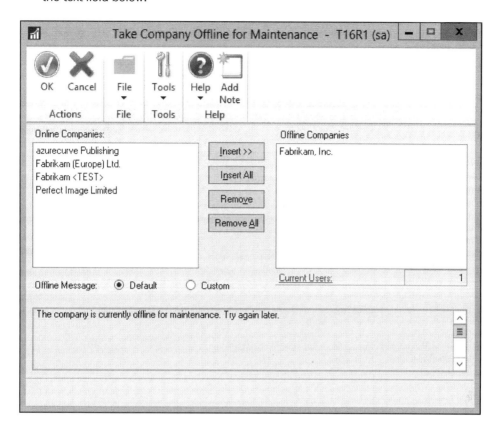

4. Click **OK**.

5. If there are users logged in you will be prompted to decide if a message should be sent to them. Click **Yes** to send a message.

6. In the list of users, unmark those who should not receive the message.

7. In the **Send message as** section, select if the message should be sent as a **Notification Message** or **Task with Reminder**.

8. Enter the message in the **Message** field.

9. Click **Send**.

How it works...

Once a database has been disabled, users who are in that company already can continue working, but users who try to log in or change company will see the company listed for selection with ***Offline*** next to the company name:

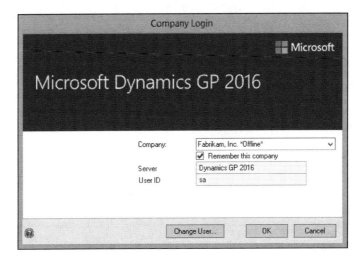

If a user tries to select the company and click **OK**, they will receive a message stating that the company is offline and that they should try again later.

The disabled company can still be accessed by a user with the POWERUSER role as normal so there is no possibility, if you only have one company, of preventing the company being brought back online.

To enable a company, simply select the company in the **Offline Companies** list and click **Remove**.

There's more...

If it's necessary to allow a non-POWERUSER user to access companies when they are offline, this can be configured in **Company Setup**:

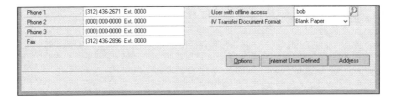

Copying and pasting journals from Excel

For many users of Microsoft Dynamics GP, there is only one way to get journals into Dynamics GP and that is to manually key them in. For those users with a license for Integration Manager Financials, they can also import them from a spreadsheet or another source file.

Dynamics GP 2013 R2 introduced a new button on the action pane of the General Ledger **Transaction Entry** window that allows data to be copied and pasted from an Excel spreadsheet, or other tab delimited data source.

Getting ready

The data for pasting into Dynamics GP must be in a specific format, as shown in the following image:

	A	B	C	D
1	Distribution Reference	Account	Debit	Credit
2	Correct posting to 000-8510-00	000-8410-00	1250	
3	Correct posting to 000-8410-00	000-8510-00		1250

The four columns can be labeled in any way but must be the order of **Distribution Reference**, **Account**, **Debit Amount**, and **Credit Amount**.

The dataset can contain as many rows as necessary, but for very large datasets a tool such as Integration Manager is still the recommended manner of getting the data into Dynamics GP.

How to do it...

To copy and paste the data from Excel to the General Ledger **Transaction Entry** window, follow these steps:

1. Open the **Transaction Entry** window in Dynamics GP by selecting **Financial** from the Navigation pane and then on the **Transactions** menu, click on **General**.

2. Configure the journal header as normal and select the dataset in Excel, not including any header rows, and click **Copy** on the Excel Action pane:

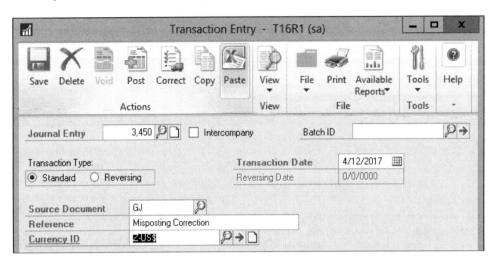

3. In **Transaction Entry**, click the **Paste** button to load the lines into the scrolling window.

There's more...

If the dataset being pasted has errors, such as non-existent accounts being present, a validation report will be generated, showing exactly which lines have an error along with a descriptive error message:

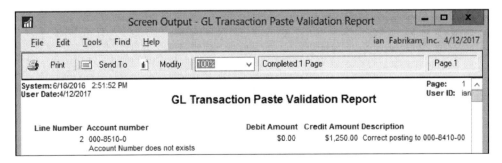

Budget Import Exception reporting

The best way of creating budgets in Microsoft Dynamics GP is to use the Budget Wizard for Excel. However, it had a large limitation in that, when a budget was imported, there was no way of knowing if there are any issues.

For example, if an account that did not exist was on the spreadsheet, the account just did not load, so the user would have problems reconciling the data in Dynamics GP with that of the source file; or, if an account was included multiple times, only the last instance of the account would be loaded.

As of Dynamics GP 2016, there is now a Budget Import Exception Report that will highlight import errors.

Getting ready

This recipe assumes that you have a budget file ready for import that has both duplicate accounts and accounts that do not exist in Dynamics GP.

How to do it...

To import a budget and see the import exception report, follow these steps:

1. Open the **Budget Selection** window in Dynamics GP from the **Cards** menu on the **Financial** area page and click on **Budget**.
2. Click **Excel** and then **Import from Excel**.
3. Click **Next** on the **Welcome** step of the **Budget** wizard for Excel.
4. Leave the selected option set to **A new Microsoft Dynamics GP budget** and click **Next**.
5. Complete the information on the **New Budget Information** step and click **Next**.
6. Click **Browse** and select the Excel file containing the budget and click **Next**.
7. Click **Finish** to perform the budget import.

8. After the import has run, a **Report Destination** window will be displayed should any errors be present. Select **Screen** and click **OK**:

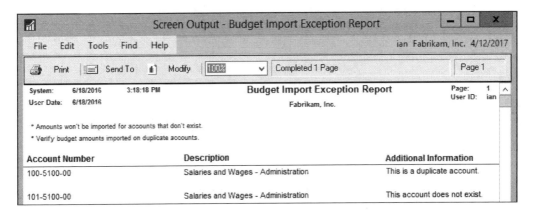

The report will list all of the errors found along with the error message in the **Additional Information** column.

Enhanced GL Year-End Closing

Year-End Close on the General Ledger is the only routine that must be performed at a year-end. This process performs several actions, such as resetting the Year To Date figures, rolling the balances of Balance Sheet accounts forward to the new year, as well as closing off the Profit and Loss accounts to Retained Earnings Account.

Dynamics GP 2013 has seen an enhancement to the **Year-End Close** window that allows inactive accounts to be maintained on the system rather than automatically deleted.

The final, and much appreciated, addition of a progress bar showing how far the year-end close has progressed serves to reassure the user that the process has not hung or crashed, which has been a regular concern due to the critical nature of the process.

How to do it...

To use the enhanced Year-End Close routine, follow these steps:

1. Open **Financial** from the Navigation pane on the left. In the center area page under **Routines**, select **Year-End Closing**.

2. To keep inactive accounts on the system, mark the **Maintain Inactive Accounts** checkbox.

3. You can either retain all inactive accounts by selecting the **All Inactive Accounts** radio button, or only those with budget amounts for the next financial year by clicking on **With Budget Amounts**:

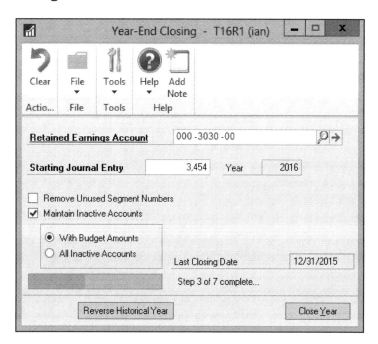

4. After clicking **Close Year**, a green progress bar will be displayed along with text to show the step, which progresses from step one to seven.

How it works...

Leaving **Maintain Inactive Accounts** unmarked will mean that the **Year-End Closing** routines will work as they always have and remove all inactive accounts from the system. Once the checkbox is marked, the selected **Inactive** accounts will be retained on the system rather than deleted.

There's more...

Closing the year now offers even more options.

Unit Account

In Dynamics GP 2010 and before, the balance of Unit Account continued to increase through year-end. A further enhancement to the **Year-End Closing** routine in Dynamics GP 2013 is the ability to that Unit Account balance.

This is done by marking the **Clear Balance During Year-End Close** checkbox in the **Unit Account Maintenance** window.

To mark this checkbox, open **Financial** from the Navigation pane on the left and in the center area page, under **Cards**, select **Unit Accounts** and mark **Clear Balance During Year-End Close**:

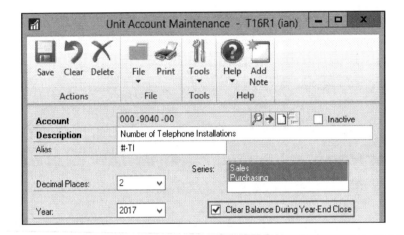

Reversing Year-End Close

Dynamics GP 2013 also saw the introduction of the ability to reverse a Year-End Closing routine. This is a function that should be handled with the utmost caution as a Year-End Close will have been done for a reason.

The reverse of the Year-End Close is performed in the **Year-End Closing** window, by clicking the **Reverse Historical Year** button:

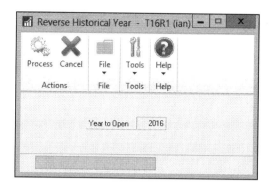

In the **Reverse Historical Year** window that opens, click **Process** to reverse the last closed year. Click **Continue** on the warning that a backup should be made before proceeding (on a live system, do make sure a backup has been made).

The year to open in the middle of the window will change back one year; this is the only sign that reversing the year has finished, so be careful not to click **Process** again.

After reversing a Year-End Close routine, a reconcile should be performed.

Fix cross-company mistakes by voiding intercompany transactions

Previously in Dynamics GP, voiding an intercompany transaction only voided the initiating side of the transaction. For example, if company A pays the bills for company B, company A could enter a payables voucher and assign the costs to expenses in company B. Dynamics GP would process an intercompany transaction and generate a journal entry with the expense on company B's ledger. If company A made a mistake and chose to void that transaction, a manual correction on company B's books was required.

With Dynamics GP 2016, this is no longer the case. Voiding the original transaction now generates an intercompany transaction to offset or void the original. This only works on the originating company. In our preceding example, only company A could void the transaction.

Getting ready

To void an intercompany payables transaction, the transaction must be open. If the voucher has been paid, the payment needs to be voided via **Void Historical Transactions**:

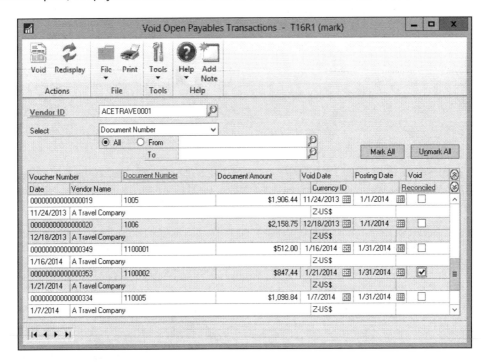

How to do it...

To void an open intercompany payables transaction, follow these steps:

1. Select **Purchasing | Transactions | Void Open Transactions**.

2. Look up or enter the vendor ID.

3. Check the box in the **Void** column next to the appropriate intercompany payables transaction.

4. If necessary, change the date in the **Void Date** and/or **Posting Date** columns to reflect the appropriate void and posting dates.

5. Click the **Void** button.

The transaction will be voided in the originating company and a reversing entry will be created in the destination company.

See also

This process does not work for entries that originate in the General Ledger since there is no option to void a posted journal entry. For posted General Ledger entries, there is a feature to back out posted journal entries. This is covered in the *Correcting errors by backing out, correcting, and copying journal entries* recipe in *Chapter 7, Preventing Errors in Dynamics GP*.

Improving cross-company visibility with Intercompany Journal inquiries

One of the improvements to the intercompany functionality in Dynamics GP is the ability to view the intercompany distributions of a journal entry from another company.

Having the **Intercompany Journal Entry Inquiry** window eliminates the need for users to switch between companies to view all originating-company and destination-company distributions of an intercompany journal entry. All distributions can be viewed from one company:

How to do it...

To view details for an intercompany journal entry, follow these steps:

1. Select **Financial | Inquiry | Journal Entry**.
2. Look up or enter the **Journal Entry** number for an intercompany transaction.
3. The window displays the portion of the transaction applicable to the current company.
4. Click the **Intercompany** button on the bottom left to see details of the intercompany transaction for the other companies.

How it works...

If the intercompany entry is viewed in the originating company, the window behind the **Intercompany** button will show the entry on the destination company. If the entry is viewed from a destination company, the **Intercompany Journal Entry** window displays the originating company's side of the transaction.

EFT Format Enhancements

The EFT for Payables Management and EFT for Receivables Management has been enhanced in Dynamics GP 2013 to provide additional functionality for setting a Settlement Date on the EFT output.

Getting ready

This recipe assumes that EFT is already configured in Dynamics GP and that the user making changes is familiar with the maintenance process.

How to do it...

To improve the visibility of required fields, follow these steps:

1. Open the **EFT File Format Maintenance** window in Dynamics GP by selecting **Financial** from the **Cards** menu on the **Financial** area page and clicking on **EFT File Format**.

2. An EFT file can be composed of multiple lines. To add a settlement date to a particular line, select the line in the header, and then, in the **Maps To** column of the scrolling window, select **Settlement Date**:

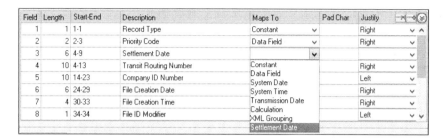

Field	Length	Start-End	Description	Maps To	Pad Char	Justify	
1	1	1-1	Record Type	Constant		Right	
2	2	2-3	Priority Code	Data Field		Right	
3	6	4-9	Settlement Date				
4	10	4-13	Transit Routing Number	Constant		Right	
5	10	14-23	Company ID Number	Data Field		Left	
6	6	24-29	File Creation Date	System Date		Right	
7	4	30-33	File Creation Time	System Time		Right	
8	1	34-34	File ID Modifier	Transmission Date		Left	
				Calculation			
				XML Grouping			
				Settlement Date			

3. Save the EFT file format.

4. Perform the standard payment run process, and, in the **Generate EFT File** step, you can set **Settlement Date**, different from **Transmission Date**, which is output on the EFT file in the field specified in the template:

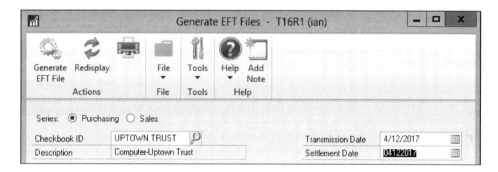

There's more...

In Dynamics GP 2013, EFT File Format Maintenance has been enhanced further to allow file types other than fixed format text files to be produced.

In the **EFT File Format Maintenance** window, a field delimiter can now be specified in the **Delimit Fields** section of the window.

Field delimiters can be set to the standard ones of comma, space, and tab with an option for a user-specified **Other**. **Text Qualifier** can also be defined, which can allow commas to be used in files that are comma delimited:

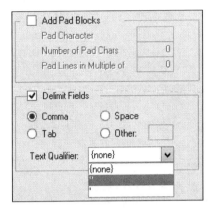

Expanding payment options with credit card payment runs

In Dynamics GP, most firms process payables with a check run that pays a batch of checks. Before GP 2016 it wasn't possible to pay multiple invoices with a credit card. A payment run could only use checks or EFT. With Dynamics GP 2016, it's now possible to do a credit card run. This doesn't actually send a credit card payment to a vendor, but records that these vouchers were all paid via credit card.

Getting ready

This recipe assumes that at least one credit card or bank card has been created in Dynamics GP. A credit card is tied to a vendor and payment is ultimately made to that vendor. A bank card is tied to a bank account and payments made using the card reduce the balance in the bank account.

Users should also be successfully generating other types of payment via batches such as checks or EFTs to ensure that the payables setup is complete:

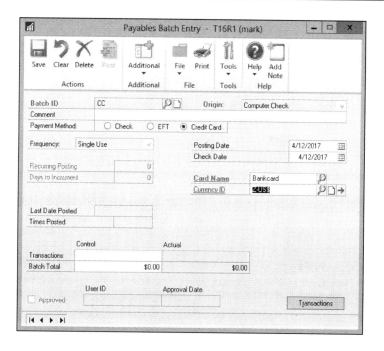

How to do it...

To create a credit card based payment run, follow these steps:

1. Under **Purchasing | Transactions**, click on **Select Checks**.
2. Enter a new batch name in **Batch ID** and press *Tab*.
3. Click **Add** to create a new batch.
4. In **Payment Method** select **Credit Card**.
5. The required field **Checkbook Name** will change to **Card Name**.
6. Enter or select the card being used for payment.
7. Click **Save** and close the batch window.
8. Select vouchers to pay as you normally would and click **Print Checks**.
   Check printing will be skipped. You will have the chance to print a remittance to indicate which vouchers were paid via credit card. You can post once these steps have been completed.

How it works...

This process is actually closer to the EFT process since no checks are created, but, unlike EFT, no file is created either. The credit card payment process is designed to clear vouchers that have already been paid via credit card.

Merging records with Customer Combiner and Modifier

In previous versions of Dynamics GP, Customer Combiner and Modifier was included in the Professional Services Tools Library as two separate tools. Dynamics GP 2013 R2 saw this tool moved to Sales and improved.

Customer Combiner and Modifier can both change customer numbers and also merge two customer records together. For example, if a duplicate customer record has been created for a returning customer, instead of the existing customer being reused, or two customers merging, Customer Combiner can be used to combine these records together into one without losing any history.

How to do it...

To combine Pacific Digital into Aaron Fitz Electrical using Customer Combiner and Modifier, follow these steps:

1. Select **Sales | Utilities | Customer Combiner and Modifier**:

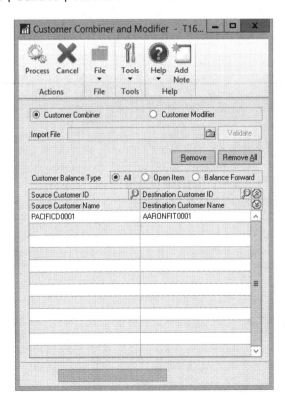

2. In **Source Customer ID**, enter PACIFICD0001.

3. In **Destination Customer ID**, enter AARONFIT0001.

4. Click **Process**.

Customer Combiner and Modifier removes customer numbers and recalculates the Summary records to include both customers' records so Pacific Digital will be merged into Aaron Fitz Electrical with no loss of information, leaving the combined transaction information in the system under the Aaron Fitz Electrical customer number.

There's more...

We've shown how Customer Combiner and Modifier can be used to combine two records together, but it can also be used to change a customer number. Not only can you do these one-by-one, but an import from spreadsheet is also available.

Modifying a customer number

In the main part of this recipe, we showed how to two customer records could be merged by combining PACIFICD0001 and AARONFIT0001, which leaves the customer number as AARONFIT0001, but this might not reflect the name of the new customer.

If Pacific Digital and Arron Fitz Electrical is merged, the resulting company may be named Fitz Digital, meaning the naming convention may require the new customer number to be FITZDIGI001.

To change the customer number, follow these steps:

1. Select **Sales | Utilities | Customer Combiner and Modifier**:

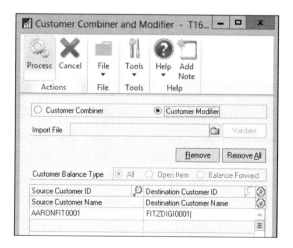

2. At the top, mark the **Customer Modifier** radio button.

3. In **Source Customer ID**, enter AARONFIT0001.

4. In **Destination Customer ID**, enter FITZDIGI0001.

5. Click **Process**.

Customer Combiner and Modifier changes the customer number in all tables so the new customer can be used without issue throughout Dynamics GP.

Import from spreadsheet

As well as being able to combine customer numbers individually, they can also be done en masse by importing from a spreadsheet. To do this, follow these steps:

1. Set up a spreadsheet with two columns, the first containing **Starting Customer Number** and the second containing **Combined Into Customer Number**.

2. Save the spreadsheet as a Tab delimited text file.

3. Open **Customer Combiner and Modifier** from the **Sales** area page under **Utilities**.

4. Click **Next**.

5. Click **Validate** and browse to and select the Tab delimited text file.

6. When prompted, select a destination for the **TA Invalid Customers** report.

7. If there are errors, address them in the file and revalidate, or click **Import**, browse to the file, and click **OK** to process the import.

Each row of the spreadsheet will be processed and the customers combined; any errors will be reported at the end.

Other Combiner functions

Combiner and Modifier functions also exist for vendors within the Purchasing series.

Modifying Sales Order Ship To Address

Sales Order Processing has been enhanced to allow Ship To Addresses to be individually named and to allow one of the customer phone numbers to be selected.

Getting ready

To use this recipe, users need basic familiarity with Sales Order Processing and maintaining customers.

How to do it...

To set a Ship To **Address Name**, follow these steps:

1. Open the **Customer Address Maintenance** window in Dynamics GP by selecting **Sales** from the Navigation pane and clicking on **Addresses** on the **Cards** menu.

2. Enter, or do a lookup and select the customer ID from the **Customer ID** field.

3. Enter, or do a lookup and select the address ID from the **Address ID** field:

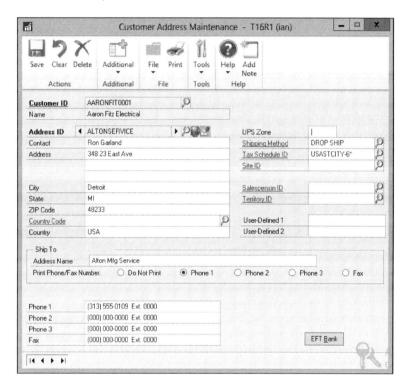

4. In the **Ship To** section of the window, enter the **Address Name** that is to be included on the **Sales** document.

5. Choose whether one of the three phone numbers or the fax number from the master customer record is to be printed, or choose **Do Not Print** if none are required for the loaded address.

How it works...

When a sales transaction is entered, the Ship To Address is entered on each line as normal. When the transaction is printed, the address name and selected phone number are printed, along with the address itself for lines where the address differs from the default address.

In the following example, the first line is being shipped to the default address for the supplier, but the second line is to be dispatched elsewhere:

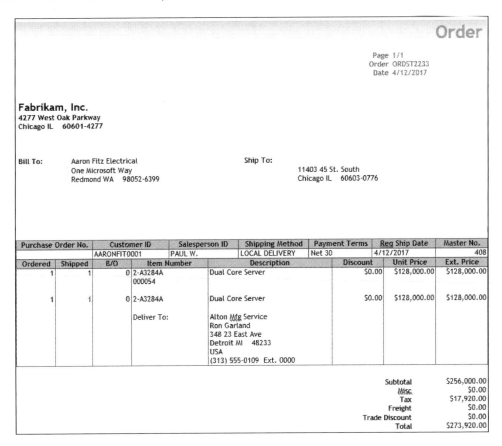

Order

Page 1/1
Order ORDST2233
Date 4/12/2017

Fabrikam, Inc.
4277 West Oak Parkway
Chicago IL   60601-4277

Bill To: Aaron Fitz Electrical
One Microsoft Way
Redmond WA   98052-6399

Ship To:
11403 45 St. South
Chicago IL   60603-0776

Purchase Order No.	Customer ID	Salesperson ID	Shipping Method	Payment Terms	Reg Ship Date	Master No.
	AARONFIT0001	PAUL W.	LOCAL DELIVERY	Net 30	4/12/2017	408

Ordered	Shipped	B/O	Item Number	Description	Discount	Unit Price	Ext. Price
1	1	0	2-A3284A 000054	Dual Core Server	$0.00	$128,000.00	$128,000.00
1	1	0	2-A3284A	Dual Core Server	$0.00	$128,000.00	$128,000.00
			Deliver To:	Alton Mfg Service Ron Garland 348 23 East Ave Detroit MI 48233 USA (313) 555-0109 Ext. 0000			

Subtotal	$256,000.00
Misc.	$0.00
Tax	$17,920.00
Freight	$0.00
Trade Discount	$0.00
Total	$273,920.00

There's more...

The same Ship To Address functionality is used on Drop Ship Orders in Purchase Order Processing. When the order is printed, the address name and phone number will be printed the same way that they are on the sales transaction.

▶ The *Relating or linking items for suggested sales* recipe in *Chapter 3, Automating Dynamics GP*

Getting a complete view with All-In-One View

A challenge with complex transactions is getting a complete view of what has gone on with a customer or vendor. Getting a global view in past versions of Dynamics GP was difficult. Tracing a vendor transaction through purchase order, receipt, invoice match, and payment required a lot of steps. Similarly, tracing a customer's sales from quote to order to invoice to receipt of payment was a complex process. Now Dynamics GP 2016 includes a new All-In-One View feature designed to make it easier to get a more complete view:

How to do it...

To use the **All-In-One View** option for vendor transactions, follow these steps:

1. Select **Purchasing | Inquiry | Purchasing All-In-One View**.

2. Look up or enter a vendor.

3. Check the box next to a transaction to see related transactions. For example, checking a box next to a purchase receipt shows the related purchase order and matched invoices.

To use the **All-In-One View** option for customer transactions, follow these steps:

1. Select **Sales | Inquiry | Sales All-In-One View**.

2. Look up or enter a customer.

3. Check the box next to a transaction to see related transactions. For example, checking a box next to an order shows the related quotes, invoices and cash receipts.

How it works...

Selecting a transaction by checking the box activates a filter limiting the information returned to just related transactions. Additional filters and sorting are available in the headers. The All-In-One viewer is a fantastic tool for digging into transactions.

Tracking serial and lot numbers on drop ship POs

Dynamics GP has long supported the tracking of serial and lot numbers for Sales Inventory items that are brought into the inventory system; Dynamics GP 2013 introduced the ability to track serial and lot numbers for drop ship purchase orders where the goods will be delivered direct to the customer and never enter the inventory system.

Getting ready

Purchase Order Processing and Inventory Control will need to be configured and items created. We also need a drop ship purchase order to receive, but as the sample company does not include one by default we will need to create one, as follows:

1. Open the **Purchase Order Entry** window in Dynamics GP by selecting **Purchasing** from the Navigation pane and clicking on **Purchase Order Entry** in the **Transactions** section.

2. Change the **Type** option to **Drop Ship**.

3. Tab or click away from the **PO Number** field to create a new purchase order.

4. Enter, or perform a lookup to select **Vendor ID** ADVANCED0001.

5. Enter, or perform a lookup to select **Customer ID** AARONFIT0001.

6. In the scrolling window, in the **Item** field, enter 100XLG.

7. Set the **Quantity Ordered** option to **10**.

8. Enter WAREHOUSE in the **Site ID** field.

9. Click **Save** on the toolbar to save the purchase order.

How to do it...

The serial or lot numbers can be recorded when receiving the drop ship purchase order:

1. Open the **Purchasing Invoice Entry** window in Dynamics GP by selecting **Purchasing** from the Navigation pane and clicking on **Enter/Match Invoices** in the **Transactions** section.

2. Tab or click away from the **Receipt Number** field to create a new invoice.

3. Enter **Document Number** of the vendor.

4. Enter **Invoice Date**.

5. Enter, or perform a lookup to select **Vendor ID** ADVANCED0001.

6. Click the **Auto Invoice** button on the toolbar (to the right of **Post**) to open the **Select Purchase Order Items** window.

7. Locate and click on the purchase order created in the *Getting ready* section in the list on the left.

8. In the scrolling window, mark the checkbox against the Purchase Order line.

9. Mark the **S/L** checkbox (next to **Quantity Invoices**):

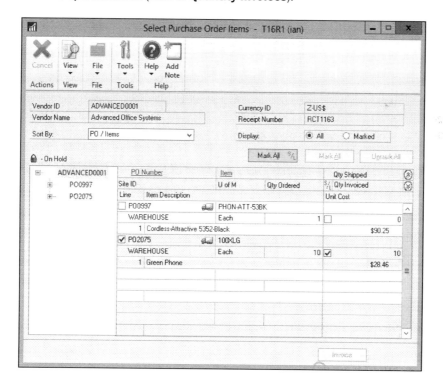

10. Click **Invoice**, which will open the **Purchasing Serial Number Entry** window.

11. In this case, item 100XLG has been set up to allow serial numbers to be auto-generated, so click the **Auto-Generate** button.

12. Click **OK** to accept the serial numbers and complete entry of the invoice as normal.

How it works...

With the serial number entered in Dynamics GP, the information is available from **Inquiries** and **Reports**, which will improve the control and tracking of items dispatched to customers.

There's more...

This new ability to track serial and lot numbers on drop ship purchase orders has been integrated with Sales Order Processing. If the drop ship PO was created from a sales order, then, when the purchase order is invoiced, the serial/lot number will automatically be assigned to the originating sales order line.

See also

▶ The *Gain Flexibility with Inventory Tolerance Handling* recipe in *Chapter 5, Exposing Hidden Features in Dynamics GP*

▶ The *Relating or linking items for suggested sales* recipe in *Chapter 3, Automating Dynamics GP*

▶ The *Preventing sales of discontinued inventory* recipe in *Chapter 7, Preventing Errors in Dynamics GP*

▶ *Selecting multiple serial or lot numbers*

Selecting multiple serial or lot numbers

One very welcome addition to Dynamics GP 2013 is the ability to select multiple serial or lot numbers when entering Sales Transaction. For each one the serial number had to be selected and the **Insert** button clicked; now several can be selected and **Insert** hit once, saving a lot of time.

How to do it...

To select multiple serial numbers, follow these steps:

1. Open the **Item Transfer Entry** window in Dynamics GP by selecting **Inventory** from the Navigation pane and clicking on **Transfer Entry** in the **Transactions** section.

2. Enter WAREHOUSE in the **From** field.

3. Enter DEPOT in the **To** field.

4. Enter 100XLG in the **Item Number** field.

5. Tab three times and enter 5 in the **Quantity** field:

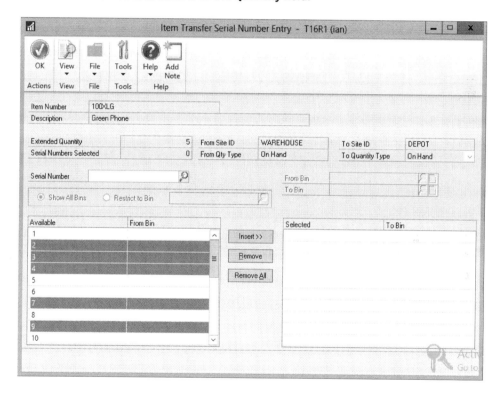

6. The **Item Transfer Serial Number Entry** window will open. Use the Windows standard of *Ctrl* or *Shift* in combination with left-clicking with the mouse to select five serial numbers from the **Available** list and click **Insert >>**.

There's more...

This multi-select works for both serial numbers and lot numbers throughout Dynamics GP 2013 wherever serial numbers can be selected.

See also

- ▸ *Tracking serial and lot numbers on Drop Ship POs*
- ▸ The *Gaining flexibility with Inventory Tolerance Handling* recipe in *Chapter 5, Exposing Hidden Features in Dynamics GP*
- ▸ The *Preventing sales of discontinued inventory* recipe in *Chapter 7, Preventing Errors in Dynamics GP*

Intercompany asset transfer

Dynamics GP has included intercompany processing in some modules for quite some time. With Dynamics GP 2013, intercompany processing has arrived in Fixed Asset Management with the introduction of intercompany asset transfers.

This new functionality can save time depreciating the asset in the current company and the time needed to create the asset and configure the depreciation in the new company.

How to do it...

To perform an intercompany asset transfer, follow these steps:

1. Open the **Fixed Asset Intercompany Transfer** window in Dynamics GP by selecting **Financial** from the Navigation pane and clicking on **Intercompany Transfer** in the **Transactions** section under **Fixed Assets**:

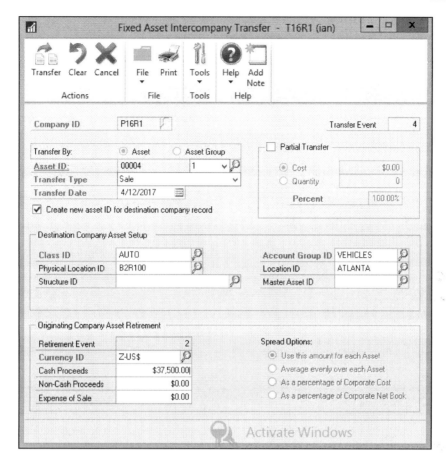

2. Enter, or perform a lookup for **Company ID**.

3. Choose whether to transfer by **Asset** or, to transfer multiple assets, **Asset Group**.

4. If entering by **Asset**, enter **Asset ID** and **Suffix**.

5. Select **Transfer Type**.

6. If a date other than the user date is required, enter or choose the required date.

7. Mark the **Create new asset ID for destination company record** checkbox if a new asset ID should be generated. Leaving this checkbox unmarked will use the same asset ID, which may cause a conflict.

8. Enter the **Destination Company Asset Setup** information.

9. Enter the **Originating Company Asset Retirement** information.

10. Click **Transfer** to create the asset in the new company and retire the original.

When the transfer is finished, the **FA Intercompany Transfer Edit List** report will print, unless printing is switched off in **Posting Setup**.

There's more...

As well as transferring a single asset, **Fixed Asset Intercompany Transfer** can transfer groups of assets by choosing to **Transfer By Asset Group**, or partially transfer an asset.

See also

▸ *Historical depreciation report*

▸ *Fixed Assets Batches*

Historical depreciation report

One of the regularly, and most frequently, requested enhancements of Fixed Asset Management is the ability to generate historical depreciation reports in order to verify depreciation expense for tax purposes.

This feature arrived with Dynamics GP 2013.

How to do it...

The option to run the historical depreciation report has been added to the standard **Fixed Asset** report options. To generate a historic depreciation report, follow these steps:

1. Open the **Depreciation Reports** window in Dynamics GP by selecting **Financial** from the Navigation pane and clicking on **Depreciation** in the **Reports** section under **Fixed Assets**.

2. Select **Depreciation Detail** the **Reports** option field.

3. Click **New** to open the **Depreciation Report Options** window:

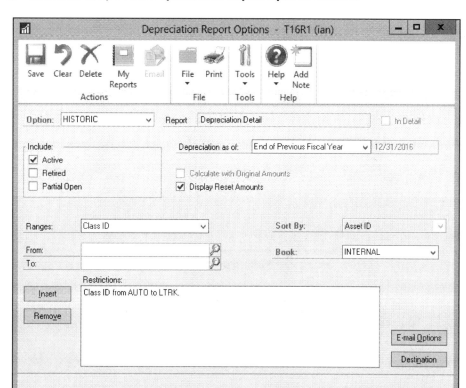

4. Enter HISTORIC in the **Option** field.

5. Choose **End of Previous Fiscal Year**, or **End of Previous Month**, in the **Depreciation as of:** field (the default option is **Current Amounts**, which reproduces functionality as it existed in previous versions).

6. Mark the **Active** box in the **Include** frame.

7. Add a range of classes from **AUTO** to **LTRK**.

8. Choose **INTERNAL** in the **Book:** field.

9. Click **Print** to print the new report option of historic depreciation.

How it works...

In previous versions of Dynamics GP there was no way to generate historic depreciation reports. In Dynamics GP 2013, by choosing a depreciation as-of date, such as End of Previous Fiscal Year, the user is able to specify the date for which depreciation will be calculated.

There's more...

Fixed Asset depreciation has been enhanced in other ways too.

Mass depreciation reversal

In previous versions of Dynamics GP, if depreciation was calculated incorrectly, then the reversal had to be done one asset at a time. In Dynamics GP 2013, the standard Depreciation Process Information window has been enhanced with an option to reverse depreciation, and this can be run against either an Asset Group or all Assets.

To mass reverse depreciation, follow these steps:

1. Open the **Depreciation Process Information** window in Dynamics GP by selecting **Financial** from the Navigation pane and clicking on **Depreciate** in the **Routines** section under **Fixed Assets**:

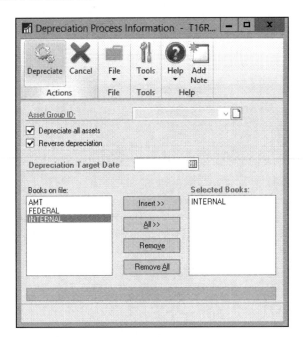

2. Mark the **Depreciate all assets** checkbox.
3. Mark the **Reverse depreciation** checkbox.
4. Choose **Depreciation Target Date**.
5. Select the books for which the depreciation is to be reversed.
6. Click the **Depreciate** button to process the mass reversal.

Reset History in Detail

In previous versions of Dynamics GP, if depreciation was reset, the depreciation for closed years was lumped into the last period of the most recent closed year. In Dynamics GP 2013, a new option has been introduced that will spread the reset transactions across all periods of the asset's life, thereby offsetting the original transactions in the respective periods.

To enable **Reset History in Detail**, follow these steps:

1. Open the **Fixed Assets Company Setup** window in Dynamics GP by selecting **Financial** from the Navigation pane and clicking on **Company** in the **Setup** section under **Fixed Assets**:

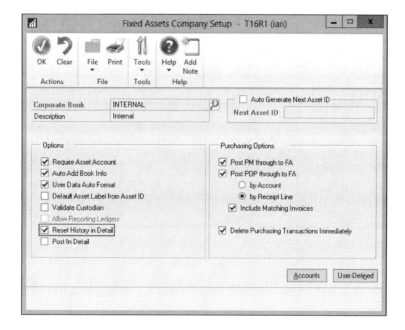

2. In the **Options** frame, mark the **Reset History in Detail** checkbox.
3. Click **OK** to save the changes to the **Fixed Assets Company Setup** window.

With this option set, any depreciation reset will have the reset value spread across all periods of the asset's life, allowing accurate inquiry and reporting of depreciation.

See also

▸ *Intercompany asset transfer*
▸ *Fixed Assets Batches*

Fixed Assets Batches

One of the main criticisms of Fixed Assets integration with the General Ledger has been the lack of transparency for the values being posted. With Dynamics GP 2013, the integration has been enhanced with the introduction of Fixed Asset Batches which allow users to review batches before they are posted.

How to do it...

To generate a batch of Fixed Assets transactions for review before posting, follow these steps:

1. Open the **Fixed Assets General Ledger Posting** window in Dynamics GP by selecting **Financial** from the Navigation pane and clicking on **GL Posting** in the **Routines** section under **Fixed Assets**.

2. Tab or click away from the **Batch ID** field to create a new batch.

3. The user date will default into the **Posting Date** field but can be overridden if required:

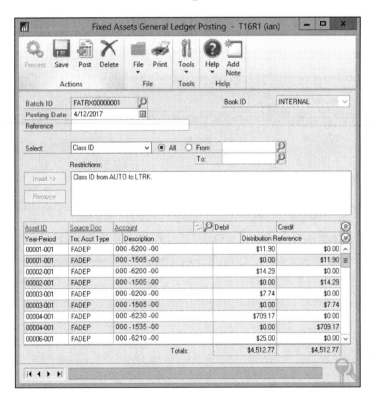

4. If all transactions from Fixed Assets which have not yet been posted need to be, then leave the **Restrictions** field blank. Otherwise, enter the required criteria.

5. Click **Process** to generate the batch lines, which will then be displayed at the bottom of the window for review.

6. The GL account can be amended if required, although the debit and credit values cannot.

There's more...

Dynamics GP 2013 also includes an **Inquiry** window where Fixed Asset Batches can be viewed after posting by following these steps:

1. Open the **Fixed Assets Batch Inquiry** window in Dynamics GP by selecting **Financial** from the Navigation pane and clicking on **Batches** in the **Inquiry** section under **Fixed Assets**:

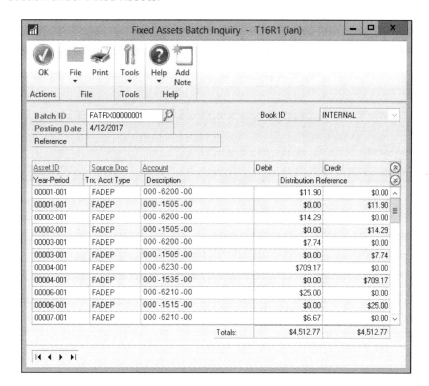

2. Enter or perform a lookup for **Batch ID** to be viewed.

See also

▸ *Intercompany asset transfer*

▸ *Historical depreciation report*

Improve year-end with the Fixed Asset Year-End Closing Report

In earlier versions of Dynamics GP, the year-end fixed asset procedure was something of a mystery. The closing process would end, but a report wouldn't print to show what the closing process had done. Dynamics GP 2016 includes a new Year-End Closing Report, making it easier to document the results of the year-end close processes.

Getting ready

The Year-End Closing Report is part of the process for closing the fixed asset year. When closing the year for fixed assets, it is important to follow the process as documented at `https://support.microsoft.com/en-us/kb/865653`:

Closed Book	System: 30/12/14 4:10:17 1		Fabrikam, Inc.		Page: 1	
	User Date: 12/4/17		FIXED ASSETS YEAR-END CLOSING REPORT		User ID: sa	
	For: AMT					
	CurrentFiscalYear: 2018					
	Asset ID	Description	Cost Basis	YTD Depr	Accum Depr	Net Book
	Pl in Svc	Depr Thru	Quantity	YTD Maintenance		Status
	00001	Office Desk	$1,000.00	$0.00	$232.82	$767.18
	1/1/15	28/2/17	1	$0.00		Active
	00002	Office Desk	$1,200.00	$0.00	$279.38	$920.62
	31/1/15	28/2/17	1	$0.00		Active
	00003	Side Chair	$650.00	$0.00	$151.33	$498.67
	1/3/15	28/2/17	1	$0.00		Active
	00004	Big Automobile	$42,550.00	$0.00	$8,436.85	$34,113.15
	1/4/15	28/2/17	1	$0.00		Active
	00005	Little Truck	$0.00	$0.00	$5,128.20	$13,421.80
	15/5/15	1/7/16	1	$0.00		Retired
	00006	PC	$1,500.00	$0.00	$650.78	$849.22
	1/7/15	28/2/17	1	$0.00		Active
	00007	Monitor 17"	$400.00	$0.00	$173.54	$226.46
	1/7/15	28/2/17	1	$0.00		Active
	00008	Duplicator	$24,000.00	$0.00	$5,587.53	$18,412.47
	1/10/15	28/2/17	1	$0.00		Active
	00009	Building 1	$100,000.00	$0.00	$3,216.61	$96,783.39
	1/11/15	28/2/17	1	$0.00		Active
	00010	Building2	$120,000.00	$0.00	$3,859.94	$116,140.06
	1/11/15	28/2/17	1	$0.00		Active

The report lists Down the assets Affected and Associated details

Report Header It is printed when Performing the Year-End closing routine

How to do it...

To generate the Year-End Closing Report for Fixed Assets, follow these steps:

1. Select **Financial** | **Routines** | **Year End** from the **Fixed Asset** section in this window.

2. Select a book and click **Insert** or click **All** to select all books.

3. Click **Continue** to complete the year end process.

4. Check the box next to one or more print options and click **OK** to print the report.

Purchase requisitions

Dynamics GP 2013 R2 saw the introduction of purchase requisitions. A purchase requisition is the stage before a purchase order.

It allows a user to enter a requisition with limited information, which is then processed and turned into a purchase order once an item and vendor have been selected. Purchase requisitions can be entered by users of any license type (Full, Limited, or Self-Serve), which can result in significant cost savings. Purchase requisitions work best when paired with approval workflows, which are covered in depth in the *Microsoft Dynamics GP Workflow 2.0* book by Ian Grieve (one of the authors of this book).

How to do it...

To enter a purchase requisition, follow these steps:

1. Open the **Purchase Requisition Entry** window in Dynamics GP by selecting **Purchasing** from the Navigation pane and clicking on **Purchase Requisition** in the **Transactions** section.

2. Tab through the **Requisition Number** field and enter New Server in the **Description** field.

3. Enter WAREHOUSE in the **Ship To Address** field.

4. Click the **Save** button:

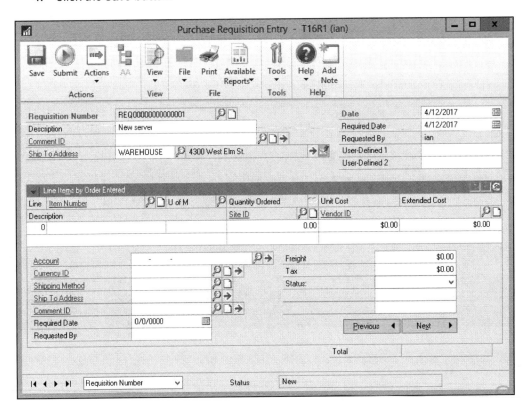

5. At its simplest level, the above is all that is required to enter the purchase requisition, but all of the fields marked with an asterisk are required before the requisition can be turned into a purchase order.

6. Once all of the required fields have been filled in, click the **Actions** button followed by **Purchase**. Ensure the site and vendor links for the item have been created and mark the checkboxes in the left pane and then click **Generate**; this will transform the purchase requisition into a purchase order:

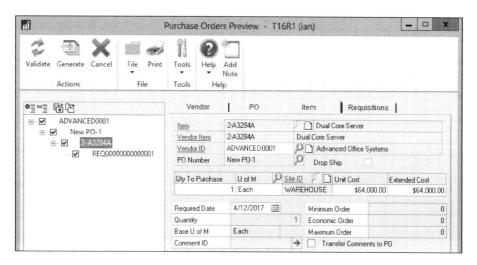

There's more...

The selected **Procurement** section that shows the status of requisitions and allows the user to interact via drill downs has been introduced to the GP home page:

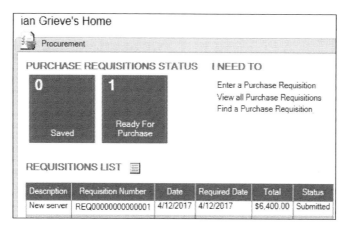

Gaining efficiency by printing or e-mailing any report with Word templates

Previous versions of Dynamics GP had limited e-mail capability for reports. Reports could be e-mailed in a text format. E-mailing PDFs required expensive, full versions of Adobe Acrobat. With Dynamics GP 2016 and the Word Template Generator, any report, not just those with prebuilt templates, can be rendered in Microsoft Word, making it easy to print or e-mail reports in Word or PDF format.

Getting ready

Prior to turning a report into a Word template, the Word Template Generator needs to be installed from the Dynamics GP installation media and Microsoft Word needs to be present on the same machine as Dynamics GP.

Additionally, a template needs to be created for that report. To create a template and assign it to a report, follow these steps:

1. Print **ANY Microsoft Dynamics GP** report to an XML file.

2. Save to your desktop or another easily accessible location:

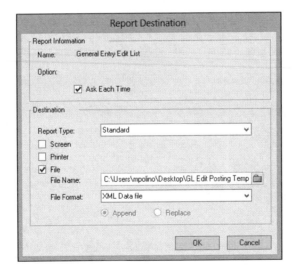

3. Left click, hold, and drag the file into the `TemplateGenerator.EXE` file within the program files folder. A small black window will display for a moment:

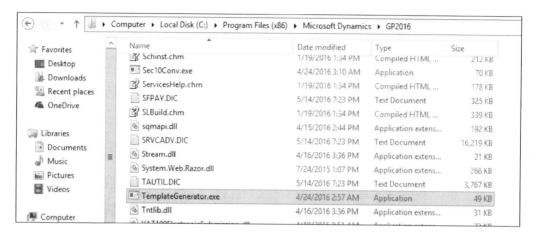

4. Now you have a Word template. The Word document is deployed to the same location that you dragged the XML file from.

5. In Dynamics GP, go to **Administration** | **Reports** | **Template Maintenance**.

6. Look up your report in the **Report Name** drop-down.list For default reports, use **Original**. For other reports, make sure you choose the correct one: **Original**, **Modified**, **Alternate**, or **Alternate Modified**.

7. Click the green plus sign (**+**).

8. Locate your file and click **Open**:

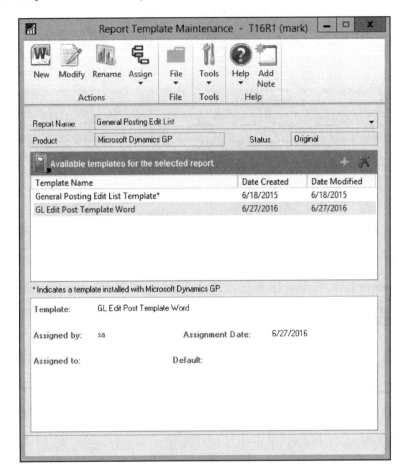

9. Click on the new template and select **Assign | Company**.

10. Check the box next to one or more companies.

11. Click the **Set Default** button to make this the default report. In the window that opens, check the box next to the report and click **Save**.

12. Click **Save** to finish.

How to do it...

1. Once a template has been set up, select **Print** to print the report as you normally would.

2. Change **Report Type** from **Standard** to **Template**.

3. Select a destination: **Screen**, **Printer**, or **File**. The output will be sent to the destination using Microsoft Word.

4. The latest versions of Word allow exporting to PDF and e-mailing directly from Word.

There's more...

More information on e-mail and Word reports is available in the, *Speeding document delivery with e-mail* recipe in *Chapter 3, Automating Dynamics GP*.

Attaching documents to records

There are full document management solutions available for Microsoft Dynamics GP, but not everyone needs a solution of this scale. As an alternative, Dynamics GP ships with a module called Document Attachment; it allows documents to be scanned and attached into GP on any window. Document Attachment integrates with almost every window in Microsoft Dynamics GP, either by having a paper clip button on the action pane or by replacing the obsolete OLE Notes functionality on the record notes.

Getting ready

Before documents can be attached into Dynamics GP, the Document Management module needs to be activated and configured by following these steps:

1. Open the **Document Attachment Setup** window in Dynamics GP by selecting **Administration** from the Navigation pane and clicking on **Document Attachment Setup** in the **Setup** section under **Company**.

2. Mark the **Allow Document Attachments** field.

3. Enter a UNC or shared drive path in the **Default Location** field; this is where **Document Attachment** will look by default when the user tries to attach a document.

4. Once attached, documents are stored in the SQL database; this requires active management by the DBA to ensure the server can hold all of the attachments. This can be helped by setting a **Maximum File Size** value:

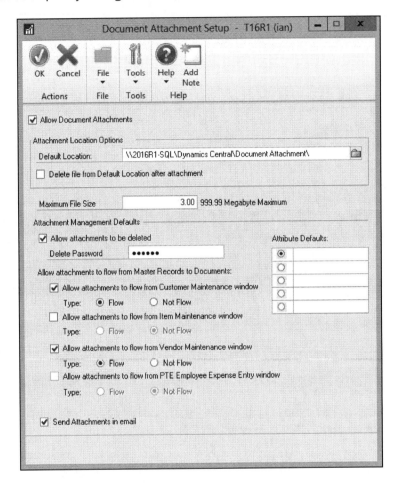

5. Mark the **Allow attachments to be deleted** checkbox.

6. Enter a password in the **Delete Password** field.

7. If attached documents are to be able to flow from the maintenance windows (such as **Vendor Maintenance or Customer Maintenance**), mark the **Allow attachments to flow from the xxx Maintenance** window.

8. Allowing the document to flow means that an attachment on the master record will also be attached to the transaction when one is created; the document on the vendor record must be individually marked to allow this.

9. Mark the **Send Attachments in email** checkbox to allow attachments to be included on the e-mail when a document is sent; for example, a quote might be attached to a purchase order and be attached to the e-mail when e-mailed to the vendor.

10. Click **OK** to save the changes and activate **Document Attachment**.

How to do it...

To attach a document to a purchase order, follow these steps:

1. Open the **Purchase Order Entry** window in Dynamics GP by selecting **Purchasing** from the Navigation pane and clicking on **Purchase Order** in the **Transactions** section.

2. Perform a lookup and select PO2072 in the **PO Number** field.

3. Click the **Attach** button on the action pane.

4. Click the **Attach** button at the bottom right of the window.

5. If the file is in the default location, select the file and click **Open** or navigate and find the file:

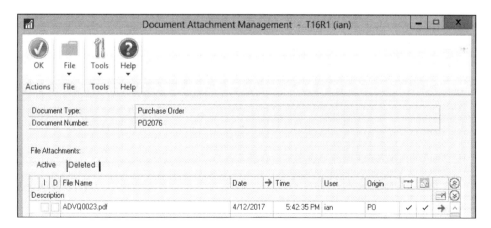

6. When finished attaching files, click **OK** to close the window.

5
Exposing Hidden Features in Dynamics GP

Hidden features are the focus of this chapter including the following:

- ► Controlling Posting Dates when not posting by batch
- ► Reducing posting steps with better printing control
- ► Improving information with tax dates in transactions
- ► Gaining the option to process taxes in general ledger
- ► Changing the Remit-To Address on a Payables transaction after posting
- ► Understanding an asset's financial information with Asset Details
- ► Speeding up entry by copying a purchase order
- ► Getting control of printing with Named Printers
- ► Speeding month-end processing with the Reconcile to GL functionality
- ► Improving budget creation with Combine Budgets
- ► Control POs with prepayments
- ► Gaining flexibility with Inventory Tolerance Handling
- ► Creating Fixed Assets with a default ID
- ► Avoid creating Payables Invoices when a PO already exists

Introduction

In this chapter, we look at some features of Dynamics GP that many users miss. Some of these features are well known to consultants but somehow users still miss the big benefits that can be gained with these recipes.

This chapter is really about leveraging features to remove obstacles. It's about those hidden settings that shave seconds off processes, seconds that build up to save hours over the course of a month. Now, it's hidden feature time!

Controlling Posting Dates when not posting by batch

Transactions in Dynamics GP can be posted individually or as part of a batch. When posting as part of a batch, the batch gets a posting date that can be different from the date of the transaction. For individual transaction posting, the posting date can also be different from the transaction but the way to accomplish that is not obvious.

When not posting in a batch, the Posting Date on a transaction is the date that the transaction will have in the General Ledger. The document date on represents, the date of the document, and is used to calculate aging for sales and purchase transactions. The posting date can be controlled separately. In this recipe, we'll take a look at posting a transaction with a posting date different from the transaction date.

How to do it...

To post a transaction with different posting and transaction dates, follow these steps:

1. In Dynamics GP, select **Purchasing** from the Navigation list. Pick **Transaction Entry** on the home page from the **Transactions** menu.

2. This opens the **Payables Transaction Entry** window. Tab to the **Doc. Date** field and click on the blue arrow:

3. The **Payables Date Entry** window will open to display the **Posting Date** field. Add thirty days to the date in the **Posting Date** field and click **OK**:

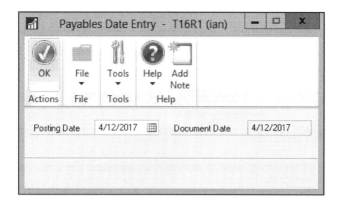

4. Now, when the transaction is completed and posted with the **Post** button, the posting date will be thirty days later than the document date.

How it works...

This is one of those exquisitely simple items that is hidden just enough that users don't find it. The ability to separate the Posting Date from the transaction date is an important accounting tool that is often not present in lower-end systems. The fact that Dynamics GP supports this in both batch and transactional posting is one small difference between an enterprise reporting system and simple accounting software.

Reducing posting steps with better Printing Control

When posting a transaction in Dynamics GP, a series of posting reports print by default. Reports are often set to ask for the type of output (printer, screen, or file) each time. In this scenario, each report opens a window allowing the user to change the report destination when the report is run. This significantly increases the amount of time it takes to simply start the printing process because the user has to make a choice multiple times. This means that it's not uncommon to have eight windows open and four reports print every time a user posts.

With this much mess, users often click through the prompts without actually reading them or they print reports that they don't really need and cancel reports they should print.

There is a better way. Reports can be turned off, routed only to the screen, or sent to file to save several minutes each time transactions are posted. In this recipe we'll see how to control printing during posting. For our example, we'll look at controlling printing when posting a payables transaction entry.

Getting ready

Prior to changing the printing of posting reports, administrators should evaluate what reports really need to be printed or saved at the time of posting. Posting reports can be reprinted at a later date and much of the data is duplicated across reports. Consequently, there is often no need to print any of the reports.

To show the range of options for our example, we will send the posting report to a file, the summary report to a printer, and we'll turn off the detail report and any other reports.

How to do it...

To get control of posting reports, follow these steps:

1. Select **Administration** from the Navigation list and **Posting** under the **Posting** heading on the **Setup** section to open the **Posting Setup** window.

2. In **Series**, select **Purchasing**. In **Origin**, select **Payables Trx Entry**.

3. In the lower section, find the report labeled **Trx Entry Posting Journal**. Check the box on the left under the **Print** heading next to **Trx Entry Posting Journal**. Uncheck all of the four center boxes then check the one under the file folder icon. Tab to the **Path** field and enter `c:\AP Posting.txt`.

4. This process sets **AP Transaction Entry Posting Journal** to default to printing to a file located on the `C:` drive and named `AP Posting.txt`. The folder icon in the top right can also be used to browse and select a file location.

5. Check the box next to **Trx Distribution Summary** under the **Print** heading. Uncheck any boxes in the middle and check the box under the printer icon.

6. This activates **Transaction Distribution Summary Report** and sends it to the printer by default.

7. Uncheck any other **Print** boxes to turn off the remaining reports and click **Save** to continue:

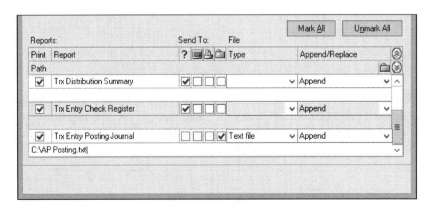

8. Now, when a payables transaction is posted, the posting report will append to a file and **Transaction Distribution Summary Report** will print to the printer.

How it works...

In most cases, there is no need to print any posting reports. But setting posting reports to ask every time they are printed is the least efficient of all the options. Since posting reports can be reprinted in Dynamics GP, once users are past the initial insecurity of using the system, posting reports should generally be turned off. However, if posting reports are required for control purposes, the number and types of automatic reports should be limited and sent to a file for easy retrieval, e-mailing, and archival.

There's more...

Printing posting reports makes less sense when users know how to reprint them on demand and there is a way to turn off the rarely used **Print Options** box.

Posting reports

Posting reports are found in the **Reports** section of each module. To continue the theme of a payables transaction, select **Purchasing** from the Navigation list. Then pick **Posting Journals** on the area page under **Reports**. The first option is **Transaction Journal** but other posting journals can be selected for printing with the drop-down menu:

The only exception to this is the posting report for **General Journal** entries. The report exists; it's just called a cross-reference report instead of a posting journal.

Print Options box

The other box that is frequently skipped during printing is the **Print Options** box. This box displays when printing to a printer. It provides the option to print more than one copy of a report or to print only certain pages of the report. This box is actually controlled via the **Named Printers** functionality that we'll look at in the *Getting control of printing with Named Printers* recipe found later in this chapter. For now, we'll just look at turning off this feature.

To turn off the print options box, follow these steps:

1. Select **Administration** from the Navigation list. Pick **Named Printers** from the area page under **Setup | System**. Enter the system password if prompted.

2. Check the box marked **Do Not Display System Print Dialog** and click **OK** twice:

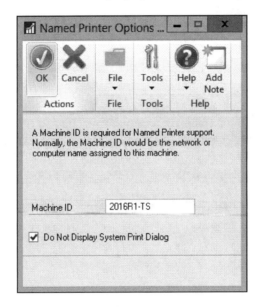

3. Select a default printer for Dynamics GP and click **OK**.

4. Click **Save** to assign the default printer to **Named Printers**. Then pick **File | Close** to close the window:

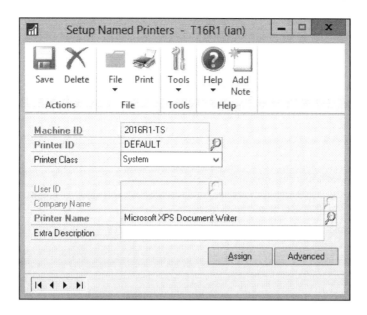

If the **Named Printers** feature has already been set up, then steps 3 and 4 won't appear as an option. This process turns off print options for this printer for all users on this workstation.

See also

▸ *Getting control of printing with Named Printers*

Improving information with Tax Dates in transactions

When working with sales tax and use tax it is often useful to set the date of a transaction for tax purposes. For example, assume a February invoice subject to use tax arrives in March. This is after February has been closed and use tax submitted. The invoice still needs to be dated in February to age properly but it needs to appear on tax reports for March to ensure that the taxing authority is paid properly. Dynamics GP includes functionality to support this but it needs to be turned on. The Tax Date functionality was originally designed to support **Value Added Tax** (**VAT**) which is popular in Europe and other parts of the world. Firms with this requirement will need to activate tax dates as well. In this recipe, we'll look at how to activate and use tax dates.

Getting ready

Prior to using **Tax Dates**, they need to be activated. To activate **Tax Dates**, follow these steps:

1. Select **Administration** from the Navigation list. On the **Administration** area page, pick **Company** under the **Company** heading on the **Setup** section.

2. Click **Options** in the **Company Setup** window.

3. Check the box marked **Enable Tax Date** and click **OK** twice:

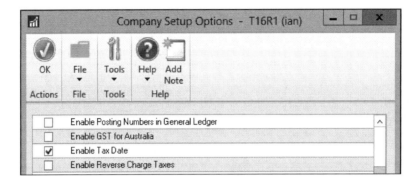

Tax Date functionality is now set up. Let's look at how to use it in a transaction.

How to do it...

To use **Tax Dates** in a transaction, follow these steps:

1. Select **Transaction Entry** from the **Purchasing** area page under **Transactions**.

2. Tab to the **Doc. Date** field, select the blue arrow next to the date and enter `4/12/2017`:

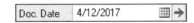

3. A new **Tax Date** field appears in this window. Enter `5/1/2017` in the **Tax Date** field and click **OK**:

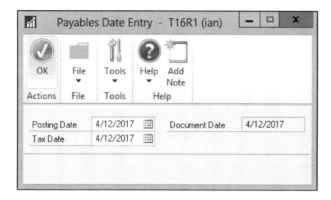

How it works...

The **Tax Date** feature is required for processing VAT but it's also very useful for sales tax and use tax reporting. Once the tax date feature has been activated, tax dates on transactions are available to add to SmartLists. This makes reporting on tax dates easy and flexible.

See also

▸ The *Tailoring SmartLists by adding fields* recipe in *Chapter 8, Harnessing the Power of SmartLists*

Gaining the option to process taxes in general ledger

There are times when companies need to process sales or use tax transactions through the general ledger rather than through a subledger such as Sales or Purchasing. Perhaps tax was incorrectly calculated or omitted on the original transaction, which is sometimes a requirement for international implementations. It's also possible that a company uses another system to feed the general ledger in Dynamics GP. For example, in one company I worked for we used a specialized accounts receivable application that was designed for our industry. Data from that application was integrated with Dynamics GP and all other transactions ran through Dynamics GP directly. This can lead to the need to process tax transactions through the GL.

Dynamics GP includes options to calculate and process taxes directly through the general ledger and that is the focus of this recipe.

Getting ready

Prior to processing tax transactions via the general ledger, this feature needs to be turned on. To activate the ability to process taxes through the general ledger, follow these steps:

1. Select **Administration** from the Navigation list. On the **Administration** area page, pick **Company** under the **Setup | Company** heading.

2. Click **Options** in the **Company Setup** window.

3. Scroll down in the window and check the box marked **Calculate Taxes in General Ledger** and click **OK** twice:

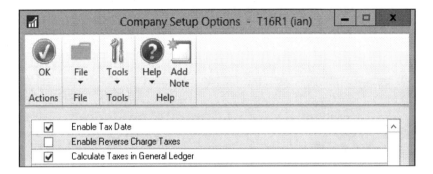

Now that tax calculations in the general ledger have been activated, let's see how they work. We'll use the sample company's tax schedules for our example.

How to do it...

To calculate taxes in the general ledger, follow these steps:

1. Select **Financial** from the Navigation list. Pick **General** under **Transactions** on the area page.

2. Select the new **Tax Entry** button on the bottom left of the **Transaction Entry** window.

3. On the **Tax Entry** window, set the **Transaction Type** option to **Credit**. Use the lookup button (magnifying glass) to select or key in the sales account 000-4100-000. Enter $1,000.00 in the **Sales/Purchase Amount** field.

4. Use the lookup button (magnifying glass) to select **USASTE-PS6N0 (State Sales Tax)** in the **Tax Detail** field. Notice that Dynamics GP will fill in the tax amount automatically:

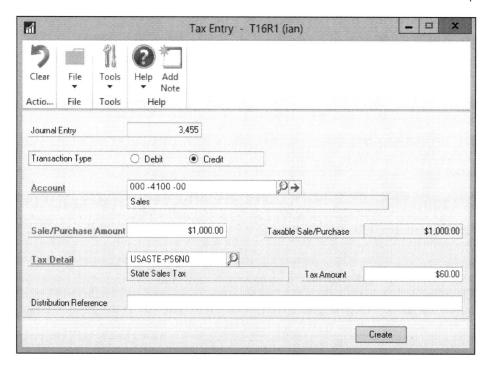

5. Click **Create** to create the transaction in the general ledger. The created transaction will have the account and amount entered along with the appropriate tax. Since this is only one side of the entry, enter 000-1200-00 (other receivables) in the next open line to make the transaction balance:

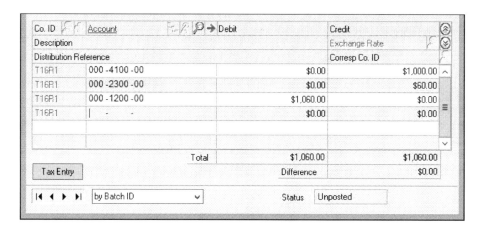

How it works...

The ability to calculate taxes as part of a general journal entry provides the ability to accommodate tax adjustments and changes in tax law. It also provides flexibility to work with other systems connected to Dynamics GP.

See also

▸   *Improving information with Tax Dates in transactions*

Changing the Remit-To Address on a Payables transaction after posting

One of the long-standing issues with Microsoft Dynamics GP was how it handled Remit-To Addresses on Payables Transactions when the vendors default Remit-To Address was changed.

The Remit-To Address on the vendor card was a used as the default on Payables Transactions when they were created. If the transaction was posted and the vendor card updated, the Remit-To Address on the transaction was left unchanged and, until the release of Dynamics GP 2013, there was no way to update it.

How to do it...

To change the Remit-To Address on a posted Payables Transaction, follow these steps:

1.   Select **Purchasing** from the Navigation list then pick **Edit Transaction Information** under **Transactions**.

2.   In the sample company, use the lookup button (magnifying glass) to select vendor **ASSOCIAT0001**:

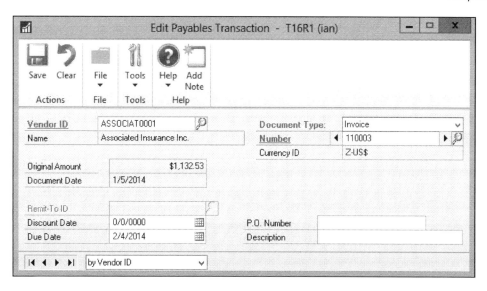

3. Enter `110003` in the **Number** field which will load the transaction details which can be amended.

4. In the **Remit-To ID** field enter or perform a lookup for the address ID to be used as the Remit-To Address for this invoice. Invoices entered prior to Dynamics GP 2013 will show a blank **Remit-To ID** field; those entered in Dynamics GP 2013 will display the Remit-To ID from Payables Transaction.

Understanding an asset's financial information with Asset Details

Dynamics GP has a nice module for tracking and maintaining Fixed Assets. However, many users have trouble figuring out the history of a specific asset. Often, users find that while reviewing fixed asset general ledger postings something looks wrong, but they can't figure out where to go in the Fixed Asset module to validate how transactions are posted.

Dynamics GP provides the ability to see every transaction for a Fixed Asset and its link back to the general ledger. This functionality can be hard to find. In this recipe we'll look at how to trace Fixed Asset transactions.

How to do it...

To get the specifics of Fixed Asset transactions, follow these steps:

1. In Dynamics GP, select **Financial** from the Navigation list. Then pick **Financial Detail** under the **Inquiry | Fixed Assets** area.

2. Use the lookup button (magnifying glass) to select asset 00001 suffix 1. Set the **Book ID:** field to **INTERNAL**.

3. The **Financial Detail Inquiry** window will open and display all of the transactions for this asset:

4. The grid at the bottom displays the Fixed Asset Period, GL Batch Number, Account Type, Date, Source Document, and Amount. The key fields are **Transaction Type** and **Source Document**. These fields provide details about the type of transaction. For example, the first two lines demonstrate the cost and clearing entry for the initial purchase of the asset.

5. The **Batch Number** column contains the batch sent to the GL. It can be reviewed using a SmartList.

6. Below that is the first depreciation entry transaction. It affected the **Depreciation** and **Reserve** accounts.

7. Select the first depreciation line and click the blue **Amount** hyperlink to get more information about this transaction line. Dynamics GP shows full details of the line including GL batch, posting date, account, and user information. Click **OK** to close this window:

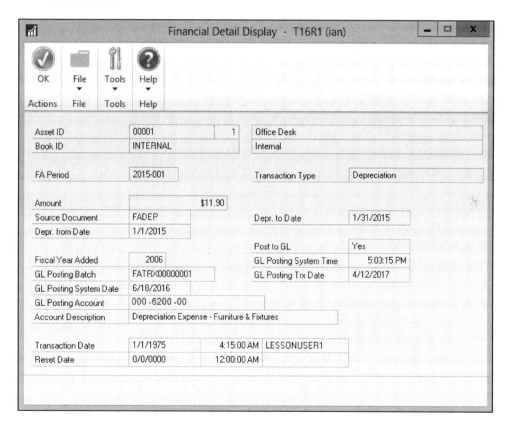

8. Back on the **Financial Detail Inquiry** screen, scroll down to the end of the transactions. Notice that there are two transaction lines without GL batches. Typically, this indicates that there is a fixed asset transaction waiting to be processed to the GL. If, however, a batch is missing for a transaction that is not at the end of the list, it can indicate a problem transaction that was not sent to the GL:

FA Period	Batch Number	Transaction Acct. Type	Trans. Date	Src Doc.	Amount
2016-011	FATRX00000001	Reserve	1/1/1975	FAXFR-C	($273.76)
2016-011	FATRX00000001	Cost	1/1/1975	FAXFR-C	($1,000.00)
2016-011	FATRX00000001	Cost	1/1/1975	FAXFR-C	$1,000.00
2016-012	FATRX00000001	Depreciation	1/1/1975	FADEP	$11.96
2016-012	FATRX00000001	Reserve	1/1/1975	FADEP	($11.96)
2017-001		Depreciation	1/1/1975	FADEP	$11.90
2017-001		Reserve	1/1/1975	FADEP	($11.90)
2017-002	FATRX00000001	Depreciation	1/1/1975	FADEP	$11.90
2017-002	FATRX00000001	Reserve	1/1/1975	FADEP	($11.90)

|◄ ◄ ► ►| by Asset ID   ▼   by FA Year & Period   ▼

How it works...

The **Fixed Asset Financial Detail Inquiry** window provides all the information necessary to trace all of the transactions related to a fixed asset. This is extremely useful for understanding what actually occurred. Any number of items can affect fixed assets including incorrect depreciation settings, wrong asset lives and problems with the fixed asset calendar. Being able to understand all the transactions that affect an asset is an important troubleshooting tool that is often overlooked.

Speeding up entry by copying a purchase order

Creating purchase orders can be a time-consuming process. It's not uncommon to have a large number of line items being ordered. Validating part numbers and prices can also take time. Dynamics GP provides a mechanism to create a new purchase order by copying information from an existing purchase order. Unlike copying an inventory item, where the copy icon is on the main window, the process to copy a purchase order is not obvious. Copying a purchase order is the focus of this recipe.

How to do it...

To copy a purchase order, follow these steps:

1. Select **Purchasing** on the Navigation list, then click **Purchase Order Entry** on the **Transactions** section of the area page.

2. Click **Actions** and then pick **Create and Copy New PO**:

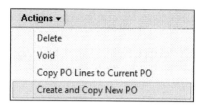

3. Use the lookup button (magnifying glass) to select **Source PO Number** to copy from. In the sample company, select **PO0997**. Dynamics GP will fill in the rest of the information:

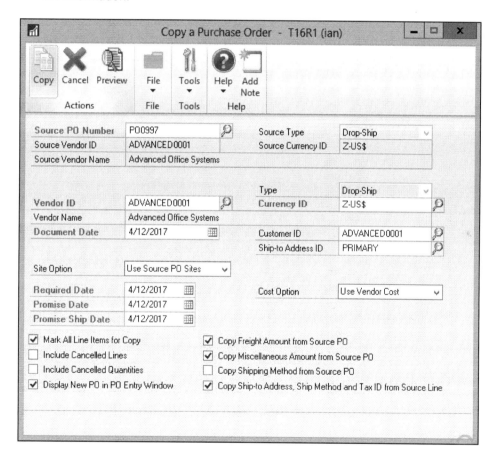

4. Users can change various settings to fine-tune the copy. To demonstrate this, uncheck **Copy Freight Amount** from source PO. Also change the **Required Date** field to 5/31/2017:

Required Date	5/31/2017	Cost Option	Use Vendor Cost
Promise Date	4/12/2017		
Promise Ship Date	4/12/2017		

5. Click **Copy** to create a new purchase order. The new PO can be changed or adjusted just like one that has been entered from scratch.

How it works...

It's unclear why Microsoft chose to hide the copy functionality for purchase orders, but it's great that this feature exists. The ability to selectively copy a PO and then adjust the end result is a huge time saver. This is a feature that definitely needs to come out from hiding.

There's more...

Creating a Sales Order can be just as time consuming as creating a Purchase Order. Fortunately, Sales Order Processing also provides a mechanism that allows a transaction to be created by copying an existing one.

Copying a sales order

Unlike when copying a purchase order, the header of the sales order needs to be created before the copy can be done. To copy a sales order, follow these steps:

1. Select **Sales** on the Navigation list, then click **Sales Transaction Entry** on the **Transactions** section of the area page.

2. Select **Type/Type ID** of **Order/STDORD**.

3. Click in the **Document No.** field so a number is defaulted.

4. Enter, or do a lookup for, **Customer ID** AARONFIT0001.

5. Enter **Currency ID** Z-US$.

6. Click **Actions** then pick **Copy**:

7. Use the lookup button (magnifying glass) to select **Document Number** to copy from. In the sample company, select sales order **ORDST2222**:

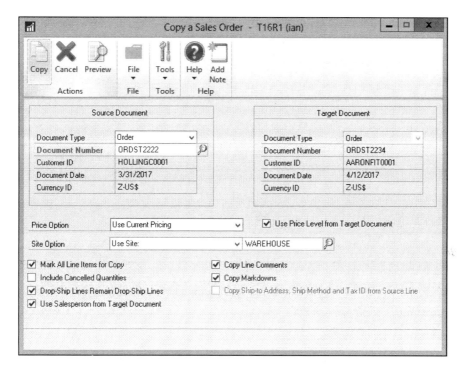

8. Users can change various settings to fine tune the copy. For example, the **Price** option can be changed to **Use Source Document Pricing** or **Zero Pricing**.

9. Click **Preview** to see the lines on the document that will be copied:

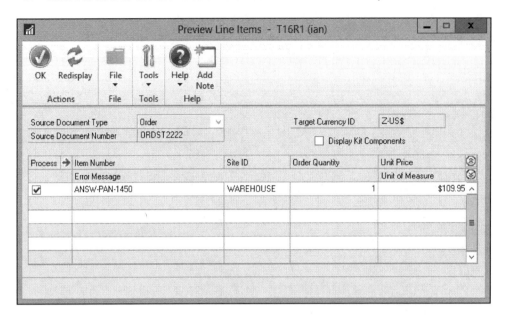

10. If dealing with a multiline order, unmark the checkbox in the **Process** column to remove lines that should not be copied.

11. Click **OK** to return to the **Copy a Sales Order** window and then click **Copy** to complete the copy process.

Getting control of printing with Named Printers

In the *Reducing posting steps with better Printing Control* recipe, we touched on the Named Printers functionality by turning off **System Print Dialog**. However, there is much more than that to Named Printers. The idea behind Named Printers is to allow the assignment of different printers to different functions in Dynamics GP. For example, check printing could be directed to a dedicated check printer or invoices could be automatically sent to a high speed printer. Even better, these settings are by workstation so there is a geographic component to the setup. Users in one building can point checks to a check printer in their building without interfering with a different set of users in another building. In this recipe, we'll look at setting up Named Printers.

Getting ready

Prior to creating Named Printers, there is some setup required; follow these steps:

1. Select **Administration** from the Navigation list. Pick **Named Printers** from the area page under **Setup**. Enter the system password if prompted.

2. Click **OK** twice.

3. Select a default printer for Dynamics GP and click **OK**.

4. Click **Save** to assign the default printer to Named Printers:

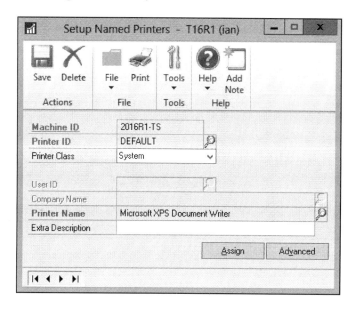

5. Create a new Printer ID named CHECKS. Use the lookup button (magnifying glass) to select a printer for checks. Click **Save** and close the window.

How to do it...

To set Named Printers, follow theses steps:

1. Select **Administration** from the Navigation list. Pick **Named Printers** from the area page under **Setup**.

2. Notice that printers for this machine ID can be set for a specific user and company. For now, we'll leave these alone. Change the **Task Series:** field to **Purchasing**:

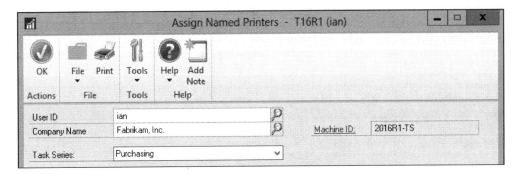

3. Click the blue **Printer** hyperlink to add another printer.

4. In **Task Description** find **Payables – Computer Checks/Cheques Printer**. Change **Printer Class** to **System**.

5. Pick the printer named CHECKS in the **Named Printers** window that opens.

6. Click **OK** to complete the assignment of a check printer to the check printing function:

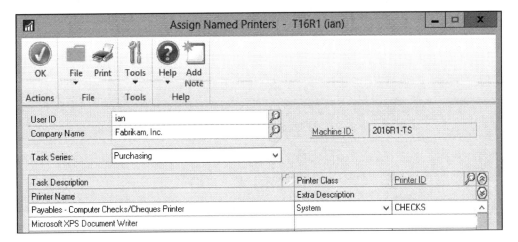

7. Now when checks are printed via the **Computer Checks** function in **Purchasing**, from this computer and by this user, the checks will print to the designated check printer. Any other printer request combination will be sent to the default printer.

How it works...

Named Printers provides fine-grained control over printing functions in Dynamics GP. It provides the ability to control printing by user, computer, and printer. This ability to control printing provides additional security as well since it can be used to control which reports print to shared printers in the organization. The Named Printers feature can provide huge time-saving and cost benefits by preventing printing to less efficient or erroneous printers.

There's more...

Even more control is available via Printer classes.

Printer classes

When setting up printers in Named Printers, the option exists to select a printer class. Printer classes are preset options controlling what users can select to print to a printer. For example, an expensive color printer might be limited to only certain users to prevent accidental printing to that printer. The available printer classes are as follows:

- **System**: These Printer IDs are available to all users and companies
- **User**: This printer ID is only available to a single user for all companies
- **Company**: All users of this company can access this Printer ID
- **User&Company**: This printer ID's use is restricted to a single user and company
- **AnyPrinterID**: Any printer available on the workstation can be used
- **ManualSelection**: This printer is selected by the user at the time of printing
- **None**: The default printer is used

See also

- *Reducing posting steps with better Printing Control*

Speeding up month-end processing with the Reconcile to GL functionality

One process that can be extremely time-consuming is balancing subledgers to the general ledger to ensure that everything in the system is in balance. An out of balance situation can occur if users change the GL account on a subledger transaction. For example, if a user changes the payables account on an AP subledger transaction, the AP subledger no longer matches the AP GL account.

Another common occurrence is that users post general ledger transactions to an AP or AR control account without going through the appropriate subledger. This means that the general ledger is updated but not the subledger, resulting in an out of balance situation.

Dynamics GP provides a feature to facilitate reconciling accounts payable and accounts receivable to the general ledger. The Reconcile to GL feature uses Microsoft Excel to provide an analysis of matched and unmatched transactions. In this recipe, we'll look at how to use the Reconcile to GL feature to balance subledger accounts to the general ledger. For our example we'll look at balancing accounts payable.

How to do it...

To use the Reconcile to GL feature, follow these steps:

1. In Dynamics GP, select **Financial** from the Navigation list and pick **Reconcile to GL** in the **Routines** area.

2. In the **Reconcile to GL** window set the **Module:** field to **Payables Management**.

3. Use the lookup button (magnifying glass) next to **Accounts:** to select accounts `000-2100-00`.

4. Repeat this process for account `000-2105-00` on the next line. Since the sample company tracks discounts, we need both accounts.

5. For the sample company, don't change the dates:

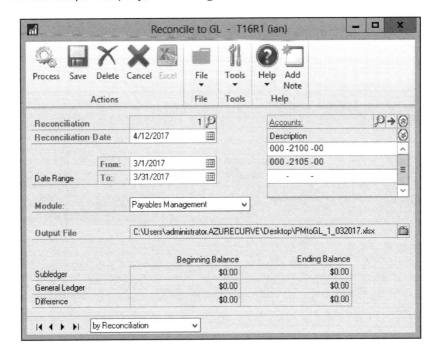

6. Set the **Output File** path for where the Excel spreadsheet will be created.

7. Click **Process** to start the reconciliation. Excel will open with a reconciliation sheet:

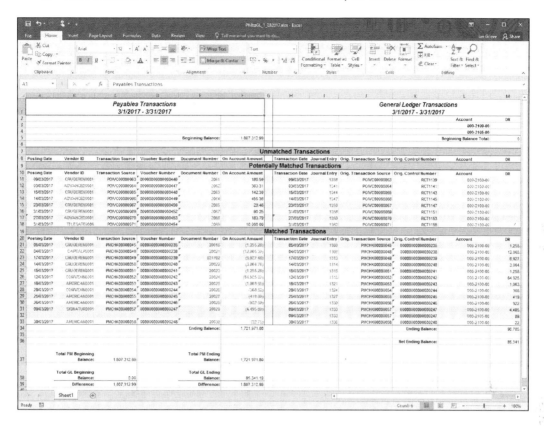

8. Subledger transactions are on the left and general ledger transactions on the right. **Unmatched** transactions are at the top followed by **Potentially Matched** transactions and **Matched** transactions. At the bottom is a reconciliation of the differences.

9. Finally, users would use the unmatched and potentially matched information to make adjusting entries in the GL or subledger to correct out of balance transactions.

How it works...

The reconcile feature for AP, AR, Bank Reconciliation, and Inventory Control fills an important role during month-end close. Balancing subledgers to the general ledger is an important step in ensuring the correctness of financial statements. The Reconcile to GL feature in Dynamics GP makes this easier than ever. The use of Excel as the balancing mechanism provides a familiar, easy-to-use interface for users.

There's more...

The Reconcile to GL routine has been in Dynamics GP for a while but has seen significant improvements in Dynamics GP 2013. Each reconciliation is numbered and can be saved for later recall; the created spreadsheet is saved to a user specified file and can be recalled by clicking the Excel button on the toolbar.

Balancing the year

Whether through inexperience or a lack of oversight, it is not unusual to find firms where the subledger and general ledger have been out of balance for most of the year. The best way to approach this problem is to start with the oldest out of balance month and work forward one month at a time. Trying to balance the entire year at once requires an overwhelming amount of data and can actually make balancing more difficult.

When AP and AR aren't enough

While the Reconcile to GL feature of Dynamics GP works well, it is limited to the accounts payable, accounts receivable, bank reconciliation, and inventory subledgers. There is a third party option named **The Closer from Reporting Central**. The Closer offers similar reconciliation functionality for AP, AR, and Inventory Control, as well as Cash, Sales Order Processing, Cost of Goods Sold, and Accrued Purchases. For companies that require more than simple AR and AP reconciliation, this is a great option. More information about *The Closer* is available at `http://www.Reporting-Central.com`.

Improving budget creation with Combine Budgets

When training new users of Dynamics GP, one of the regular issues raised is the creation of budgets and how they want to be able to send out separate files to each of the budget holders and have an easy way of combining them. Prior to Dynamics GP 2013 this wasn't possible; however, Dynamics GP 2010 introduced Combine Budgets, which provides this functionality.

How to do it...

This example assumes you have two budgets created on the system, `MASTER2017` and `SALES2017`, where the latter needs to be combined into the former:

1. In Dynamics GP, select **Financial** from the Navigation list and pick **Budgets** in the **Cards** area.
2. In the list of available budgets, click on `MASTER2017`.

3. Click the **Open** button and then select **using Microsoft Dynamics GP**:

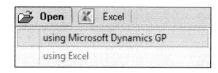

4. This will open the **Budget Maintenance** window and populate with the
   MASTER20017 budget:

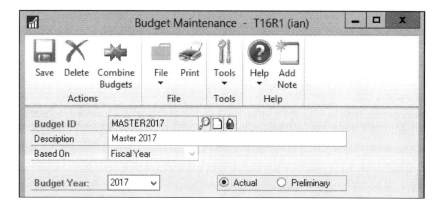

5. Click the **Combine Budgets** button on the toolbar.
6. The **Master Budget ID** field will prepopulate with MASTER2017 from the previous
   window.
7. Enter SALES2017 in the **Combine with Budget ID** field:

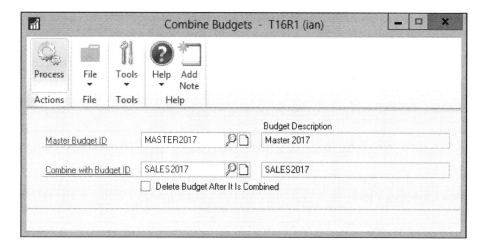

8. If the budget being combined with Master Budget is no longer needed, mark the **Delete Budget After It Is Combined** checkbox.

9. Click **Process** to combine the budgets.

How it works...

Combine Budgets performs a merge of all the figures on the second budget with those on the Master Budget; for example, if account 000-2100-00 has $20,000 on the Master Budget and $12,500 on the Combine Budget, the resulting figure after combination on the Master Budget will be $32,500.

By combining budgets in this way, a separate budget can be created for each budget holder and then combined together into a single Master Budget for use in reporting tools such as Management Reporter or for Commitment accounting.

Controlling POs with prepayments

Dynamics GP has the ability to apply prepayments to purchase orders directly in the PO window making it easy to deal with orders that require payment or deposits up front, including tax amounts.

Getting ready

There is some setup associated with prepayments. To activate PO prepayments, follow these steps:

1. Select **Purchasing | Setup | Purchase Order Processing**.

2. Check the box next to **Allow Purchase Order Prepayments**:

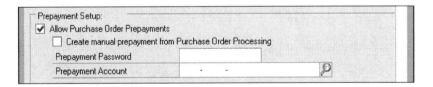

3. There are a few other optional selections as follows:

   ❑ The **Create manual prepayment from Purchase Order Processing** box permits manual payments in addition to payments via the payable computer check process. If this box is not checked, the payment must be generated using the computer check process. Manual payments are appropriate for payments made outside of Dynamics GP, such as wire transfers.

❑   Entering a password in **Prepayment Password** requires users to enter the password to create a prepayment.

❑   The **Prepayment Account** field sets the account used to hold the prepayment. This account is cleared when the payment is processed. If the **Prepayment Account** field is not set, the prepayment account entered in the **Posting Account Setup** window for the **Purchasing** series will be used as the default entry.

How to do it...

To apply a prepayment, follow these steps:

1.   Open **Purchase Order** or create a new one using **Purchasing | Transactions | Purchase Order Entry**.

2.   In the **Prepayment** box, enter the prepayment amount up to the amount of the total:

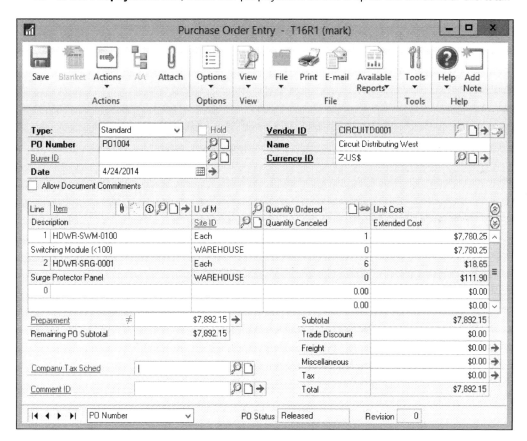

3.   Save the transaction and close the window to post the prepayment.

4. To process a payment, create a check batch and check the box marked **Purchasing Prepayment Batch** to include prepayments with other payables checks:

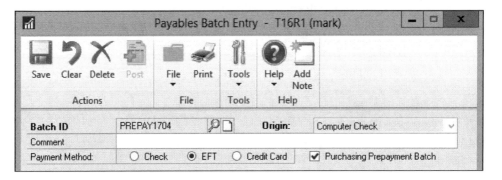

There's more...

Next to the **Prepayment** field, on **Purchase Order Entry**, is an expansion button marked by a blue arrow. Selecting this opens the **Purchasing Prepayment Entry** window. From this window, a user can set the prepayment account if it doesn't default. If **Create Manual Prepayments** from **Purchase Order Processing** is checked in setup, the option to select **Manual Prepayment** and provide the appropriate information is available:

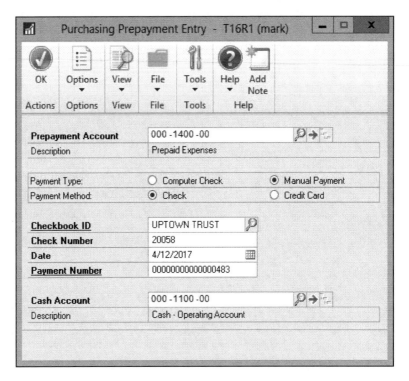

Gaining flexibility with Inventory Tolerance Handling

For many kinds of inventory items, there is flexibility in the quantity of goods delivered within a reasonable threshold. For example, contracts for wiring often have overage and underage clauses where the vendor can deliver 10% more or less than the contracted amount. In the case of wire, this is because wire comes on a spool, and it is inefficient to leave a small amount on a spool or start a new spool for an order that an existing spool can't quite fulfill.

Without a mechanism to deal with this, Purchase Order's for these items have to be closed manually for short orders or adjusted upward for overages. Dynamics GP 2016 has features in place to handle tolerances such as this.

How to do it...

To set up inventory tolerances, follow these steps:

1. Open **Item Card** using **Inventory | Cards | Item**.
2. Look up or enter an inventory item.
3. Select the **Go To** button from the ribbon at the top.
4. Pick **Purchasing** from the **Go To** menu.
5. To allow a shortage tolerance, check the box next to **Shortage** and enter a percentage.

6. To allow an overage tolerance, check the box next to **Overage** and enter a percentage:

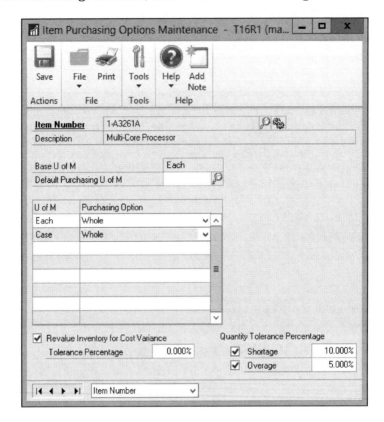

How it works...

Once a tolerance is set up, purchase order receiving will respect the tolerances. If a shortage is set and a quantity is received that is less than the full quantity, but within the shortage percentage, the PO line will be considered completely received and will close. If the amount is less than the full quantity, but still less than the shortage percentage, the line will stay open.

Similarly, if an overage tolerance is set and the quantity received is greater than the P.O. quantity, but still within the tolerance percentage, Dynamics GP will allow receiving more than the PO quantity.

P.O. tolerance is great for items where the quantity varies naturally, including products such as cable, wire, fabric, and items sold by weight.

Creating Fixed Assets with a default ID

Fixed Asset Management can either have the asset ID defaulted from the company setup or one that is manually entered by the user when the asset is created. Dynamics GP 2013 R2 saw a new option introduced; the ability to default the asset ID from the class.

Getting started...

To set a Next Asset ID on a class, follow theses steps:

1. In Dynamics GP, select **Financial** from the Navigation list and pick **Class** in the **Setup** area under **Fixed Assets**.

2. Perform a lookup on the **Class ID** field and select **COMP**.

3. Mark the **Default Asset ID from Class** checkbox.

4. In the **Default Next Asset ID** field, enter FAC000001:

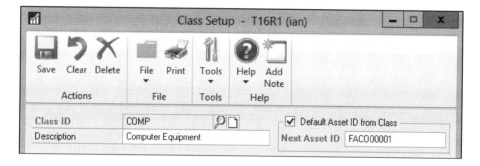

5. Click the **Save** button and close the window.

6. Repeat the preceding steps for each of the Fixed Asset classes that should have a unique asset ID.

How to do it...

With the classes configured with unique asset IDs, the next step is to start creating assets:

1. In Dynamics GP, select **Financial** from the Navigation list and pick **General** in the **Cards** area under **Fixed Assets**.

2. In the **Class ID** field perform a lookup and select **COMP**.

3. Tab to the next field and the Asset ID will be set to the next value:

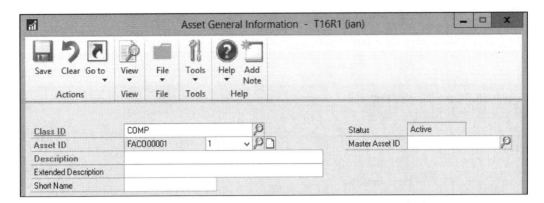

Avoid creating Payables Invoices when a PO already exists

Many users of Dynamics GP use both Purchase Order Processing and Payables Management invoices. There are different transaction types for different types of transaction; the former is used when creating a PO for items such as stationery or consultancy services, and the latter for items such as rent or rates.

One issue that plagues customers is getting the invoice entered in the correct one of two windows: **Enter/Match Invoices** for when a PO was involved and **Payables Transaction Entry** for the remainder.

As of Dynamics GP 2015, it is now possible to get a warning when entering a Payables Management invoice when there is an outstanding purchase order.

How to do it...

For the warning to work, it needs to be enabled. To enable the warning, follow these steps:

1. In Dynamics GP, select **Purchasing** from the Navigation list and pick **Transaction Entry** in the **Transactions** area.

2. Mark the **Warn if Vendor has Existing Purchase Order** checkbox.

3. Click **OK** to save changes and close the window:

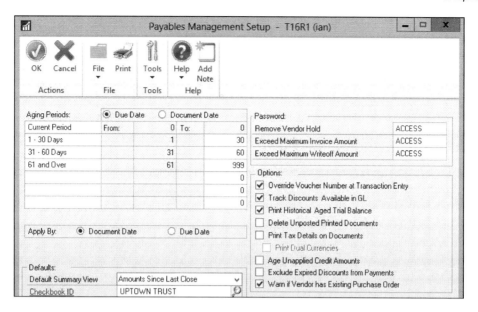

When a user enters an invoice in the **Payables Transaction Entry** window, a warning message will be displayed when the user clicks either **Save** or **Post**:

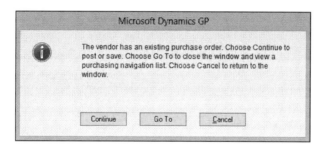

How it works...

Once the warning is enabled, Dynamics GP checks the vendor for open Purchase Order transactions when the user tries to either save or post the invoice. If at least one open PO is found, the warning triggers giving users the option to continue with the transaction, cancel and delete the transactions, (presumably to enter an invoice match instead), or drill to open Purchase Orders via GoTo to decide if this really belongs on a PO.

A simple warning like this can save hours of work fixing errant invoices.

6
Improving Dynamics GP with Hacks

In this chapter, we'll look at the following recipes:

- ▸ Using comments without needing a comment name
- ▸ Keeping the chart of accounts clean by reactivating Account Segment warnings
- ▸ Reducing licensing needs by preventing multiple company logins
- ▸ Turning on more features with Dex.ini settings
- ▸ Tackling self-assessed taxes such as Use Tax with the Reverse Tax functionality
- ▸ Correcting a lost system password by resetting the system password
- ▸ Getting greater journal entry control by clearing recurring batch amounts

Introduction

Hacking computer systems is a time-honored tradition, and by hacking I mean finding ways to make a system do more and go farther than its creators ever intended—not using a system in an inappropriate way.

Microsoft Dynamics GP is incredibly flexible. Over the years, users have found that there are ways to use Dynamics GP to solve business problems by applying conventional features in unconventional ways. This can include using a different feature to supply missing functionality, applying best practices to improve clarity, exposing hidden settings, or applying some simple code to add functionality to the system.

In this chapter, we'll look at ways to improve the usability of Dynamics GP by hacking the system with a few changes, some unconventional uses of features, and a little free code.

Using comments without needing a comment name

Comments can be used on a number of different transaction types, such as Sales Transactions or Purchase Orders, by entering or selecting a Comment ID, which allows a predefined piece of text to be added to an order line. However, it is sometimes useful to be able to add an ad hoc comment such as "6 of the 10 items have shipped; the remainder will ship on Tuesday."

Ad hoc comments are used by not adding a comment ID; this is useful as it prevents one-off comments from polluting the list of recurring comments.

How to do it...

To create comments without using a comment ID, follow these steps:

1. Select **Sales** from the Navigation list, then from under **Transactions** pick **Sales Transaction Entry**.

2. Click the right arrow in the lower left of the screen to select the first available Sales Transaction:

3. Leave the **Comment ID** field blank and click the blue arrow next to the **Comment ID** field:

4. In the **Comment** box, type This is a comment without an ID and click **OK**.

5. Notice that a new indicator appears between the **Comment ID** prompt and the **Comment ID** field to show that there is a comment without an ID:

6. Any documents that already show comments will include comments entered without an ID. The documents don't have to be changed at all.

How it works...

This recipe is the perfect solution for ad hoc comments without polluting comment IDs. As a plus, it allows the use of traditional comments with an ID. The biggest problem with this process is that it is hidden so deeply that most users don't find it.

There's more...

This works for all **Comment ID** boxes, including line item comments; however, only the first four lines of a comment appear on a document by default.

You can also add additional comments when a comment ID has been selected.

Line item comments

Our example showed a transaction level comment that would appear at the bottom of a document. However, each line in a document such as a Purchase Order or Invoice can also use comments without an ID in the same way.

Clicking on a line item in a document and selecting the blue arrow key opens up additional details about that line and exposes another **Comment ID** field. This works exactly like transaction level comments, except that the comments appear below each line item on the document by default.

Keeping the chart of accounts clean by reactivating Account Segment warnings

When creating a new account, where user keys in a segment without an associated description, they get an informational message providing the opportunity to add a description. Included in that informational message, the choice **Do not display this message again**, is the option to turn off the message:

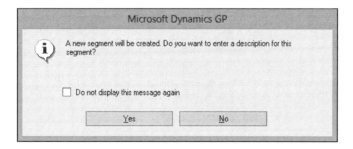

Once this box is checked for a user, the feature to allow the entry of a segment description on the fly is completely disabled for that user.

Since Microsoft does not include a switch to turn this feature back on, administrators will need to hack their way through some simple SQL code to make this available again.

How to do it...

To re-enable Account Segment warnings, follow these steps:

1. Open Microsoft SQL Server Management Studio and connect to the SQL Server used for Dynamics GP. Use either a username and password or Windows authentication to connect.

2. Because of the way that security is implemented between Dynamics GP and SQL Server, a Dynamics GP user login will not work here. The exception is the sa user, which is also the SQL Server system administrator login.

3. Click on **New Query** and select the appropriate company from the drop-down box on the top left. The sample company is named TWO. In the query area on the right, enter the following script:

    ```
    Delete from SY01401
    where coDefaultType = 13
    ```

    This will enable Account Segment warnings for all users.

4. To turn on Account Segments for a single user, add this third line, and change myUserID to the appropriate USERID:

    ```
    and USERID = 'myUserID'
    ```

5. Click **Execute** to run the script:

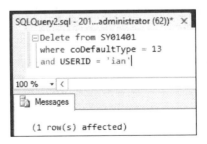

How it works...

Fixing features that the developer left out is what hacking is all about. In this case, Microsoft simply missed the option to turn this feature back on for a user and it can be very painful if the primary account entry user accidently turns it off. Fortunately, an administrator can re-enable the Account Segment warning with just a few lines of SQL code.

Reducing licensing needs by preventing multiple company logins

Dynamics GP is licensed on a concurrent user basis; a company might have 50 users, but only ten at a time can log in. With multiple companies in Dynamics GP, users have a tendency to log in to more than one company at a time to make switching between companies faster. However, each company login uses up a concurrent license.

There is no built in functionality to prevent users from logging in multiple times, so in this recipe we have a hack designed to prevent users from logging in to multiple companies at once. One point to note is that this hack will only work with the Dynamics GP desktop client; it will not work with the web client.

How to do it...

Follow these steps to prevent users from logging in to multiple Dynamics GP companies simultaneously:

1. Open Internet Explorer and navigate to `http://azrcrv.co.uk/zdBps`.

2. Download and save the `Prevent User Logging In To Multiple Companies.zip` file to your desktop.

3. Right-click on the downloaded file and pick `Extract`. Then click the **Extract** button.

4. After the files extract, repeat this process with the new file named `v10.00 Prevent User Logging In To Multiple Companies.zip`. Despite the `v10.00` designation in the filename, this file works just fine in version 2013.

5. Back in Dynamics GP, select **Microsoft Dynamics GP | Tools | Customize | Customization Maintenance**.

6. Click **Import** then **Browse**. Navigate to the location where you extracted **v10.00 Prevent User Logging In To Multiple Companies** on the desktop and pick the `MicrosoftActiveXDataObjects 2.8 Reference.package` file. Click **OK** to install.

7. Repeat Step 5 and 6 using the `SwitchCompany.Package` file.

8. Apply this customization to each user's workstation using Step 5, 6, and 7.

9. Once applied, users will be prevented from logging in to multiple companies simultaneously. If they try, users will get a message and an indication of what company they are already logged in to:

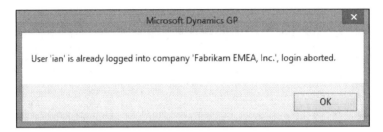

How it works...

This hack uses a free, unsupported **Visual Basic for Applications** (**VBA**) file created by David Musgrave. David was kind enough to release this code for free, for the benefit of the Dynamics GP community.

If there are any issues with installation, there are additional troubleshooting steps in the included `Installation Instructions.txt` file.

Turning on more features with the Dex.ini settings

Dynamics GP contains a number of features that can't be controlled via the interface; the controls for these features reside in an initialization file known as the `Dex.ini` file, which is loaded when Dynamics GP starts. The `Dex.ini` settings affect only the computer on which the file is installed.

As an example, `Dex.ini` settings can be used to control the date warning that appears when midnight passes, or force Dynamics GP to open full screen. If a particular setting is not present in the `Dex.ini` file, a user can simply add it to the end of the file.

If there are errors in the `Dex.ini` file, it can prevent Dynamics GP from opening, so users should make a copy of the `Dex.ini` file before making changes. In this recipe, we'll look at how to apply some of the most common and useful `Dex.ini` settings.

Getting ready

Before we can change `Dex.ini` settings, we need to open up the file. To open and modify the `Dex.ini` file, follow these steps:

1. Open the Notepad utility provided with all copies of Microsoft Windows.

2. In Notepad, select **File | Open**. Navigate to the `GP install` folder, which is typically found in `%ProgramFiles(x86)%\Microsoft Dynamics\GP2013` on a 64-bit machine (or `%ProgramFiles%\Microsoft Dynamics\GP2013` on an x86 machine).

3. Open the `Data` folder and select `Dex.ini` to open the file (if the `Dex.ini` file is not visible, type `*.ini` in the **File name** field to show files with an `.ini` extension):

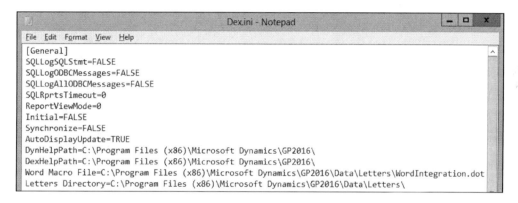

How to do it...

To demonstrate how to change the settings in the `Dex.ini` file, we'll start by turning on an alternative setting to dramatically speed up exporting SmartLists to Excel, and then we'll look at other common settings:

1. To force Dynamics GP to always open in a full screen, go to the `Dex.ini` file, find the setting named `WindowMax`, and set it to `WindowMax=True`.

2. To suppress sounds in Dynamics GP but not in other applications, find the setting `SupressSound` and set it to `SupressSound=True`. If `SupressSound` doesn't exist, key it at the end.

3. Prevent the warning that appears when adding new code or modules to Dynamics GP by finding `AutoInstallChunks` and setting it to `AutoInstallChunks=True`. If doesn't exist, simply key it at the end.

4. One of the problems that occur when exporting Report Writer-based reports is that long sets of data wrap to the next line in the export. This makes opening and analyzing exported data in Excel difficult. To prevent text report lines from wrapping when exporting, find the `Dex.ini` setting named `ExportOneLineBody` and set it to `ExportOneLineBody=True`. As with the others, simply key it at the end if it isn't in your `Dex.ini` file.

5. In *Chapter 5, Exposing Hidden Features*, in Dynamics GP, in the *Reducing posting steps with better printing control* recipe, we looked at how to turn off the print dialogue box via the interface. The same result can be accomplished by finding or keying the `NoPrintDialogs` setting and changing it to `NoPrintDialogs=True`.

6. Finally, when the computer time passes midnight, Dynamics GP displays a message indicating that the date has changed and asking the user if they want to change the date in Dynamics GP. This message can be turned off by setting `SuppressChangeDateDialog=True`. The date in the open Dynamics GP session won't automatically change to the next day; the warning is simply suppressed.

7. When finished, save the `Dex.ini` file to the desktop. Copy the desktop version to same location as the original, overwriting the original `Dex.ini` file. Restart Dynamics GP to see the changes. The save and copy process is required because Windows doesn't allow direct saving of this file since it's in a program files subfolder.

There's more...

These settings are just a sample of common changes that can be made via the `Dex.ini` file. There are lot more settings available.

Additional Dex.ini settings

Some of the other additional `Dex.ini` settings are as follows:

▶ `OLEPath=\\server\folder\ole`: This sets the path for linked and embedded files and should be the same for all users. When using a **Universal Naming Convention** (**UNC**) path such as `\\server\`, the complete folder structure must exist. Dynamics GP will not create it with the first note. If a mapped drive is used, such as `F:\`, the folder structure does not have to be created beforehand.

It is recommended that UNC paths rather than mapped drives are used, as UNC paths will work on all machines on the domain, whereas mapped drives need to be configured identically on each machine (either manually or via a logon script)

▶ `ShowAdvancedMacroMenu=True`: This setting turns on an additional menu for working with macros.

▶ `DPSInstance=1`: This setting allows the use of multiple process servers on a single physical machine. Process servers can be used to move the load of certain functions, such as posting, off a user's machine and onto a central process server.

Popular Dex.ini resources

By their very nature, `Dex.ini` switches are not easily discoverable. Fortunately, the MVP Leslie Vail has a comprehensive list of available `Dex.ini` switches on her blog, *Dynamics Confessions* (`http://azrcrv.co.uk/6dVnQA`).

See also

▶ The *Troubleshooting issues with a* recipe in *Chapter 11, Maintaining Dynamics GP*

Tackling self-assessed taxes such as Use Tax with the Reverse Tax functionality

In some jurisdictions, companies are subject to self-assessed purchase taxes. An example of this in the United States is Use Tax. Use tax is a variation of sales tax that is paid by a company when it retains untaxed goods instead of passing them through to customers. Since the company is the final user, they are responsible for paying the tax.

Dynamics GP doesn't handle self-assessed taxes automatically, but built-in Purchase Tax functionality and negative taxes can address this. In this recipe, we'll show how to use these features to handle these types of tax.

Getting ready

This process has some setup that needs to be done. The nice part about this option is that the burden on the user is pretty small. Setting up the basic tax schedules and details is well covered in the GP manuals and is not covered in this recipe. Make sure to set up at least one tax schedule and tax detail as a Purchase schedule before you start. Mine is named `IL State Tax`. Follow these steps to make this work:

1. Turn on **Reverse Tax Schedule** functionality in **Administration** | **Setup** | **Company** | **Company** | **Options**.

2. Check the box for **Enable Reverse Charge Tax**:

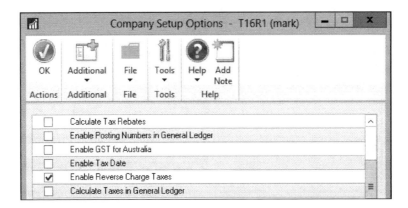

3. Create a tax detail for a purchase tax that includes a negative amount. This negative is the same percentage as the corresponding positive tax details. You can use one negative tax percentage to offset multiple positive tax percentages:

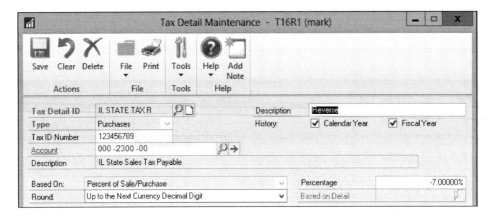

4. Add the tax detail to the corresponding tax schedule and to the **All Details** schedule if you are using that.

How to do it...

Follow these steps to apply Use tax this way:

1. Start an AP transaction via **Purchasing | Transactions | Transaction Entry**.

2. Set the **Shipping Method** option to **PICKUP** and pick the **Tax Schedule** setup earlier that included a negative tax assignment:

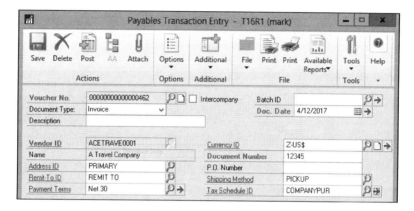

3. It appears that no tax is assigned. Click the **Expansion** button (blue arrow) next to **Tax**. Both tax schedules are assigned:

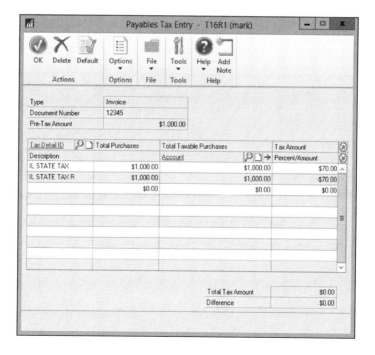

4. Click **OK** to close the **Payables Tax Entry** window.

5. Click **Distributions** to view the distributions. Notice that in this transaction, tax is expensed to a specific expense account and an offsetting liability is created:

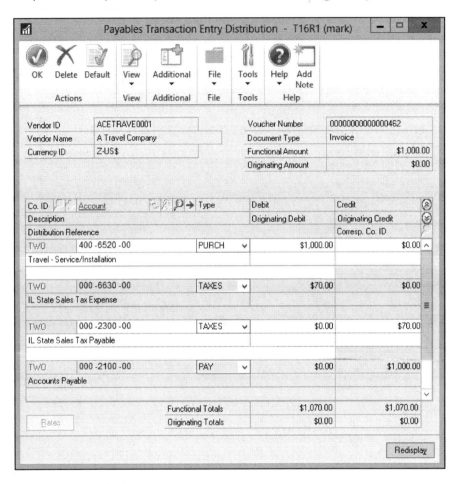

How it works...

The positive and negative tax details cancel each other out, making payment to the vendor correct and leaving a liability for later payment to the taxing authority. SmartLists can be used for reporting to support the ultimate payment to one or more tax authorities.

There's more...

Credit for this option goes to Gina Hoener of Summit Group Software. She first detailed this option in a blog post at `http://azrcrv.co.uk/jHx9EH`.

In our example, we directed the tax expense to its own account. In practice, many companies want the tax expense to apply to the same account as the transaction. Follow these steps to accomplish this:

1. Activate an **Australian** or **Canadian** tax option by selecting **Administration | Setup | Company | Company | Options** and checking either **Enable Canadian Tax Detail** or **Enable GST for Australia**. Canada is recommended as there are fewer dependencies.

2. Accept the warning message about setting up a Canadian tax ID or accept the warning message to activate effective tax dates for the Australian option.

3. Click **OK** to save the setting and restart Dynamics GP.

4. Open the tax detail pointed to expense by selecting **Administration | Setup | Company | Tax Details** and choosing the appropriate tax detail.

5. Clear the account from the **Account** field.

6. A new field is now available, labeled **Post to**. Change the drop-down menu in this field to select **Vendor Purchase Account**:

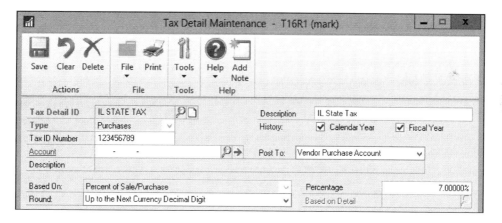

7. With this change, future expenses will be redirected to the same account that was used for purchases.

Correcting a lost password by resetting the system password

Part of the security matrix of Dynamics GP is the system password, which provides another layer of protection after users have already logged in to Dynamics GP by requiring the system password to be entered before certain system windows can be accessed.

While the use of a system password is technically optional, it is typically used, but often it used infrequently, and then typically by administrators. Consequently, the system password can be lost or forgotten as people leave or change roles.

Fortunately, there is a process available for administrators with access to SQL Server to reset the administrator password. In this recipe, we'll look at how to do just that.

How to do it...

To reset the system password, follow these steps:

1. Open Microsoft SQL Server Management Studio and connect to the SQL Server used for Dynamics GP. Enter a username and password, or use windows authentication to connect.

2. Because of the way that Dynamics GP maintains security with SQL Server, a Dynamics GP username can't be used here. The only exception is the SQL system administrator (sa) user.

3. Click the **New Query** button. Select the **System Database** (typically called DYNAMICS) from the drop-down box on the top left. Enter the following script in the code area on the right:

```
Use Dynamics
Go
Update SY02400 Set Password =
   0X002020202020202020202020202020
Go
```

4. Click **Execute** to run the script. This resets the system password to blank.

5. Open Dynamics GP and select **Administration** from the Navigation list. Pick **System Password** from the area page under **System**.

6. Enter a new system password. Re-enter the new system password as confirmation and click **OK** to save.

How it works...

The long line of numbers after `Set Password` simply sets the password back to being blank. The password isn't encrypted, it's simply masked. With enough time, energy, and access to a company's SQL Server, it would be possible to decode the masking. Then again, if a troublemaker has access to a firm's SQL Server, they don't need the system password to make a mess. This tip should be reserved for a company's database administrator. Ordinary users should be prevented from running queries that update information via SQL.

There's more...

In addition to resetting the system password, a similar script can be used to reset a lost budget password:

1. Click the **New Query** button and select the company database containing the budget that needs its password reset from the drop-down box on the top left. Enter the following script in the code area on the right, replacing `myBudgetID` with the budget ID to be reset:

```
Update GL00200 Set BUDPWRD =
   0X0020202020202020202020202020202020
Where BUDGETID = 'myBudgetID'
Go
```

2. Click **Execute** to run the script to reset the budget's password.

Getting greater journal entry control by clearing recurring batch amounts

The recurring batch functionality in Dynamics GP provides the batch and approval functionality that many companies need, but until version 2010 the only option to change the amounts was to overwrite each line. There was no option to have a template style entry and batch approval. This process left a lot of room for user error, making it an imperfect solution.

Dynamics GP 2010 introduced the ability to clear the amounts from a recurring batch after it is posted. This allows a user to build a journal entry but not be locked into the same amounts each time. It also allows the use of batch approval. In this recipe, we'll setup a recurring batch where the amounts clear after each posting.

How to do it...

Follow these steps to set up recurring batches to clear after posting:

1. Select **Financial** from the Navigation list, then **Batches** under **Transactions**.

2. In **Batch ID** enter Z TEST RECUR.

3. Set **Origin** to **General Entry**.

4. Change **Frequency** to **Monthly** to set up a recurring batch.

5. Check the box marked **Clear Recurring Amounts**:

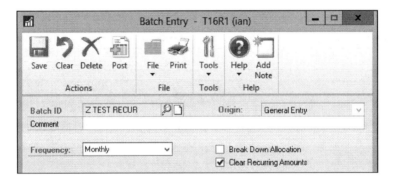

6. Click **Transactions** to add recurring journal entries.

After the recurring batch is posted, the amounts will clear, allowing users to enter new amounts the next time.

7
Preventing Errors in Dynamics GP

Microsoft Dynamics GP is a robust **Enterprise Resource Planning** system. However, any software system is vulnerable to the possibility of errors. Errors can be caused by user actions, software bugs, network issues, hardware failures, or other sources. In this chapter we'll look at some ways to prevent errors in Dynamics GP:

- ▶ Preventing posting errors by managing Batch Date
- ▶ Reducing out of balance problems with Allow Account Entry
- ▶ Ensuring entry in the correct company by warning about test companies
- ▶ Protecting Dynamics GP with key security settings
- ▶ Providing clean vendor information by properly closing Purchase Orders
- ▶ Preventing account selection errors with segment names
- ▶ Ensuring proper year-end closing by checking Posting Types
- ▶ Preventing sales of discontinued inventory
- ▶ Correcting errors by backing out, correcting, and copying journal entries

Introduction

The longevity and popularity of Microsoft's Dynamics GP Enterprise Resource Planning software is a testament to the system's robustness, but any system is vulnerable to errors. There are times when users make entry mistakes, network outages occur, and computer hardware fails, and any of these events can cause errors in Dynamics GP. For a Dynamics GP administrator, some of the most common and most controllable errors are those related to user activities. For example, an administrator can't control when a network switch is going to fail, but they can ensure that proper security is in place to prevent users from deleting tables.

Preventing errors frees up administrators' and users' time to focus on more important things. In this chapter we'll look at some common setup and procedural changes that administrators and users can make to help prevent errors in Dynamics GP. Additionally, we'll take a look at how to fix erroneous transactions that managed to make it to the general ledger.

Preventing posting errors by managing Batch Date

In most modules, Microsoft Dynamics GP provides the option to post transactions individually or to collectively post a group of transactions in a batch. The common best practice when implementing Dynamics GP is to use Batch Posting, not individual transaction posting.

The reasoning behind this preference is that batches and batch posting provide a number of benefits over transactional posting. These benefits include the ability to save transactions without posting them, improved error handling, and the ability to post multiple transactions or multiple batches at once. Additionally, batches can be used to control the date that transactions are posted on, thereby making it easy to ensure that transactions are posted in the right period.

In this recipe we will look at batch naming and posting techniques along with error handling options designed to minimize posting errors.

Getting ready

To set up the process to post transactions by batch, follow these steps:

1. In Dynamics GP, select **Administration** from the Navigation pane, then pick **Posting** under the **Setup | Posting** section on the **Administration** area page.

2. Select the **Series** to change the settings of. For our example, select **Purchasing**.

3. Select a posting **Origin**. In this example, select **Payables Trx Entry** to control posting settings for accounts payable voucher entry:

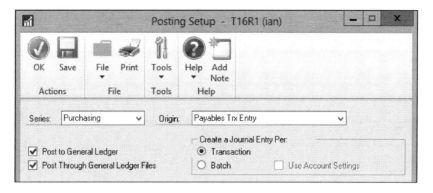

4. Uncheck **Allow Transaction Posting** to force posting to the general ledger by batch.

5. Check **Transaction** under **Create a Journal Entry Per** to avoid rolling up transactions in the general ledger.

6. Sending batches of subledger transactions to the general ledger as a single transaction has its roots in ledger paper accounting. This practice moved to software when disk space was at a premium. It is almost never needed now and complicates tracing subledger transactions through the general ledger.

7. Click **Save**, then **OK** to finish.

How to do it...

To set up a batch using best practices, follow these steps:

1. Select **Purchasing** from the Navigation pane, then pick **Batches** under the **Transactions** section on the **Purchasing** area page.

2. Name the batch with your initials and today's date. In my example batch is named IG-2017-04-17:

3. By naming batches this way, users searching for a batch will see the available batches sorted in order by user initials and then date.

4. Typically, firms either let users post their own batches or they use a designated individual or group to post batches from multiple users:

   ❏ If users post their own batches, start the batch name with initials followed by the date, such as IG-2017-04-17. This will cluster a user's batches together when posting, making it easier to post multiple batches for a single user.

   ❏ If a different individual posts transactions for multiple users, start the batches with the date followed by the initials, such as 2017-04-17-IG. This clusters batches together by date making it easier to select the right batches across multiple users.

5. Dates in batch names should start with the year and then the period, such as 2017-04. This naming convention clusters batches together when approaching year-end or period-end. For example, it's typical at period end to have some left-over transactions from the previous period and new transactions for the current period. Starting dates with the year and period helps ensure that users pick the correct batch to post.

6. Single digit periods and days should use a zero in front since Dynamics GP sees batch names as text. Not using a leading zero will cause a batch for period 10 to come before a batch for period 9.

7. Select **Payables Trx Entry** in the **Origin** field.

8. Set **Frequency** to **Single Use** for our example. Recurring batches have a frequency other than single use (monthly, weekly, and so on). They are designed to be posted multiple times. For recurring batches, the following recommendations apply:

   ❏ Start recurring batches with the letter z to cluster them at the bottom of lookup windows. It may make sense to date recurring batches with their end date instead of creation date to make it easy to identify when this batch will stop recurring.

   ❏ Provide a complete description and notes for recurring batches since the rationale for the recurring batch may fade from memory over time.

   ❏ If there are multiple transactions in a recurring batch, ensure that they are all designed to stop repeating at the same time.

9. Enter today's date as **Posting Date** for the batch following these recommendations:

   ❏ **One period per batch**: Users shouldn't mix transactions from multiple periods in a single batch as this makes it impossible to post the transactions in the proper period since the entire batch will post in one period.

   The only exception to this is **general ledger** (**GL**) batches, which always use the date on the transaction for posting; there is no option to post GL batches by date.

❑ **Post using the batch date**: Posting using the batch date ensures that all the transactions in the batch post using the same date and the date is visible with a glance at the batch. This contrasts with individual posting where the posting data could be different on each transaction.

For transaction posting, the true posting date is hidden behind an expansion arrow on the date field, making it difficult to validate the posting date on multiple transactions.

10. Click the **Transactions** button to add transactions to a batch.

11. Once transactions are entered, batches can be posted from the same window.

The following items should be considered when posting batches:

▸ Non-recurring batches should disappear when posted. In the event that this doesn't happen, users need to select the printer icon in the upper right to print the batch edit list either to paper or to the screen. Printing the batch edit list prior to posting is a best practice, but this process can be impractical for batches with large numbers of transactions.

▸ **Transaction Edit List** will show batch level errors at the top and transaction level errors below any problem transactions. The most common batch level error is a closed fiscal period preventing batches from posting. For transaction level errors, missing accounts or account-related problems are seen most often.

▸ Batches that contain errors may fail posting and end up in **Batch Recovery**. **Batch Recovery** is found in the **Administration** area page under **Routines**. **Batch Recovery** will either resolve minor errors and continue the posting or return the batch to a state where **Transaction Edit List** can be printed and reviewed for corrections:

How it works...

Following these batch level posting techniques simplifies batch management by providing a standard process and naming convention for all users. Posting errors are reduced by managing posting dates at the batch level and ensuring that batches only cover a single period.

Years of experience have shown consultants and advanced users that transactions posted in a batch have a better chance of recovery in the event of a catastrophic posting error such as a network outage during posting. This isn't acknowledged explicitly in any of the software documentation but there is a wealth of painful stories illustrating that transactions posted by batch recover from errors better than individually posted transactions.

See also

- ▸ The *Controlling Posting Dates when not posting by batch* recipe in *Chapter 5, Exposing Hidden Features in Dynamics GP*
- ▸ The *Preventing entry to wrong dates by closing periods* recipe in *Chapter 11, Maintaining Dynamics GP*

Reducing out of balance problems with Allow Account Entry

Balancing subledgers such as accounts payable or accounts receivable to the GL can be a time consuming process at period end. A common reason that a subledger doesn't match the corresponding account in the general ledger is that a user has made an entry directly to the general ledger.

Transactions in Dynamics GP generally flow down from subledgers into the general ledger. With rare exceptions, transactions made in the general ledger do not flow back upstream to a subledger. This means that when users make an entry directly to a general ledger account, the information doesn't flow back up to a related subledger, resulting in an out of balance situation.

A scenario like this is easily prevented by disabling an often overlooked feature known as **Allow Account Entry**. Disabling the **Allow Account Entry** setting prevents entries directly to the general ledger for certain accounts. When this feature is deactivated for an account, transactions must flow from a subledger; direct entries to that account from the general ledger are blocked by the system.

In this recipe we will look at how to deactivate the **Allow Account Entry** feature and we'll see how it works in practice.

How to do it...

To require transactions to flow through a subledger for a particular account, follow these steps:

1. Select **Financial** from the Navigation list then pick **Accounts** under the **Cards** section.

2. Use the lookup button (magnifying glass) to select account `000-2100-000`, the **Accounts Payable** account in the sample company.

3. Uncheck the box marked **Allow Account Entry** and click **Save** to finish:

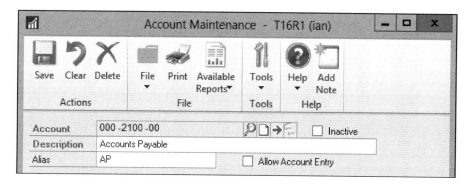

To see what happens when this feature is deactivated for an account, follow these steps:

1. Back on the **Financial** area page, select **General** under **Transactions**.

2. Use the lookup button (magnifying glass) in the **Account** field to select account `000-2100-000` in the **Account** field on the bottom of the window.

3. Dynamics GP responds with a message that **Account 000-2100-00 does not allow account entry.**:

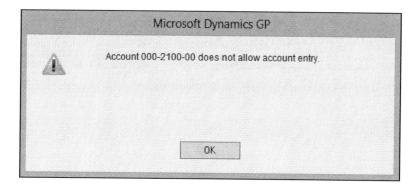

How it works...

This feature is simple to implement but extremely powerful. A simple checkbox can dramatically improve the process of balancing transactions at period end. There are a number of accounts that can benefit from turning off Allow Account Entry; common accounts that are prime candidates for preventing direct general ledger entry include **Cash, Accounts Payable, Accounts Receivable, Inventory, Payroll Accounts, Fixed Assets, Accumulated Depreciation**, and **Depreciation Expense**.

There's more...

There can be valid reasons for adjusting some of these accounts in the general ledger so administrators need to understand the process to accomplish this.

Adjustments

There are times when an adjustment to one of these accounts is needed in the general ledger. Perhaps a network outage happened during posting that resulted in a transaction properly posting to the subledger but not moving to the general ledger. In a scenario like this, an administrator can temporarily check the box to allow account entry and uncheck the box as soon as the correction is posted. This is an occasional inconvenience when compared to the benefits of smoother monthly balancing. Because of the potential effects on balancing, the ability to adjust this setting should be limited to select users.

See also

> ▸ The *Speeding up month-end processing with the Reconcile to GL functionality* recipe in *Chapter 5, Exposing Hidden Features in Dynamics GP*

Ensuring entry in the correct company by warning about test companies

Most companies using Dynamics GP set up a test company. This is normally a copy of the live, production, and GP database, and may reside on its own server. A test company may be used for testing things such as new processes, modules, or even, if it resides on a separate server, test upgrades.

A test company is used in addition to the sample company because it contains a copy of the firm's actual data. Consequently, they have different uses. For instance, the sample company is great for learning about new modules that a firm is not yet licensed for since unlicensed modules aren't available in a test company. A test company is great for trying out the process to close a year or providing training to new users.

A common problem occurs when a user mistakenly logs into the test company and enters a transaction. When they find their mistake they have to enter it again in the production database and even more problems can occur if a user mistakenly enters a test transaction in the production company.

Dynamics GP provides a feature to help prevent these scenarios from occurring. There is a small trick that can be used to warn users when they log in to a test company; this is similar to the message that users get when they open the sample company. Warning users when entering a test company is the focus of this recipe.

How to do it...

To warn users that they are opening a test company, follow these steps:

1. Sign in to a test company in Microsoft Dynamics GP. This recipe will not work with the sample company because of the way it is set up.

2. In Dynamics GP, select **Administration** from the Navigation list. Pick a company under the **Setup | Company** section on the home page.

3. Next to the company name in the text box, type `<TEST>` in all caps:

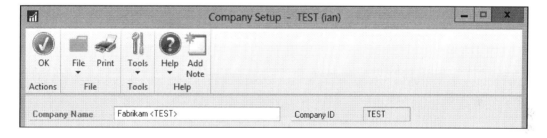

4. Click **Save** to save the settings.

5. Restart Microsoft Dynamics GP and log in to the same test company.

6. A warning message will appear alerting the user that this is a test company:

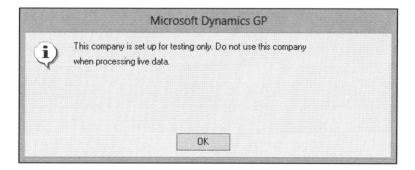

How it works...

Warning users about test companies is a great way to prevent errors. I've seen it be a real lifesaver when a user realized that they didn't see the warning and were entering test data in the production company. This recipe is so simple to implement that everyone should use it.

Protecting Dynamics GP with key security settings

Security is an important part of any ERP system, and Dynamics GP provides a robust security model which rolls up individual item access into tasks and tasks into roles. Roles can then be applied to individual users, providing fine-grain control of security with minimal work after the initial setup.

While the set up and maintenance of security in Dynamics GP could fill a book by itself, there are a couple of critical settings that every administrator needs to be aware of.

Dynamics GP security contains a master switch that turns all security on or off. The original purpose of this switch was to allow set up and testing of the system while security was still being configured. Then, like Chevy Chase's Christmas lights in the movie National Lampoon's Christmas Vacation, a master switch could be flipped and security would be active.

Located below the **Security** master switch is an **Account Security** switch. What account security does is limit access to accounts based on an organizational structure that needs to be set up first. If an organization structure is not set up, when this box is checked, all users are denied access to the chart of accounts, and it appears that the chart of accounts has been deleted. Few checkboxes in Dynamics GP can induce the stomach dropping fear that comes with inadvertently checking the account security box. This is easily one of the most panicky support calls I see and certainly it is the one with the easiest fix.

Setting up security and account security aren't recipes, they are more like Thanksgiving dinners. For this recipe, we'll trim it down to a snack and show how to ensure that security is on and account security is off.

How to do it...

To activate security and deactivate account security in Dynamics GP, follow these steps:

1. Select **Administration** from the Navigation list. Pick a company under the **Setup | Company** section on the **Administration** area page.

2. Check the **Security** box on the middle right to activate security. If it is already marked, security is on, congratulations!

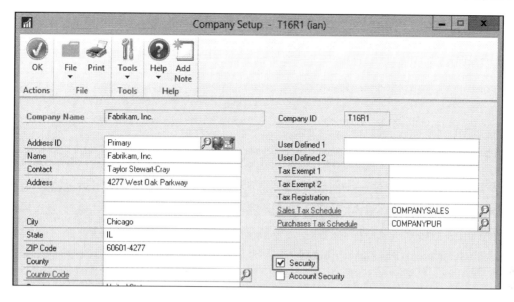

3. Below that is the **Account Security** box. Simply uncheck the box to ensure that account security is off.

How it works...

These are two very basic settings that often trip up administrators. It's maddening to see a very detailed security model with a lot of work put into it and then find the security box unchecked. Don't even think about the effect on an administrator's career if an auditor finds this box unchecked. It's also career limiting to have the CFO asking where the chart of accounts has disappeared to because someone accidently turned on account security. Don't misunderstand, account security is a great feature, it's just not one that should be turned on lightly.

There's more...

Given the power of these check boxes, access to them should be secured as well. For complicated security setups and additional security features, consider third-party solutions.

Security for security

The **Security** and **Account Security** checkboxes are powerful. Once they are set correctly it is important that security be restricted to the **Company Setup** window to prevent a user from disabling security entirely by simply unchecking a box.

Security solutions

There are several third party solutions that build on Dynamics GP security making security management easier and adding additional features. For example, FastPath's Configurator AD product synchronizes user passwords with Windows Active Directory passwords, allowing multiple single sign-on options. Additionally, Configurator AD provides an interface outside of Dynamics GP to assign security roles to users. This allows a central security manager to assign Dynamics GP security to users without using up a Dynamics GP license or providing excessive access to the security manager. More information is available at `http://www.gofastpath.com`.

Providing clean vendor information by properly closing Purchase Orders

It's not unusual for a **Purchase Order** (**PO**) to be left open in Dynamics GP due to a vendor's inability to deliver goods. However, when the time comes to close an incomplete PO, too many users simply change the PO line quantity to match the quantity delivered and close the PO. The problem with this process is that it reduces visibility into the performance of a vendor. By changing the quantity ordered there is no way to track the fact that the vendor didn't deliver goods.

A better way to close a PO is to put any undelivered amounts in the quantity canceled line. This makes performance information available to SmartLists and Excel reports, making it possible to analyze the performance of a vendor over time. As an example, an analysis may show that it may make sense for a firm to pay a little more to a reliable supplier instead of dealing with the frustration of product outages.

In this recipe, we'll look at the right way to close a partially received PO using the sample company.

How to do it...

To properly close a partially received PO, follow these steps:

1. Select **Purchasing** from the Navigation list. Pick **Purchase Order Entry** under the **Transaction** section on the **Purchasing** area page.

2. Use the lookup button (magnifying glass) to select **PO Number** PO1016. Change the **Quantity Canceled** to 5 to out this PO:

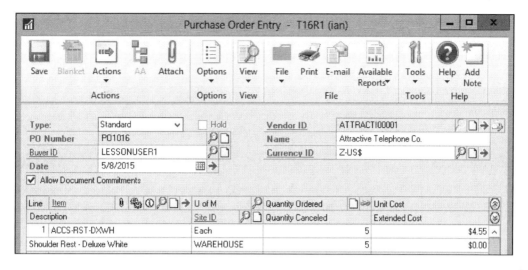

3. Click **Save** to save the changes. The PO closes automatically when the last line is canceled.

How it works...

Properly closing POs in Dynamics GP allows a company to make intelligent sourcing decisions about which vendors are able to meet the firm's needs. Companies gain the data necessary to analyse vendor performance and make decisions based on factors beyond just price. After all, having a cheaper product to sell isn't very helpful if it never arrives.

Preventing account selection errors with segment names

Given the typical meticulous tendencies of most accountants, it's a little bit of a surprise that the descriptions in an average chart of accounts are a complete mess. Most charts of accounts are initially pristine but as accounts are added by various people over time, their descriptions become inconsistent. This makes it very difficult to ensure that users select the right account.

As an example, assume that the first segment in the chart of accounts represents the company, the second is the natural account, and the third is a department. An account description would ideally be something like ABC Co.-Cash-Marketing. In reality, accounts tend to look like Marking Cash, ABC, or AP Ops. This makes it hard for users to find and select the right account.

Dynamics GP provides a mechanism to ensure that new accounts follow a set naming pattern. Rather than adding a description to the chart of accounts, every unique option in each segment is given a name in a setup screen. When that item is selected, Dynamics GP provides the name of that segment from the setup.

We'll use the sample company to set up and use **Account Segment** descriptions to cook this recipe.

Getting ready

To set up account segment descriptions, follow these steps:

1. Select **Financial** from the Navigation list. Pick **Segment** under the **Setup** section.

2. Set **Segment ID** to **Division**. Use the lookup button (magnifying glass) in the **Number** field to find number **300**. Add or change the **Description** field to `Sales and Marketing`:

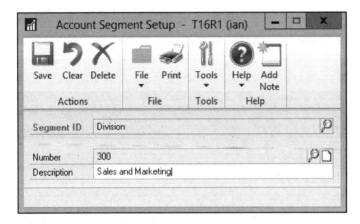

3. Set **Segment ID** to **Account**. Use the lookup button (magnifying glass) in the **Number** field to find number **1100**. Add or change the **Description** field to `Accounts Receivable`.

4. Set **Segment ID** to **Department**. Use the lookup button (magnifying glass) in the **Number** field to find number **02**. Add or change the **Description** field to `Marketing`.

How to do it...

To create an account description using account segments, follow these steps:

1. Select **Financial** from the Navigation list. Pick **Account** under the **Cards** section.

2. In the **Account** field, enter `300-1100-02` and press *Tab*.

3. The name will be automatically built in the **Description** field from the descriptions of the three segments in the account number:

How it works...

Having consistent account descriptions prevents errors by providing clear and consistent account naming, making it easy for users to select the right account. This recipe also makes it easy for users who create accounts. They no longer have to wrestle with the right naming order. Unfortunately, it does not provide a mechanism to fix existing accounts. Users will have to cook up that recipe on their own.

See also

- The *Keep the chart of accounts clean by reactivating Account Segment warnings* recipe in *Chapter 6, Improving Dynamics GP with Hacks*

- The *Importing data with Microsoft Word and a Dynamics GP macro* recipe in *Chapter 10, Connecting Dynamics GP to Microsoft Office 2016*

Ensuring proper year-end closing by checking Posting Types

When setting up accounts in Chart of Accounts, users are required to select a posting type of either Balance Sheet or Profit and Loss. These selections correspond to their respective financial statements, the Balance Sheet and the Profit and Loss statement, also known as Income Statement. Asset, Liability, and Equity accounts should have a posting type of Balance Sheet. Revenue and Expense accounts need the Profit and Loss Posting Type. This is important because the Posting Type controls the behavior of year-end closing for these accounts.

The year-end closing routine in Dynamics GP zeros out the accounts with a Posting Type of Profit and Loss and updates the selected Retained Earnings account. This process resets the Profit and Loss accounts to prepare for a new year and uses the ending balance in Balance Sheet accounts to create the beginning balance in the new year.

If accounts are incorrectly set up as Profit and Loss accounts, their year-end balance will be erroneously cleared to retained earnings. Similarly, accounts incorrectly set up as Balance Sheet accounts will not get cleared to Retained Earnings to reflect prior-year net income. In short, if the Posting Type is not correct during year-end closing, companies end up with a mess that can be difficult to fix.

Because of this, validating that the Posting Type is set correctly is an important step prior to closing the year. There are two typical processes to validate Posting Types, using a SmartList to view exceptions and using a report to review all accounts. In this recipe we will cook up both options.

Getting ready

The two main options for validating Posting Types are an exception-based SmartList and a built-in dynamics GP report. Many firms use a standard, generalized numbering system for their chart of accounts based on the first digit of the natural account. When a schema such as this is followed, it makes it possible to double check that accounts have the correct posting types. A typical scenario uses accounts starting with one, two, or three as balance sheet accounts representing assets, liabilities, and equity respectively. Those starting with four or higher are used for the Profit and Loss statement.

The benefit of this type of setup is that users can create a SmartList that only shows the exceptions. This makes it very easy to find and correct errors. If there is no pattern or identifier designed into the account structure a report built into Dynamics GP can still be used to review account Posting Types.

Once incorrect posting types have been identified, they can be corrected using the **Account** window on the **Financial** area page under **Cards**:

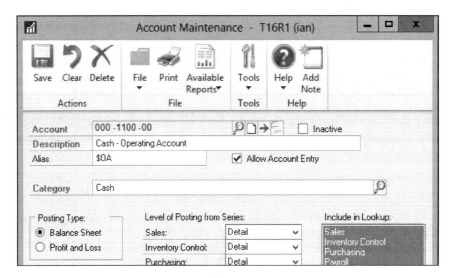

For our example, we use the sample company that is set up with the last **Balance Sheet** account as 3999 and the first **Profit and Loss** account as 4000.

How to do it...

To review **Account Posting Types** with a SmartList, follow these steps:

1. Click the SmartList icon to open the SmartList window.

2. Select the **Accounts SmartList** under the **Financial** section.

3. Click the **Search** button.

4. Set **Search Definition 1** equal to **Account Number** (or Segment 2 if the segments in the sample company were not renamed during deployment) is less than 4000.

5. Set **Search Definition 2** equal to **Posting Type** equals **Profit and Loss**:

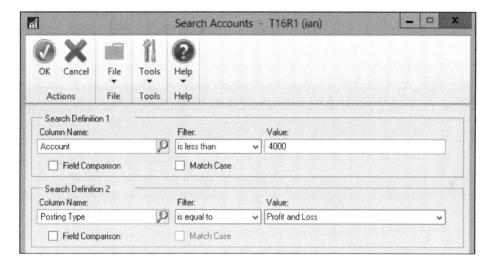

6. Click **OK** to display low-numbered accounts that are improperly listed as **Profit and Loss** accounts.

7. Press the **Print** button to print this report to make the appropriate corrections in the **Account Maintenance** window later.

8. Click **Favorites** and save this SmartList as **Favorite** named YE BS Errors.

9. Click **Search** again.

10. Change **Search Definition 1** to **Account Number** (or Segment 2 if the segments in the sample company were not renamed during deployment) is greater than 4000.

11. Change **Search Definition 2** to **Posting Type** equals **Balance Sheet**:

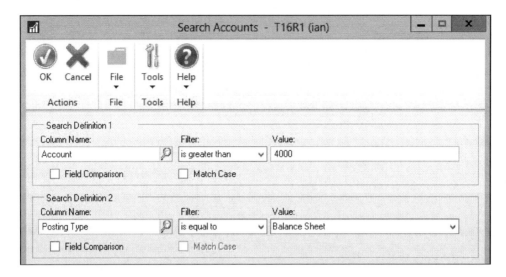

12. Click **OK** to display high numbered accounts that are improperly listed as **Balance Sheet** accounts.

13. Press the **Print** button to print this report and allow a user to make the appropriate corrections in the **Account Maintenance** window later.

14. Click **Favorites** and save this SmartList as **Favorite** named `YE PL Errors`.

If a firm's chart of accounts is not set up in way that makes identifying exceptions possible, a user still needs to print the chart of accounts and review the account Posting Types individually prior to year-end.

To print and review the chart, follow these steps:

1. Select **Financial** from the Navigation list. Pick **Account** from the **Financial** area page under the **Reports and Financial** sections.

2. Under the **Reports** header, pick **Posting**. Click the **New** button.

3. In the **Option** box, type `Posting Type`:

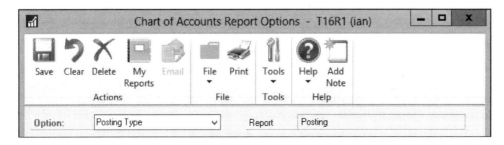

4. Click **OK** to finish.

5. Select the **Print** button and review the report for Posting Type corrections:

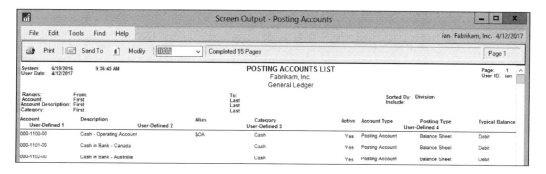

How it works...

Reviewing Posting Types prior to running year-end close is a simple solution to preventing an embarrassing situation. Firms that are able to use exception-based reporting get a fast, easy validation that Posting Types are correct. Even when exception reporting is not available, reviewing Posting Types is an important procedure to prevent a year-end disaster.

See also

▶ *Chapter 8, Harnessing the Power of SmartLists*

Preventing sales of discontinued inventory

Companies frequently discontinue inventory items. Perhaps an item's sales volume is too low, it has been replaced with a new model, or the item is no longer available from a supplier. By default, in Dynamics GP, discontinued inventory items can still be sold. The reasoning is that companies would still want to sell these items and clear out the inventory if the opportunity arose but they don't want to purchase more of a discontinued item.

The problem comes when companies need to prevent the sale of discontinued items. There could be a safety or health issue contributing to the importance of not selling a particular item. The typical advice in cases like this is to write off the discontinued inventory to prevent the sale. But that removes visibility to inventory that might be returnable for credit in the case of a safety recall. Additionally, in the event of a health issue, the inventory may need to be retained for inspection or proof of proper disposal. Writing the items off or moving them to a different item number may not be appropriate in these cases.

There is a mechanism to reduce errors by preventing the sale of discontinued inventory. In this recipe we'll look at how to do just that.

How to do it...

To prevent Dynamics GP from allowing sales of discontinued inventory, follow these steps:

1. Select **Sales** from the Navigation list. Pick **Sales Order Processing** under the **Setup** section on the **Sales** area page.

2. Click the **Options** button.

3. In the bottom grid, scroll down and uncheck **Allow Sale of Discontinued Items**. Click **OK** to finish:

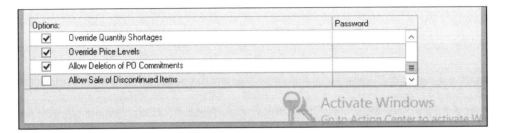

When a user enters a discontinued item in **Sales Order Processing**, the system presents an error message and requires the user select an active item as a replacement.

How it works...

Preventing the sale of discontinued inventory items is easy but since the setting is buried in Sales, not Inventory, most administrators never find it. One important point about this setting is that it is universal for a company; if the sale of discontinued items is prevented then it's prevented for all discontinued items.

There's more...

Prior to Dynamics GP 2013, there was no individual control; you could block the sale of all discontinued items, or allow the sale of all. Dynamics GP 2013 saw the introduction of the Inactive flag on individual items.

When an item is inactive it can be neither purchased nor sold; existing transactions for the inactive item can still be processed, although the quantity cannot be changed. This means an order that has been shipped can be transferred to invoice even if the item is now inactive.

To discontinue an item and set it as inactive, follow these steps:

1. Select **Inventory** from the Navigation list. Pick **Item** under the **Cards** section on the **Inventory** area page.

2. Type `24XIDE` to load the item **24x CD-ROM**.

3. Set the **Item Type** field to **Discontinued**.

4. Mark the **Inactive** checkbox:

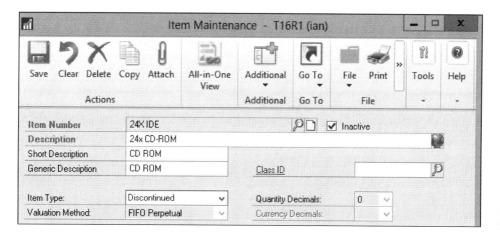

5. Click **Save**.

Once the item has been deactivated, the only transaction types that can be entered for an inactive item are as follows:

▸ Returns from sales or for purchases

▸ Inventory transfers between sites or bins

▸ Increase or decrease variances

▸ Decrease adjustments

Correcting errors by backing out, correcting, and copying journal entries

This chapter is dedicated to preventing errors but for this recipe we want to look at fixing errors, specifically, the Correct Journal Entry functionality in Dynamics GP. The occurrence of errors is inevitable. The recipes in this chapter are designed to help users and administrators minimize errors, but once an error occurs, quickly fixing it is the next priority.

A common problem happens when users post journal entries to an incorrect period. They create a transaction using the current date and forget to change it to post the entry in the previous period.

Dynamics GP includes functionality to fix journal entry errors by backing out a journal entry and optionally presenting a duplicate journal entry for the user to change and repost. This same functionality allows copying a journal entry for users who forgot to use a recurring batch.

In this recipe, we'll use the sample company to look at fixing errors by backing out, correcting, and copying journal entries.

How to do it...

To back out and correct a journal entry, follow these steps:

1. Select **Financial** from the Navigation list. Pick **General** under the **Transactions** section.

2. Select **Correct** from the top right.

3. In the **Action** field, pick **Back Out a Journal Entry and Create a Correcting Entry**. Set the year to **2017** and enter 1549 as the **Original Journal Entry**. Click **OK** to continue:

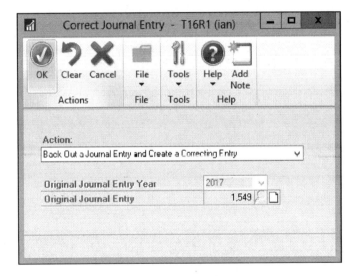

4. Click **OK** to acknowledge that this is a recurring entry and click **Select** to choose the only option. The sample company has a very limited number of journal entries that didn't originate in a subledger, and this is the best example.

5. The back out transaction will open in the **Transaction Entry** window with the debit and credit amounts switched. This reverses the effect of the original entry.

6. Dynamics GP also provides a connection to the original entry in the **Reference** field:

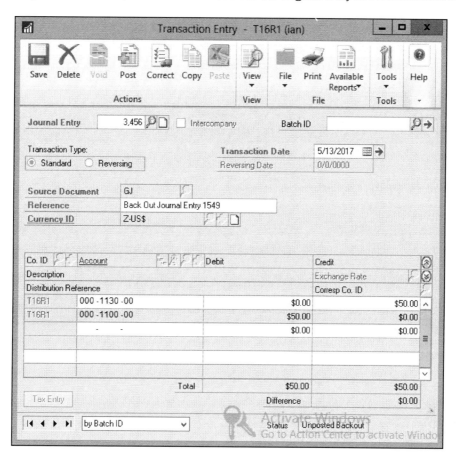

7. In the **Batch ID** field enter CORR and click *Tab*. Pick **Add** to add the batch and **Save** to save the batch. Click **Save** on the transaction to save it. Dynamics GP will create the correcting entry once the back out entry is saved.

8. Change the **Date** on the correction transaction to 11/30/2017 to simulate correcting a transaction posted in the wrong period. At this point, transaction lines can be added or deleted and amounts can be changed. Users can adjust any part of the transaction to correct the entry:

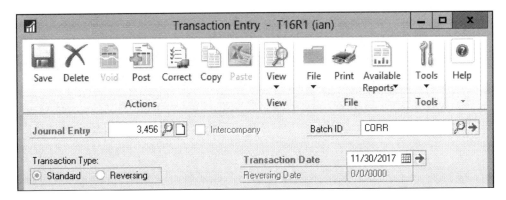

9. Click **Save** to save the transaction. Both the back out transaction and the correction are now in the CORR batch waiting to be posted.

10. Because this is a general journal entry, the entry is posted based on the transaction date so mixing different dates in a single batch is ok.

The process for copying a journal entry is similar and works like this:

1. On the **Transaction Entry** window, select **Copy**.

2. Set **Year** to **2014** and enter 27 as **Original Journal Entry**. Click **OK** to continue.

3. The user now has a copy of the original journal entry which can be changed or adjusted as necessary.

How it works...

Backing out and correcting journal entries provides an easy mechanism to fix errors. Because the original transaction is retained and a reversing transaction is used, it's easy to audit the process and address questions about these corrections. Since copying a journal entry starts with a posted entry, these transactions are also less likely to contain errors.

There's more...

For our example we used an entry that originated in the general ledger. There is also a setting that allows the correction of entries that originated in subledgers.

Subledger corrections

Generally, corrections to a subledger transaction should be made in the originating module. For example, AP transactions should typically be voided and re-entered in Purchasing, not just corrected in the general ledger. However, if a transaction needs to have only the general ledger portion corrected, subledger transactions can be backed out, corrected, and copied via this method as well. In order to make this work, there is a setting that must be activated. To activate the ability to back out, correct, and copy transactions that originated in a subledger, follow these steps:

1. Select **Financial** from the Navigation list. Pick **General Ledger** under the **Setup** section.

2. Check the box marked **Voiding/Correcting of Subsidiary Transactions** and click **Save**:

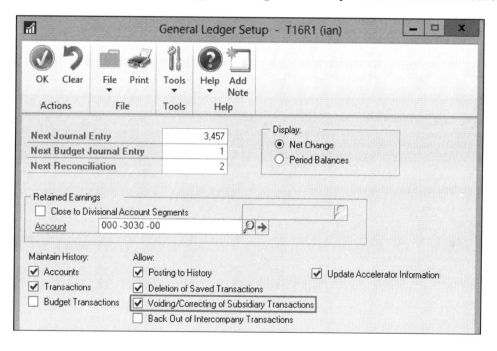

8

Harnessing the Power of SmartLists

In this chapter, we will look at ways to leverage the reporting power of SmartLists in Dynamics GP, including the following topics:

- Changing the Favorites pane size and visibility
- Sorting data to get the information you want
- Improving information returned with SmartList Search
- Tailoring SmartLists by adding fields
- Renaming fields for clarity
- Controlling data with SmartList record limits
- Speeding up access to information with SmartList Favorites
- Getting warnings with SmartList alerts
- Controlling access by sharing or restricting SmartList Favorites

Introduction

In previous chapters, we've looked at a number of recipes that touch on **SmartLists**. This powerful, user friendly reporting tool has become a foundational feature in Dynamics GP. Reminders and Favorites, which underpin most of the Lookup windows throughout the system, rely on SmartLists. Because SmartLists are so easy to use, many users never delve deeper than the surface. In this collection of recipes, we'll dig deeper into SmartLists to see how to better leverage both their simplicity and their power.

Changing the Favorites pane size and visibility

The user interface of SmartList was improved greatly in Microsoft Dynamics GP 2013 SP2 by adding the ability to both resize and hide the Favorites pane. By default, the Favorites pane hides when a favorite is selected and needs to be expanded to select a different favorite; additionally, the pane is quite narrow to begin with, which means more data can be seen once a favorite has been selected. However, a narrow Favorites pane means the names of many favorites are wider than the pane, meaning you need to scroll to the right to see the end of the name.

The new functionality allows both of these behaviors to be changed.

How to do it...

To resize or hide the Favorites pane in SmartList, follow these steps:

1. Select **Administration** in the Navigation pane, and under **Reports** click on SmartList or select the **Microsoft Dynamics GP** menu from the top and click on **SmartList**, or click on the SmartList icon on the toolbar.

   If the SmartList icon is not shown at the top, right-click on the blue bar next to the menu and select the standard toolbar to turn it on.

2. Click the **SmartList** button on the Actions pane and then select Favorites pane.

3. To switch off auto-hide, click on **Enable Auto-hide** to unmark it. This will keep the Favorites pane visible when a favorite is selected.

4. The left pointing chevron at the top right of the Favorites pane will hide it; the chevron turns into a right pointing one which, when clicked, will unhide the Favorites pane:

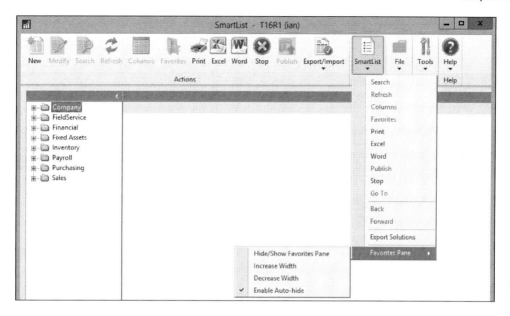

5. The width of **Favorites Pane** can be increased or decreased from the same menu. This way of changing the width of **Favorites Pane** is not very efficient.

6. Instead, you can right-click on the Navigation pane itself, and then, on the popup menu, click on **Increase Width** or **Decrease Width**:

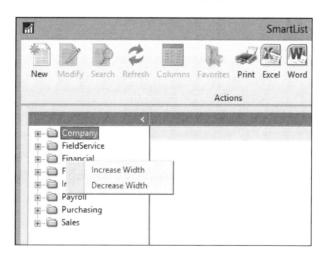

7. Repeating Step 7 might be necessary to make the pane of the required width.

Sorting data to get the information you want

At their core, SmartLists are rows and columns of data, similar to an Excel spreadsheet. They provide a powerful, friendly way to interact with information in Dynamics GP. One of the simplest SmartList features found by most users is the ability to sort a SmartList simply by clicking on a column header. However, SmartLists provide advanced sorting features that are even more powerful, just a little harder to find.

In this recipe, we'll take a look at all of the sorting options for SmartLists, both simple and advanced.

How to do it...

To sort a SmartList, follow these steps:

1. Select the **Microsoft Dynamics GP** menu from the top and click on **SmartList.**

2. Select **Financial** in the left pane then **Account Summary** below it:

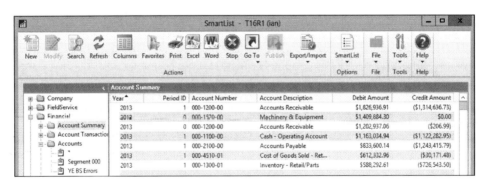

3. Simple sorting is accomplished by clicking on the column name. Select the **Debit Amount** column title to sort by debits. The arrow next to the column name shows whether the sort is ascending or descending:

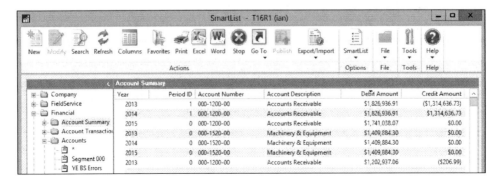

4.   Click **Debit Amount** again to change the sort order.

5.   For more advanced sorting, select **Search** from the SmartList toolbar and click on the **Order By** button at the bottom of the window. This window allows sorting by multiple fields, including fields that are included but not displayed on the SmartList:

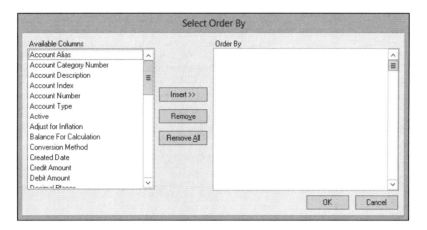

6.   Select **Year** and click **Insert**. Set **Order By** to **Descending**.

7.   Select **Period ID** and click **Insert>>**. Set **Order By** to **Ascending**:

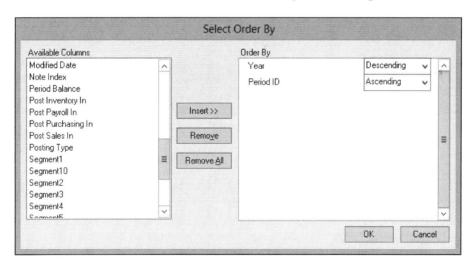

8.   Select **Account Number** and click **Insert**. Set **Order By** to **Ascending**.

9. Select **Debit Amount** and click **Insert**. Set **Order By** to **Descending**:

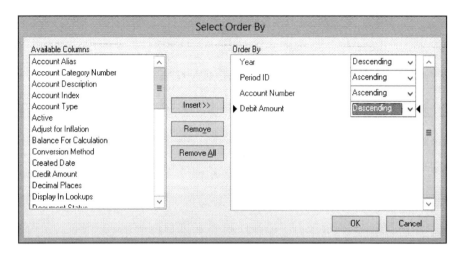

10. Click **OK** twice to return to the SmartList.

11. Notice that the SmartList has now been sorted by **Year**, **Period ID**, **Account Number**, and **Debit Amount**, following the sorting rules set up in the example:

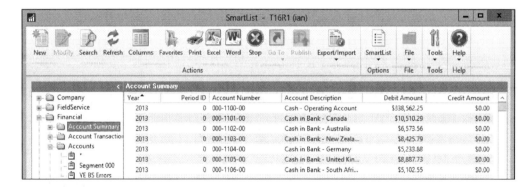

How it works...

Complex sorting in a SmartList can often bring clarity to information by providing a better arrangement of data. Frequently users who don't know about this feature take the extra step of exporting the data to Microsoft Excel and then sorting it there. With advanced sorting, this step is unnecessary and can eliminate the potentially time-consuming effort of sending a large amount of data to Excel just for sorting.

Additionally, even when the SmartList is selected with the intention of sending it to Excel, pre-sorting the information can speed up the analysis once the data is exported to a spreadsheet.

See also

▸ The *Building analyses by exporting SmartLists to Microsoft Excel* recipe in *Chapter 10, Connecting Dynamics GP to Microsoft Office*

▸ The *Getting fine-grain control of Excel exports from SmartLists* recipe in *Chapter 10, Connecting Dynamics GP to Microsoft Office*

Improving information returned with SmartList Search

The basic SmartLists included with Dynamics GP are great but they really shine once companies figure out how to fine tune and filter the records that are returned. The Search feature in SmartLists does just that, making it easy to see which invoices were generated on a particular date or which transactions affected a certain general ledger account during the month.

In this recipe, we'll look at how to better control the results that are returned using the Search feature in SmartLists. For our example, assume that auditors want to see any checkbook transactions over ten thousand dollars ($10,000) during the month of April 2017. We'll use the Dynamics GP sample company for this recipe.

How to do it...

To limit the results of a SmartList with the Search feature, follow these steps:

1. Select the SmartList icon from the menu bar at the top or select **Microsoft Dynamics GP** menu from the top and click on **SmartList**.

2. Select **Financial**, then **Bank Transactions**.

3. Select **Search**.

4. In **Search Definition 1** set **Column Name** to **Checkbook ID**, **Filter** to **is equal to**, and **Value** equal to **Uptown Trust**:

5. In **Search Definition 2** set **Column Name** to **GL Posting Date** and **Filter** to **is between**.

6. This opens up two date boxes. Set the dates to **4/1/2017** and **4/30/2017**:

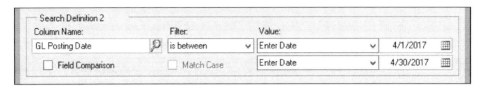

7. In **Search Definition 3** set **Column Name** to **Checkbook Amount**, **Filter** to **is greater than**, and **Value** equal to **10000**:

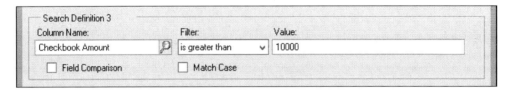

8. Click **OK**.

9. The resulting SmartList is limited to **UPTOWN TRUST** transactions in April 2017 with amounts over $10,000:

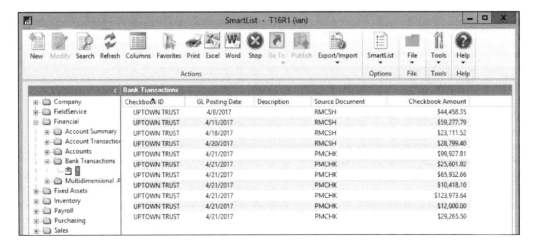

How it works...

By default, there are four available search boxes used to narrow results. However, with the **is between** option shown in the example, it's possible to effectively have more criteria than just the four boxes. The **is between** option adds two options in a single search box, meaning that users don't have to use up two boxes with the greater than and less than criteria.

There's more...

The **Field Comparison** and **Match Case** settings provide additional search features and the **Search Type** option changes the way that results are returned.

Field comparison

The **Field Comparison** checkbox changes the **Value** field to a lookup field allowing the comparison of two values. This is useful for comparing fields in the system. For example, if a user wanted to find cases where the sub-ledger posting date is not equal to the GL posting date, **Field Comparisons** would be a perfect tool.

Match case

The **Match Case** checkbox makes a search case sensitive. Sometimes it is important to find situations where data been entered in all caps. This is a great way to use the **Match Case** option.

The **Match Case** option can be removed or set as the default via the **SmartList Options** window. This window is available by picking **Administration** from the Navigation pane and selecting **SmartList Options** under **Setup | System**.

Search type

SmartLists default to **Search Type** of **Match All**. This returns results that meet all of the criteria. From a technical standpoint, this is an AND search. In our example, we found transactions for a specific checkbook, between two dates, and over a certain amount.

Switching **Search Type** to **Match 1 or More** changes the search to an OR search. Our example would return transactions for a specific checkbook regardless of date or amount. In short, it would return a mess. However, if I wanted transactions that were orders or invoices, **Match 1 or More** would be perfect since a document can't be both an order and an invoice.

Wildcard search

In addition to all the SmartList features described above, there is also the ability to search with wildcards, which can be an incredibly powerful enhancement to the search; it is also a feature that is not documented in the SmartList manual or Help within Dynamics GP. There are four wildcards available for use:

%	Zero or more characters
_	Exactly one character
[charlist]	Single or multiple characters in the list
[^charlist]	Single or multiple characters not in the list

The following screenshot shows an example using the SmartList wildcard search to search for vendors with a name beginning with A, B, C, or D and where the city they're located in does not begin with a C:

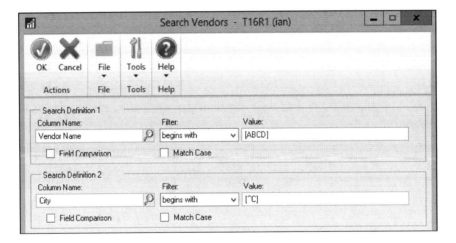

Wildcard searches are often used when reviewing information to be included on a tax return when a check is done for the **Tax Return ID** field being blank, which means it has not been included. This is done by using the [^charlist] wildcard, which shows where the character is not in the list:

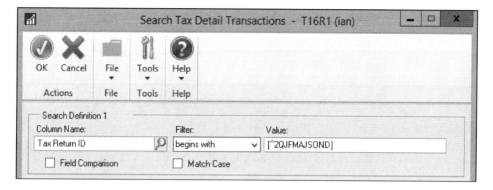

See also

▸ *Speeding up access to information with SmartList Favorites*

Tailoring SmartLists by adding fields

Default SmartLists contain predefined sets of fields. However, users always want to add additional fields or rearrange existing columns. Fortunately, Dynamics GP provides this functionality out of the box.

Users can add fields to SmartLists, remove fields or rearrange their order, allowing users to fine tune SmartLists to meet their needs. In this recipe, we'll look at adding and rearranging fields in SmartLists.

How to do it...

To add a field to a SmartList, follow these steps:

1. Select the SmartList icon from the menu bar at the top or select **Microsoft Dynamics GP** menu from the top and click on **SmartList**.

2. Select **Financial** then **Account Transactions** in the left pane.

3. Click **Columns**:

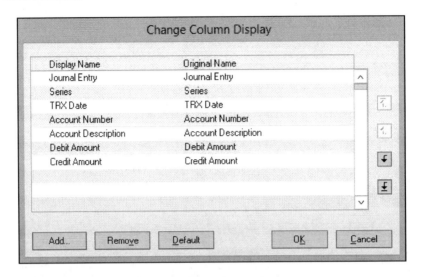

4. Click **Add**. This exposes all of the available fields for a SmartList, not just the defaults:

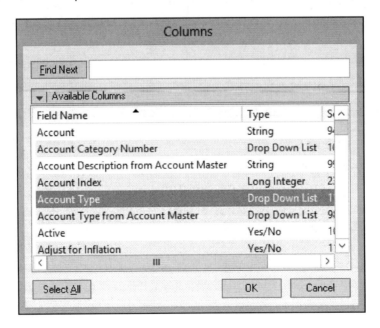

5. Select **Account Type** and click **OK** to add this field to the SmartList:

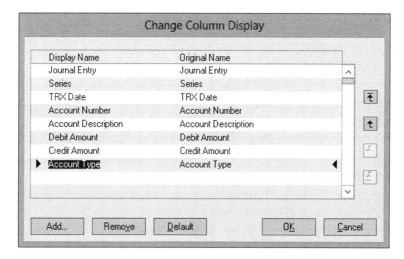

To rearrange fields on a SmartList, follow these steps:

1. Continue on the current screen and select **Account Type**.

2. Click the up arrow twice to move **Account Type** above **Credit Amount**:

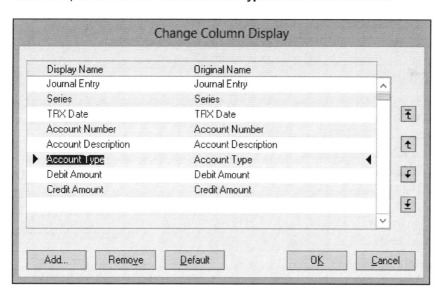

3. Click **OK** to finish.

The ability to add, remove, and rearrange fields on a SmartList gives users even more control over SmartList reporting. When users can satisfy their own custom reporting needs, it significantly reduces the reporting burden for administrators.

Theres more...

Sometimes, users need to remove fields from SmartLists as well. Also, field changes are NOT saved from one session to another, so saving the SmartList as Favorite after the changes are made is important. Finally, it is possible to add, remove, and rearrange fields on the default SmartLists.

Removing fields

Sometimes a SmartList just has more information than needed. To remove fields and clean up a SmartList, click **Columns**, select the column to delete, and hit **Remove**.

Favorites

Field changes to SmartLists are not saved. Clicking on another SmartList or otherwise moving off of a SmartList will cause field changes to reset. Saving the SmartList as a Favorite after the changes is the only way to preserve field changes. The *Speeding up access to SmartLists with Favorites* recipe has specifics on saving SmartLists.

Default SmartLists

The default SmartLists can also be modified to include or exclude columns and adjust the order as well. This is done by selecting **Administration** from the Navigation pane and then picking **SmartList Options** under **Setup | System**.

In this window, fields are added or removed by checking or unchecking the box next to a column. They can be reordered using the arrows at the right.

See also

  ▸   *Renaming fields for clarity*

Renaming fields for clarity

SmartLists are full of cool features and they are great for throwing together a report quickly, but sometimes the column names don't mean much to an average user, or the way that a company uses a field is different from its original intent.

It's not only possible, but easy to change the **Display Name** column that shows up on a SmartList. In this recipe, we'll look at how to do that.

How to do it...

To change the name of a SmartList column, follow these steps:

1. Select the SmartList icon from the menu bar at the top or select **Microsoft Dynamics GP** menu from the top and click on **SmartList**.

2. Select **Financial** then **Account Transactions** from the pane on the left.

3. Click **Columns**.

4. Click on **TRX Date** under the **Display Name** heading. Type `Journal Date` right over the old name and click **OK**:

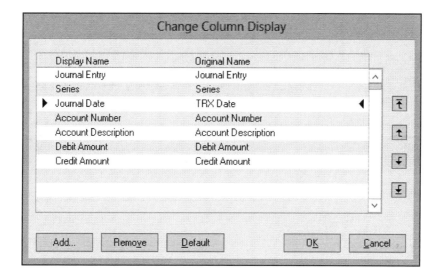

How it works...

Changing the column names in a SmartList doesn't change the name in the database; it uses the new name as an alias to overlay the database name for reporting. Notice that the title in the **Original Name** column doesn't change. This means that there is no way to save the new column name to the default SmartList from this location in GP. However, the new column names can be saved as part of a Favorite.

Additionally, when exporting a SmartList to Excel, the new column name is passed to Excel. This means that this recipe can be a great timesaver for users who regularly export SmartLists to Excel and then rename columns.

There's more...

Column names can be changed for default SmartLists, just not while working in them.

Default SmartList column names

The column names can be changed for the default SmartLists as well. Follow these steps to see how to do this:

1. Click **Administration** on the Navigation pane on the left.

2. In the **Administration** area page, select **SmartList Options** in the **Setup | System** area.

3. Select **Accounts** for the **Category** option.

4. Select **Account Category Number** and type **Category Description** in its place:

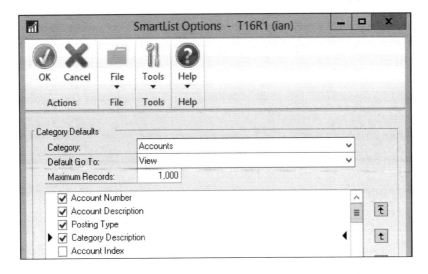

5. Click **OK** to save the new default description.

This example is quite a relevant one as the **Account Category Number** field actually contains the description of the **Account Category** field.

See also

▸ *Tailoring SmartLists by adding fields*

▸ *Speeding up access to SmartLists with Favorites*

Speeding up access to information with SmartList Favorites

SmartLists are designed for individual users to tailor reporting to their needs. This is important because users have the ability to save their unique SmartLists and make them available to be reused over and over again.

Default SmartLists are represented by an asterisk and can be customized by moving fields around, adding or removing fields, filtering the data to be returned, and sorting data in interesting ways. However, the time and effort required to do all of that is lost if a user can't save and reuse those unique settings. Saved SmartLists are called Favorites and they are the focus of this recipe.

How to do it...

In this recipe, we'll set up a SmartList and save it as Favorite:

1. Select the SmartList icon from the menu bar at the top or select the **Microsoft Dynamics GP** menu from the top and click on **SmartList**.

2. Select **Financial**, then **Accounts** from the list on the left.

3. Click on the **Account Number** column heading to sort by account numbers.

4. Click **Favorites**. In **Name:**, enter the Favorite, Account Number.

5. Leave **Visible To:** equal to **System**.

6. Click **Add**, then add Favorite to save the SmartList:

How it works...

SmartList Favorites provide a way to save a group of SmartList settings, much like options do for built-in reports. This provides a simple way to return to the same SmartList settings over and over. Favorites are saved under the category they are created in on the left. Consequently, our **Account Number** Favorite is saved under **Financial | Accounts**.

There's more...

SmartList Favorites can also be modified, and there are even more SmartList recipes to come. Favorites provide fast access to preset SmartLists, and Go Tos provide a path back to source data.

Modifying SmartList Favorites

It is possible to change a SmartList Favorite by selecting that Favorite, making changes, and clicking **Modify** instead of **Add**.

Go To

Double-clicking on a row in a SmartList drills back to the source data. Sometimes, there is more than one possible source. For example, should a sales row drill back to **Sales Transaction** or to **Customer Master Record**? Well, the **Go To** button displays more drill back options beyond the default double-click selection:

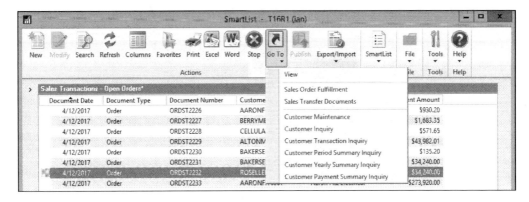

Additionally, the default Go To can be changed in the **SmartList Options** window. This window is reached by selecting the **Administration** button on the Navigation pane and then clicking **SmartList Options** under **Setup | System** on the **Administration** area page.

See also

▸ *Getting warnings with SmartList Alerts*

▸ *Controlling access by sharing or restricting SmartList Favorites*

Controlling data with SmartList record limits

When running a SmartList, the number of records returned by the SmartList is shown in the bottom left. By default, SmartLists have a record limit of one thousand (1,000) records. When the number of transactions matches the maximum, it's likely that there are more transactions not being shown. If the SmartList shows 1,000 bank transactions returned and the criteria shows first 1000 records, it's unlikely that there are exactly 1,000 bank records. In almost all cases, there are more than 1,000 records and the limit should be raised:

The idea behind this default limit is to prevent long-running SmartList queries from slowing down the system. However, sometimes it makes sense for queries to return more than a thousand records.

There are a few options for increasing or decreasing this record limit, including adjusting it on the fly, adjusting the limit for Favorites, and setting a new default limit. We'll take a look at all of these options in this recipe.

How to do it...

To adjust record limits on the fly, complete the following steps:

1. Select the SmartList icon from the menu bar at the top or select **Microsoft Dynamics GP** menu from the top and click on **SmartList**.

2. Select **Financial**, then **Bank Transactions**.

3. Select **Search**.

4. Increase **Maximum Records**, located on the bottom left, to 10,000 and click **OK**:

Adjusting limits on the fly only works for that session; the changes aren't saved. The easiest way to save new record limits is to save the SmartList as Favorite. To adjust record limits for Favorites, follow these steps:

1. Select the SmartList icon from the menu bar at the top or select the **Microsoft Dynamics GP** menu from the top and click on **SmartList**.

2. Select **Financial** then **Accounts**.

3. Select the **Account Number** Favorite setup as shown in the *Speeding up access to information with SmartList Favorites* recipe.

4. Select **Search**.

5. Increase **Maximum Records** to 10,000 and click **OK**.

6. Click **Favorites** then click **Modify** to save the new record limit.

7. The next time the **Account Number** Favorite is run, the record limit will be 10,000.

Finally, if the number of records returned is consistently over a thousand, it makes sense to adjust the default record limit for a particular SmartList category. To adjust the default limit, follow these steps:

1. Click **Administrator** on the Navigation pane, then select **SmartList Options** under **Setup | System**.

2. Pick the appropriate category. For our example, select **Accounts**.

3. Change **Maximum Records** to 10,000 and click **OK**:

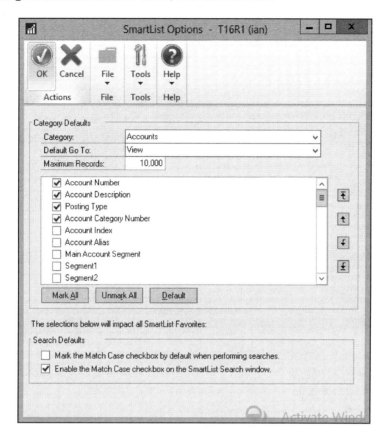

How it works...

By adjusting record limits, users and administrators gain improved productivity. If record limits are consistently too low, users waste time running SmartLists, adjusting record counts, and then running them again. If record limits are consistently set too high, users may create unacceptably long-running queries, slowing the system down for all users.

Getting warnings with SmartList alerts

In the previous recipe, we saw how to save SmartLists as Favorites. Now we can look at how to use a Favorite to build a custom reminder. SmartList Favorites actually make up the core of the reminder feature in Dynamics GP.

A custom reminder is a warning or alert generated by Dynamics GP and displayed on the **Reminder** window at login. It's used to alert a user about situations that exist in Dynamics GP. For example, reminders can display the number of invoices sixty days or more past due. They can also include the ability to drill back into the transactions that generated the reminder. The basic process takes a SmartList Favorite and builds criteria used to drive the reminder.

Built-in Reminders were covered earlier in the *Using Reminders to remember important events* recipe in *Chapter 3, Automating Dynamics GP*. In this recipe, we'll take a look at creating custom reminders.

Getting ready

The first step in creating a custom reminder is to create a SmartList Favorite. That topic was covered in detail in the last recipe, *Speeding up access to SmartList Favorites*, so this should be easy for everyone. We'll keep this example simple and assume that we simply want to be alerted about debit transactions over $1 million.

How to do it...

Once a SmartList Favorite has been created, it can be turned into a custom Reminder by following these steps:

1. Select the SmartList icon from the menu bar at the top or select **Microsoft Dynamics GP** menu from the top and click on **SmartList**.

2. Select **Financial** then **Account Transactions**.

3. Click **Search**.

4. In **Search Definition 1**, set **Column Name** to Trx Date. Set **Filter:** to **is between** and **Value:** to **Beginning of Period** and **End of Period**.

5. In **Search Definition 2**, set **Column Name** to Debit Amount. Set **Filter:** to **is greater than** and **Value:** to 1000000:

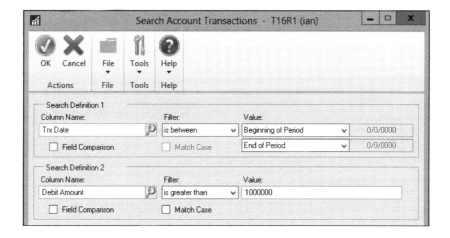

6. Click **OK**.

7. Click **Favorite** to save this as Favorite.

8. Name the Favorite Debit > $1m and leave **Visible To:** field as **System**:

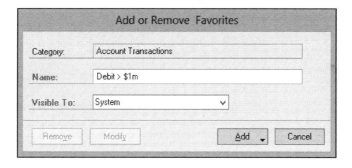

9. Click **Add | Add Favorite and Reminder**.

10. Click **Number of records**. Select **is greater than**. Leave the amount equal to 0. Check the **Display as a Cue** box and click **OK**:

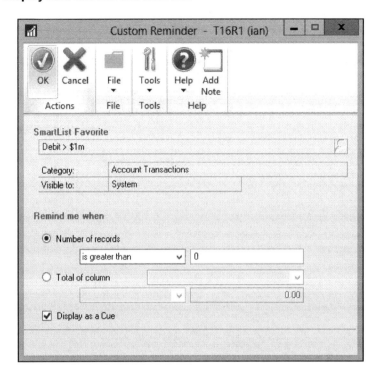

11. On the Home page, click the refresh button. The refresh button is two swirling arrows in the upper right near the **Help** button. This refreshes the current page.

12. In the Reminder pane you should see the Debit > $1m reminder with the number of debit transactions over a million dollars:

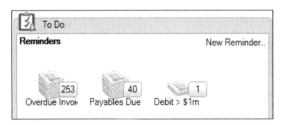

13. Click on the **Debit > $1m** line to drill back into the SmartList Favorite:

How it works...

Custom Reminders start with SmartList Favorites as their base and let users build Reminders based on those results. This increases the power of Reminders because the core SmartList can be narrowed down to provide very targeted results that can then be used to drive the alert.

Different users will need to be reminded about different things. SmartList Favorites provide opportunities to deliver relevant information to the right people in time for them to take action.

There's more...

Custom Reminders can also be modified and removed. Users aren't locked in after creating them.

Modifying and removing custom Reminders

It is possible to change a custom Reminder by selecting **New Reminder** from the Home page, highlighting a Reminder to change, and clicking **Modify** instead of **New**. This reopens the **Custom Reminder** window allowing changes.

Additionally, selecting **Remove** instead of **Modify** will delete that reminder.

See also

▶ *Improving information returned with SmartList Search*

▶ *Tailoring SmartLists by adding fields*

Controlling access by sharing or restricting SmartList Favorites

In the *Speeding up access to SmartLists with Favorites* recipe earlier in this chapter, we looked at the benefits of saving SmartLists as Favorites, along with how to make it happen. A key component of saving a Favorite that is often overlooked is setting the visibility of the Favorite.

The **Visibility to** field defines who has access to use and modify a particular SmartList Favorite. Since there are only a couple of options, it is sometimes more difficult to get the visibility right. For example, consider a user who crafts a SmartList to meet their particular needs but sets the visibility to **System**, making the SmartList available to everyone. They could find that another user has made changes and modified the Favorite to save those changes. Now our original user has to figure out how to put their Favorite back together.

In this recipe, we'll look at how to set the default visibility for SmartLists at a system level, set the visibility of a Favorite, and how to determine the right visibility to set.

Getting started...

Microsoft Dynamics GP 2015 R2 introduced the ability to change the default visibility of SmartLists at the system level. The process to set the default visibility of Favorites is as follows:

1. Select **Administration** in the Navigation pane and select **System Preferences** from under **Setup and System**.

2. Set the **Default SmartList Visibility:** property to **Company** from **System**:

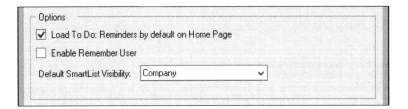

3. Click **OK** save the change and close the window.

How to do it...

The process to set the visibility of a Favorite is as follows:

1. Select the SmartList icon from the menu bar at the top or select **Microsoft Dynamics GP** menu from the top and click on **SmartList**.

2. Select **Financial**, then **Account Transactions**.

3. Select **Favorites** and name the Favorite `Account Trx`:

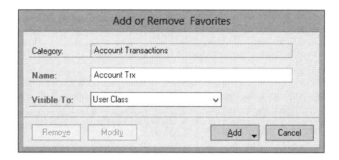

4. Set the **Visible To:** property to **User Class** and click **Add | Add Favorite**.

How it works...

The **Visible To:** property of a Favorite controls who has access to both run and modify a Favorite.

There are four options for setting visibility:

- **System**: This Favorite is available to all users with access to this SmartList category across all Dynamics GP companies.

- **Company**: This Favorite is available to all users with access to this SmartList category but only for the company it was created in.

- **User Class**: This Favorite is available to all users in the same user class as the creator. Starting with Dynamics GP 10, user classes are no longer connected to user security, so it's easier to use classes for other groupings, such as sharing Favorites, without risk of breaking security. This works well for limiting access to a small group of users.

- **User**: This Favorite is only available to the user who created the SmartList.

Too many users default to picking **System** every time, but this exposes the Favorite to everyone with access to that SmartList category. In many cases, **User Class** is the best option to select because it limits access to a much smaller list and that list is most likely to be commonly shared. For critical SmartLists, selecting **User** will ensure that no one else can change it.

There's more...

Visibility isn't the only security control on SmartLists but it is the most commonly used, and the only user-controllable, option. In addition, there are some best practices for naming Favorites.

SmartList security

Dynamics GP provides security options for administrators to control access to SmartLists. This only controls who can access a SmartList category, not individual SmartList Favorites. For example, this controls which users have access to payroll-related SmartLists, but a user with access to the payroll category would have access to all of the information in that SmartLists category.

Favorite naming best practices

A best practice for naming SmartLists is to include the user's initials at the beginning of the name. This doesn't prevent another user from using or renaming this Favorite, but it does remind users that they aren't the creators. It also makes it easy to change the name when modifying a Favorite. Simply change the initials to avoid overwriting the original favorite and click **Modify**.

9
SmartList Designer

In this chapter we will look at how new SmartList objects can be created with SmartList Designer. We will cover the following topics:

- ► Creating a new SmartList
- ► Creating a new SmartList a SQL View
- ► Adding a filter to a SmartList
- ► Exporting a SmartList object
- ► Importing a SmartList object
- ► Creating a refreshable Excel report from a SmartList

Introduction

In the previous chapter we took an in-depth look at the standard functionality of SmartLists. In Dynamics GP 2013 SP2, Microsoft introduced SmartList Designer. This new tool allows new SmartList Objects to be created and existing ones modified.

Creating a new SmartList

SmartList Designer allows entirely new SmartList objects to be created. For example, by default there is no SmartList that will allow a Purchasing SmartList to show the e-mail addresses or EFT details of a vendor. However, SmartList Designer allows these SmartLists to be created.

How to do it...

To create a SmartList object that shows the vendor EFT details, perform the following steps:

1. Select **Administration** in the Navigation pane and under **Reports** click on **SmartList Designer**; click on **SmartList** and then click the **New** button.

2. In the **List Name** field, enter Vendor EFT.

3. Leave the **Product** set to **Microsoft Dynamics GP** and set the **Series** field to **Purchasing**:

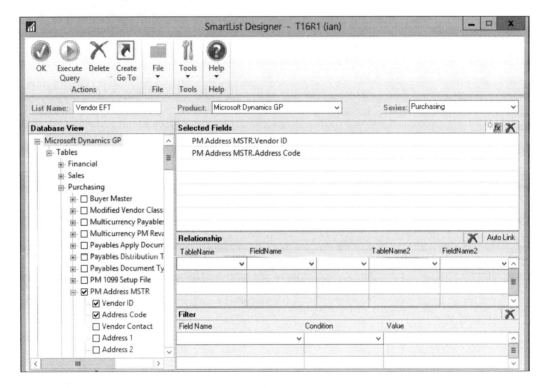

4. In the **Database View** pane, expand **Tables and Purchasing**.

5. Find **PM Address MSTR** in the list and expand it.

6. Mark the checkboxes next to **Vendor ID**, **Address Code**, **Address 1**, **Address 2**, **Address 3**, **City**, **State**, and **Zip Code**; this will add the fields to the **Selected Fields** list. The order items are selected is the order they will display in the SmartList by default.

7. Back in the **Database View** pane, minimize **Purchasing** and expand **Company**.

8. Find and expand **Address Electronic Funds Transfer MSTR**.

9. Mark the checkboxes next to **EFT Bank Code** and **EFT Bank Account**:

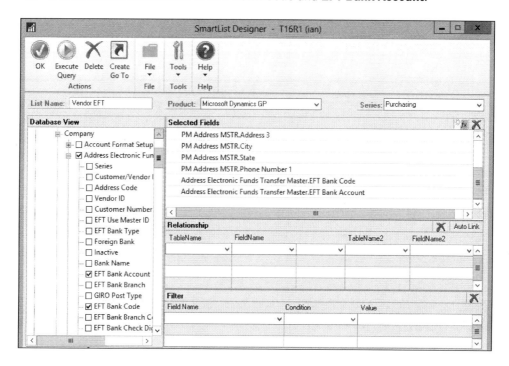

10. The last step we need to undertake, is to configure the relationships between the two tables selected in previous steps. In the **Relationship** field, set the **TableName** to **PM Address MSTR** and the **FieldName** to **Vendor ID**:

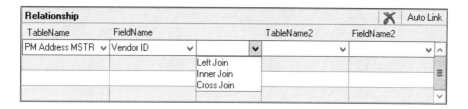

11. There are three types of join available with Left Join and Inner Join being the most commonly used. In this example, we want to return vendors whether or not they have bank details in Dynamics GP; this will allow us to verify the existing bank details and also see which vendors still need to provide them. To do this, select Left Join; an Inner Join will only return data where the data in both tables exists.

12. In **TableName2** select **Address Electronic Funds Transfer MSTR** and set **FieldName2** to **Vendor ID**:

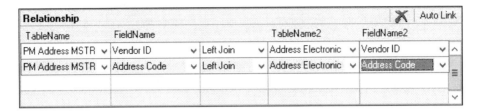

13. The relationship between the PM Address Master and Address Electronic Transfer Funds Master tables is what is known as a composite key; in other words, it is made up of two fields, **Vendor ID** and **Address Code**.

14. To complete the relationships, hit the *Tab* key to move the cursor to a new line.

15. Set **TableName** to **PM Address MSTR**.

16. Set **FieldName** to **Address Code**.

17. Set the join to **Left Join**.

18. Set **TableName2** to **Address Electronic Transfer Funds Master**.

19. Set **FieldName2** to **Address Code**.

20. Save the new SmartList object by clicking **OK** and then close the SmartList Designer.

The SmartList will need to have security configured before it will be available to users, but once this has been done it will be available in SmartList under the **Purchasing** node in the **Favorites** pane:

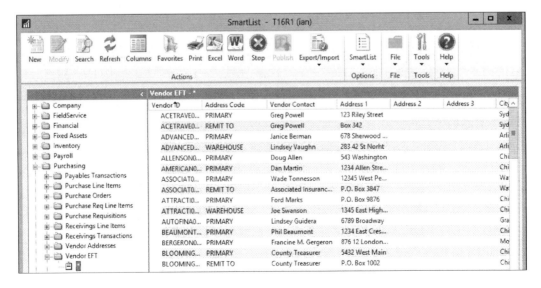

There's more...

There are a couple more things you will probably want to do when creating a new SmartList.

Preview the SmartList

While creating a new SmartList, it is possible to preview the query which will be executed to return the data. This is useful as it allows you to verify that the relationships have been correctly configured.

When working on a SmartList in SmartList Designer, preview it by clicking on the **ExecuteQuery** button on the Action pane:

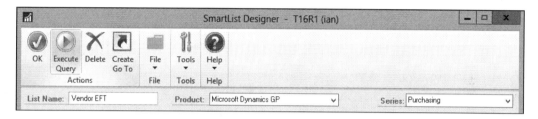

The returned data is shown at the bottom of the window in the **Result's Preview** table:

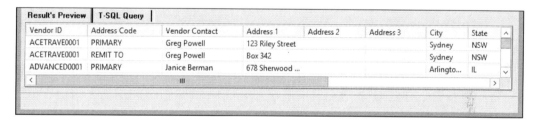

You can also click **T-SQL Query** to get access to the SQL which is being executed. This is sometimes useful to debug in SQL Server Management Studio or to use in other reporting tools:

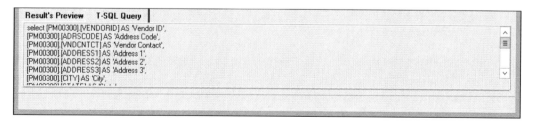

Configuring default columns for new SmartLists

The default column order for SmartList objects created using SmartList Designer is the order in which the columns were selected. This is not usually the order in which the user will want to view the columns, as to get the columns in the correct order would require jumping around in the Database View to select the columns in the correct order. Fortunately, the **SmartList Options** window can be used to amend the default column order.

To change the default column order, using SmartList Options, for the Vendor EFT SmartList object created in the previous recipe:

1. Select **Administration** in the Navigation pane and under **Setup** and **System** click on **SmartList Options**.

2. Change the **Category** to **Vendor EFT**:

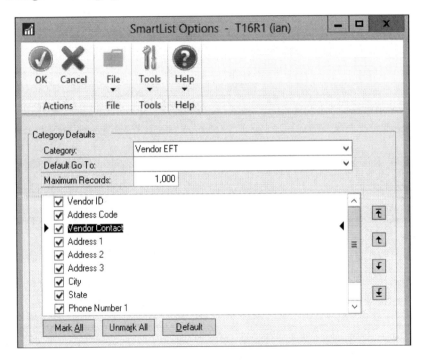

3. Select **Vendor Contact** and click the up arrow button to the side of the scrolling window.

4. Repeat Step 3 to move any other columns.

5. Click **OK** to save the changes.

Columns can be removed from the default display by unmarking the checkbox next to the field name; this means the field can be added should a user want to see them, but are not on a SmartList by default.

Creating a new SmartList from a SQL View

In the *Creating a new SmartList* recipe, we created a new SmartList object using GP tables. SmartList Designer also allows SmartLists to be created from SQL Views, which allows for more flexibility in how SmartList Designers work.

One example of this, and one used by many of my clients, are SmartLists that report on the security configuration; these were created as SQL Views to make them easy to transfer between systems.

Getting ready

Before the SmartList can be created, the SQL View needs to be loaded into the relevant database; for security data, this is the system database (typically called `DYNAMICS`), but for many SmartLists, the SQL View will need to be loaded into all company databases.

The security-related SQL View (`uv_AZRCRV_UserAccessAndGrantedSecurityViews`) that we will use in this recipe is the User Access and Granted Security Roles, `http://azrcrv.co.uk/y7xXlZ`

Download the view and load it into SQL Server in the system database, making sure the `DYNGRP` is granted `SELECT` permissions.

How to do it...

To create the SmartList from the SQL View, follow these steps:

1. Select **Administration** in the Navigation pane and under **Reports** click on **SmartList** or select the **MicrosoftDynamics GP** menu from the top and click on **SmartList**, or click the SmartList icon on the toolbar.

2. Click the **New** button on the toolbar.

3. In the **List Name** field, enter `User w Company and Role`.

4. Set the **Product** field to **Microsoft Dynamics GP** and the **Series** field to **Company**:

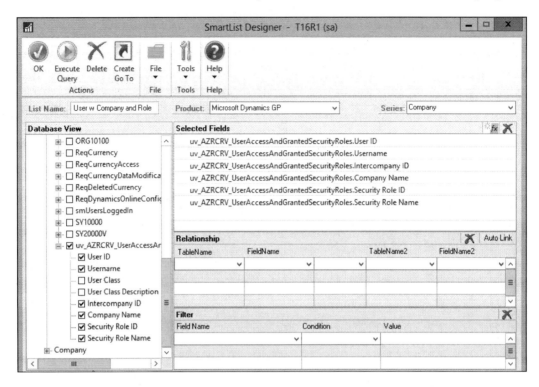

5. Scroll down to the bottom of the **Database View** field.

6. Expand the **Views** node.

7. Expand the **System** node.

8. Scroll down and find the `uv_AZRCRV_UserAccessAndGrantedSecurityViews` view.

9. We want all columns from the view within the SmartLists so click the checkbox next to the view.

10. Click **OK** and close SmartList Designer.

The SmartList will be available under the **Company** node in the **Favorites** pane.

There's more...

While you are able to create any SQL view you want to use with Dynamics GP, there is a number of resources already available from the Dynamics GP community.

The main resource for SQL views is Victoria Yudin's blog, at `http://azrcrv.co.uk/4XmFtO`, which has a number of very useful views for different areas of Dynamics GP.

In addition, Ian's azurecurve blog has a number of SQL views available at `http://azrcrv.co.uk/RGHJGn`.

Adding a filter to a SmartList

The SmartLists created so far have returned all of the data and would require the user to use search to filter it down. While this usually works, there are times when having certain information already pre-filtered is preferred, such as when the user wants to use all four available Search Definitions. To facilitate this, SmartList Designer allows filters to be defined.

How to do it...

To add a filter to the `Users w Company and Roles` SmartList, created in the previous recipe, object to exclude **Test** companies:

1. Select **Administration** in the Navigation pane and under **Reports** click on **SmartList** or select the **Microsoft Dynamics GP** menu from the top and click on **SmartList**, or click the SmartList icon on the toolbar.

2. Expand the **Company** node in the **Favorites** pane.

3. Click on **Users w Company and Roles** and click **Modify**:

4. In the **Filter** section, below **Relationships**, select the **uv_AZRCRV_ UserAccessAndGrantedSecurityRoles.Company Name** field. Due to the fixed size of the drop-down list you may need to select several fields, viewing the tooltip for each one before getting the correct field:

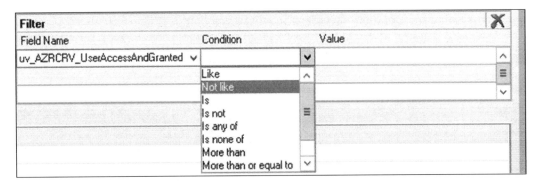

5. Set the **Condition** column to **Not Like**:

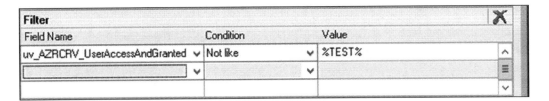

6. Enter `%TEST%` in the **Value** column. The percentage signs are required to tell SmartList Designer that the word TEST can be anywhere in the field; if we only put a % sign at the end, SmartList Designer would look for values where the field began with `TEST`.

7. Click **OK** to save the filter on the SmartList.

Exporting a SmartList object

Many clients using Dynamics GP will have entirely separate development/testing and production environments. So when a new SmartList is created, it is created on one environment and migrated to production after testing.

How to do it...

To export a SmartList object, follow these steps:

1. Select **Administration** in the Navigation pane and under **Reports** click on **SmartList** or select the **MicrosoftDynamics GP** menu from the top and click on **SmartList**, or click the SmartList icon on the toolbar:

2. Click **Export/Import** on the Action pane and then click **Export**:

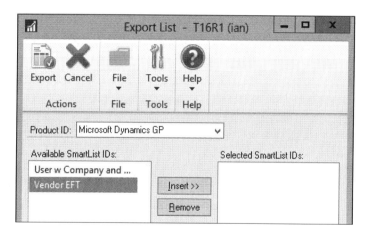

3. The **Export List** window will show all available SmartLists which can be exported (this is everything created using SmartList Designer). Ensure **Product ID** is set to **Microsoft Dynamics GP**.

4. In the **Available SmartList IDs** field, select **Vendor EFT**.

5. Click the **Insert >>** button to move the SmartList to the **Selected SmartList IDs** column:

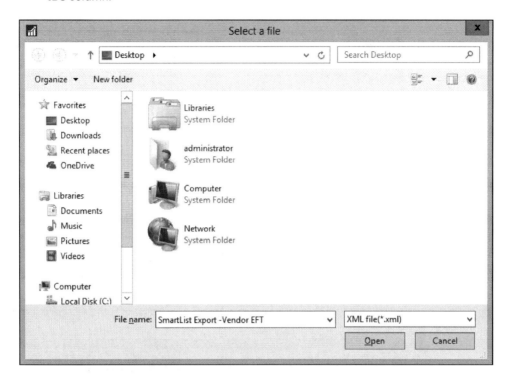

6. In the **Select a file** dialog, choose a location to save the exported file, enter a name in the **File name** field, and click the **Open** button.

7. Click the **Export** button on the Action pane.

8. Once the export is complete, click **OK** on the confirmation dialog:

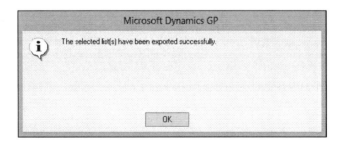

Importing a SmartList object

In the last recipe we covered the export of a SmartList object. Once we have the exported file, this can be imported into another installation of Dynamics GP.

How to do it...

To import the SmartList object, follow these steps:

1. Select **Administration** in the Navigation pane and under **Reports** click on **SmartList** or select the **MicrosoftDynamics GP** menu from the top and click on **SmartList**, or click the SmartList icon on the toolbar:

2. Click the **Export/Import** button on the Action pane and then click **Import**:

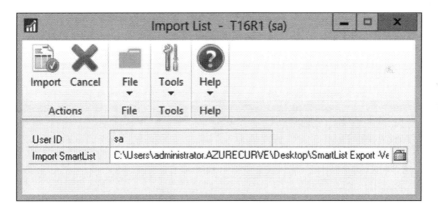

3. Click the folder icon next to the **Import SmartList** field and select the file to import.

4. Click the **Import** button on the Action pane to begin the import:

5. Confirm the location for **Import SmartList Exception Report** and then click **OK**:

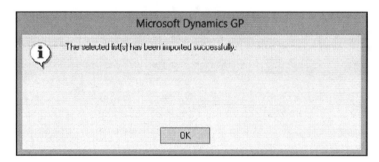

6. Once the import has finished, click **OK** on the confirmation dialog.

If there was a problem with the import, **Import SmartList Exception Report** will be generated showing details of the error:

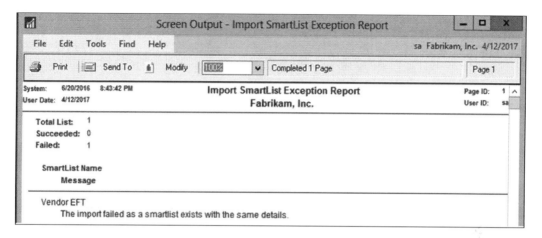

Creating a refreshable Excel report from a SmartList

The ability to create new SmartList objects using SmartList Designer is an invaluable one. The one drawback of this type of SmartList is that they can be very slow to run; one way of getting a faster version of the report is to create a refreshable Excel report from the SmartList.

Getting ready

Before a refreshable Excel report can be created, the Excel Reports need to be configured in **Reporting Tools Setup**:

1. Create or select a file location. For our example, ensure that the location `C:\XLReports` exists.

2. Select **Administration** from the Navigation pane on the left. On the **Administration** area page, select **Reporting Tools Setup** under **Setup**. Enter the system password if prompted.

3. Select the **Excel Reports** tab, set a location of network share and enter
   `C:\XLReports` in the **Reports Directory** field:

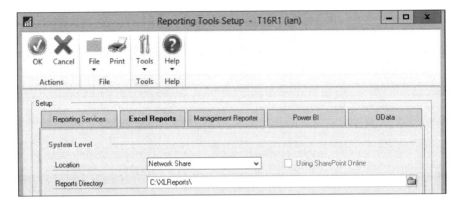

4. Click **OK** and close the window.

How to do it...

To create a refreshable Excel report from a SmartList, follow these steps:

1. Select **Administration** in the Navigation pane and under **Reports** click on **SmartList**
   or select the **Microsoft Dynamics GP** menu from the top and click on **SmartList**, or
   click the SmartList icon on the toolbar:

2. Expand the **Company** node in the **Favorite** pane and click on **User w Company and
   Role** created in an earlier recipe of this chapter.

3. Click the **Publish** button on the toolbar:

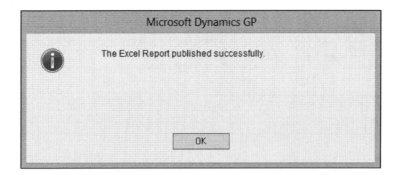

4. Once the refreshable Excel report has been created, click **OK** on the confirmation dialog.

5. To use the Excel report, click **Administration** on the Navigation pane of the main Dynamics GP window.

6. Click on **Excel Reports** in the area page list.

7. Find the T16R1 User w Company and Role Excel report, where T16R1 is the name of the database, and either double-click or mark the checkbox and click on **View**:

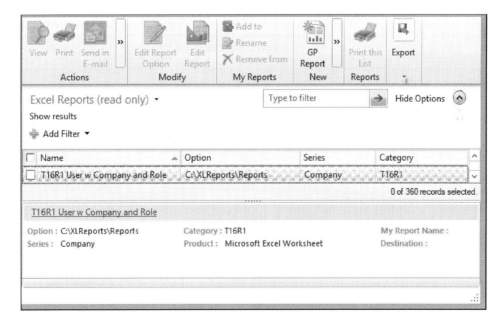

8. This will launch Excel and load the report. Click on **Enable Content** to allow the report to connect to the database:

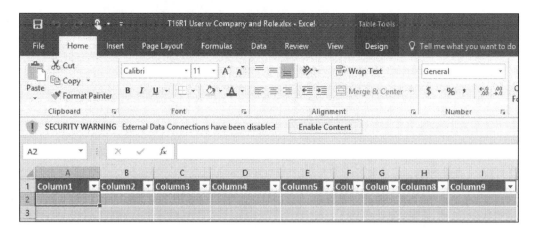

9. The report will populate with data and can be used as any other Excel spreadsheet:

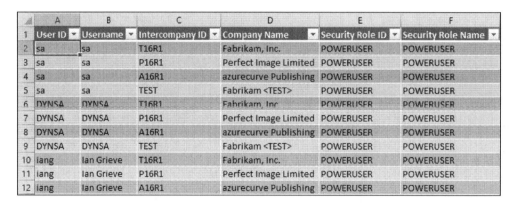

10. Any changes made to a SmartList that has been published as a refreshable Excel report will, when amended in SmartList Designer, produce a message stating that the report needs to be republished:

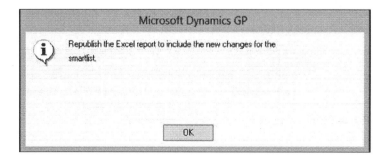

10
Connecting Dynamics GP to Microsoft Office 2016

Dynamics GP provides tight integration with Microsoft Office 2016 across multiple integration points. *Chapter 5, Exposing Hidden Features in Dynamics GP,* looks at the options for connecting Dynamics GP with Office. We will see the following recipes:

- Building analysis by exporting SmartLists to Microsoft Excel
- Getting fine-grained control of Excel Exports from Navigation lists to Excel
- Improving reports by sending SmartLists to Word
- Communicating with customers using Letters from Microsoft Word
- Skipping the exports by using pre-built Excel Reports
- Delivering the goods with Excel-based dashboards
- Reporting on any Dynamics GP data with direct Excel connections
- Importing data with Microsoft Word and a Dynamics GP Macro
- Getting fine-grained control of Excel Exports from SmartLists
- Gaining flexibility by printing documents from Microsoft Word

Introduction

With this chapter, we move out of working only in Dynamics GP and look at connecting Dynamics GP with Microsoft Office 2016. Dynamics GP provides a number of interaction points with Office and we'll look at ways to connect Dynamics GP with Word and Excel. This chapter also covers some ways to use Office applications to improve processes in Dynamics GP.

The connection between Dynamics GP and Office 2016 provides a platform for using all of the great functionality found in Office to leverage the data in GP for analysis, reporting, and communication. Let's go play with Office!

Building analyses by exporting SmartLists to Microsoft Excel

Continuing a simple to complex theme, we move on to another straightforward process, exporting SmartLists to Microsoft Excel. Dynamics GP allows users to export any SmartList to Excel with the simple push of a button. In this recipe, we'll look at how to export SmartLists and some of the considerations surrounding exports.

How to do it...

Exporting a SmartList to Excel is easy to do. Here are the steps to do it:

1. Select the SmartList icon from the menu bar at the top or select **MicrosoftDynamics GP** menu from the top and click on **SmartList**.

2. Select **Financial | Account Summary** from the **SmartList** window.

3. Once the SmartList finishes loading, click the **Excel** button.

4. Dynamics GP will export the data to Excel in the same order and with the same columns as the SmartList.

5. Once the export is complete, Excel will open with the completed data:

	A	B	C	D	E	F
1	Year	Period ID	Account Number	Account Description	Debit Amount	Credit Amount
2	2013	0	000-1100-00	Cash - Operating Account	338,562.25000	0.00000
3	2013	0	000-1101-00	Cash in Bank - Canada	10,510.29000	0.00000
4	2013	0	000-1102-00	Cash in Bank - Australia	6,573.56000	0.00000
5	2013	0	000-1103-00	Cash in Bank - New Zealand	8,425.79000	0.00000
6	2013	0	000-1104-00	Cash in Bank - Germany	5,233.88000	0.00000
7	2013	0	000-1105-00	Cash in Bank - United King	8,887.73000	0.00000
8	2013	0	000-1106-00	Cash in Bank - South Afric	5,102.55000	0.00000
9	2013	0	000-1107-00	Cash in Bank - Singapore	3,772.87000	0.00000
10	2013	0	000-1110-00	Cash - Payroll	925.44000	0.00000
11	2013	0	000-1120-00	Cash - Flex Benefits Progra	345.32000	0.00000
12	2013	0	000-1130-00	Petty Cash	175.00000	0.00000

How it works...

The simplicity of the export to Excel process belies the power of this feature. Other applications often require saving the export to a file and then opening that file in Excel. Dynamics GP provides a simple push button connection to Excel. Each time the **Excel** button is pushed, a new Excel file is created to hold the exported data.

One potential drawback to this feature is that once the data is in Excel, it is static data. Changes to the data in Dynamics GP require a new export. The Excel file is not updated automatically.

See also

> ▶ The *Turning on more features with the Dex.ini settings* recipe in *Chapter 6, Improving Dynamics GP with Hacks*

Getting fine-grained control of Excel Exports from Navigation lists to Excel

The big Excel button on the **SmartList** window provides a visual cue that SmartLists can deliver flexibility by exporting to Microsoft Excel. That same blinding flash of the obvious is not available for Navigation lists. Navigation lists provide another way to interact with information in Dynamics GP and they can be filtered and limited like SmartLists. Navigation lists don't have a big Excel button, so in this recipe we will look at how to export Navigation list data to Excel.

How to do it...

To export a Navigation list to Excel, follow these steps:

1. Select **Financial** from the Navigation pane.

2. At the top of the Navigation pane, select **Accounts** to open up the Accounts list.

3. Mark the checkbox in the header next to **Account Number** to select all accounts.

4. On the ribbon at the top, select **Go To** and then **Send to Excel**:

5. Excel will open with the data from the list.

How it works...

Navigation lists provide another way to work inside of Dynamics GP by blending data with a ribbon-like interface. This setup is designed to allow users to perform associated entries, inquiries, and reporting from a single screen for a series in Dynamics GP. The ability to export SmartList from the Navigation list interface means that there is one less reason to leave these consolidated screens.

See also

▸ The *Turning on more features with the Dex.ini settings* recipe in *Chapter 6, Improving Dynamics GP with Hacks*

Improving reports by sending SmartLists to Word

Microsoft Excel isn't the only Office product that SmartLists can be exported to. They can also be exported to Microsoft Word. This can be useful for exporting records for inclusion into a report, financial statement footnotes, or any other type of Word document.

Like the export to Excel feature, export to Word is very easy to do. In this recipe, we'll take a look at how and why you would want to export SmartLists to Word. For our example, we'll use a very small set of records showing retained earnings beginning balances for several years from the sample company.

This type of data could be useful for inclusion in financial statement footnotes, for example.

How to do it...

To send a SmartList to Microsoft Word, follow these steps:

1. Select the SmartList icon from the icon bar at the top or select **MicrosoftDynamics GP** from the top and click on **SmartList**.

2. Select **Financial | Account Summary** in the left pane of the **SmartList** window.

3. Click **Search**, Set **Search Definition 1** to **Period ID is equal to 0** (zero):

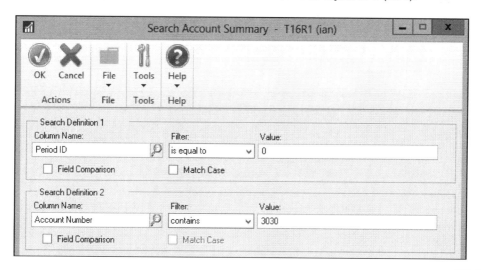

4. In **Search Definition 2**, set **Account Number** containing **3030** and click **OK**.

5. **Period 0** contains the beginning balances for each year and account **3030** is the retained earnings account in the sample company.

6. Click the **Word Excel** button to send this data to Microsoft Word.

7. Word will open a new document with the SmartList data included in a Word table format:

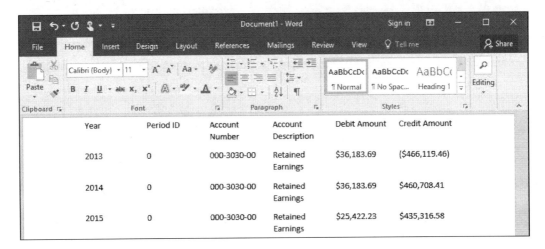

Year	Period ID	Account Number	Account Description	Debit Amount	Credit Amount
2013	0	000-3030-00	Retained Earnings	$36,183.69	($466,119.46)
2014	0	000-3030-00	Retained Earnings	$36,183.69	$460,708.41
2015	0	000-3030-00	Retained Earnings	$25,422.23	$435,316.58

How it works...

The nature of Word makes this feature less useful than Excel for processing large amounts of tabular data. However, if users need to insert small amounts of data into a much larger document, then exporting the data to Word is an easy way to get tabular data into a report. Typically, once exported to Word, the data would be cut and pasted into the larger report document, keeping the table intact.

Saving the related Excel SmartList as a favorite makes this process easily repeatable and provides a consistent data set.

See also

▸ The *Improving information returned with SmartList search* recipe in *Chapter 8, Harnessing the Power of SmartLists*

▸ The *Tailoring SmartLists by adding fields* and *Renaming fields for clarity* recipe in *Chapter 8, Harnessing the Power of SmartLists*

▸ *Getting fine-grained control of Excel Exports from SmartLists*

Communicating with customers using Letters from Microsoft Word

SmartList exports to Word are useful, but the Letter Writing Assistant feature is where the connection between Dynamics GP and Microsoft Word really shines. The Letter Writing Assistant uses built-in, or user-developed Word templates to create letters using information in Dynamics GP. Since the letters are based on the mail merge feature in Word, creating and manipulating templates follows the Word mail merge standards. Even better, the Letter Writing Assistant uses a wizard-style interface to build letters.

Dynamics GP comes with a selection of prebuilt letters for Collections, Customers, Vendors, Employees, and Applicants. In this recipe, we'll look at using the pre-built letters to create the most common type of mailing, collection letters.

How to do it...

To use Letter Writing Assistant, follow these steps:

1. From the menu bar, select **Reports | Letter Writing Assistant** to start the wizard and click **Next** to get started.

2. Select **Prepare the letters using an existing letter** and click **Next**.

3. Select **Collection** then click **Next**.

4. Check the **181 and over** box and pick **Next**. Ranges of customers can also be selected here but we'll limit our example to just clients over 180 days past due for simplicity.

5. Select **Final Notice** and click **Next**.

6. The next screen provides the ability to unmark certain customers to prevent them from getting a collection letter. Click **Next** to continue:

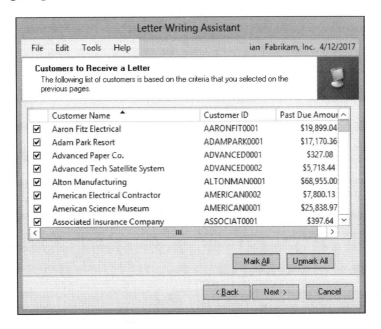

7. Finish the assistant by adding the name and contact information for the company representative and click **Finish**. Enter your name and contact information for our sample.

8. Microsoft Word will open and each letter will have its own page.

The Dynamics GP Letter Writing Assistant uses a GP wizard and mail merge functionality to insert information from Dynamics GP into letters in Word. The wizard-driven nature of this feature makes a complex process extremely simple to complete.

There's more...

In addition to our example, SmartList Favorites can be created and used to select information for letters. Additionally, users are not confined to built-in letters but can modify letters or build their own. Finally, there are other starting points for the Letter Writing Assistant, not just the **Reports** menu.

SmartList Favorites

On the **Prepare a Letter** screen of the Letter Writing Assistant, the selection box can be changed to **SmartList Selection** allowing the use of a SmartList Favorite for letter selection and population.

Letter customization

Selecting **Customize the letters by adding new letters** or changing existing letters on the second screen of the wizard changes the wizard path and walks a user through modifying existing letters and creating new letters.

Other starting points

Reports | Letter Writing Assistant is not the only place that the Letter Writing Assistant can be started from. Various windows, including Customer Maintenance, Vendor Maintenance and Employee Maintenance, include a **Write Letters** button with the Word logo. Selecting this button drops down a set of options to start the Letter Writing Assistant at the appropriate point in the wizard.

See also

▸ The *Speeding up access to information with SmartList Favorites* recipe in *Chapter 8, Harnessing the Power of SmartLists*

Skipping the exports by using pre-built Excel reports

The connections we've looked at so far between Dynamics GP and Excel have been one way and static. Data moved from Dynamics GP to Excel. Once in Excel, users could analyze and manipulate data, but when information in Dynamics GP changed, the user would need to re-export the data and re-run any analysis.

Microsoft Dynamics GP provides a new set of Excel-based reports. These reports use the **Office Data Connection** (**ODC**) to provide a live connection into Dynamics GP. Unlike exports, when data changes in Dynamics GP, these Excel reports can be easily refreshed to include the new data.

In this recipe, we look at how to deploy and use Excel reports in Microsoft Dynamics GP.

Getting ready

Prior to using Excel reports, they need to be deployed. This can be done to a simple shared file location on the company's network or to **Microsoft SharePoint Server** (**MSS**). We'll look at deploying Excel reports to a shared file location:

1. Create or select a file location. For our example, ensure that the location `C:\XLReports` exists.

2. Select **Administration** from the Navigation pane on the left. On the **Administration Area** page, select **Reporting Tools Setup** under **System | Setup**. Enter the system password if prompted.

3. Select the **Excel Reports** tab, set **Location** to **Network Share** and enter C:\XLReports in the **Reports Directory** field. Check the company the Excel Reports should be deployed to and redeploy data connections for all existing companies. Click **Deploy Reports**.

4. For our example, we are deploying system-level reports to a network location. We are not deploying user-level reports to a local directory:

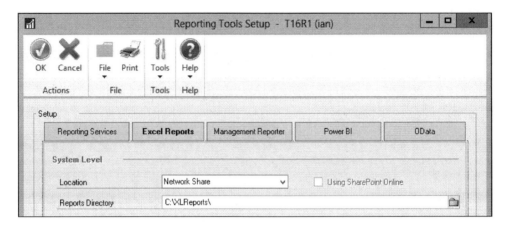

5. Click **Print Status Report** to view Deployment Report, check screen, and click **OK**.

6. Validate that the **Deployment Status** field shows **Deployed**

This process has now deployed the Excel reports and the appropriate data connections. Now let's look at how to use them.

How to do it...

There are two options to run Excel reports. They can be run from within Dynamics GP or from Excel. Let's see how to do both.

To start an Excel report from within Dynamics GP, follow these steps:

1. Select **Financial** from the Navigation pane. In the top section of the Navigation pane, select **Excel Reports**.

2. If Excel Reports does not appear after deploying the reports, restart Dynamics GP.

3. Double-click the **Account Summary** report (it will be preceded by the company identifier. For our sample company, it's `T16R1 AccountSummary`):

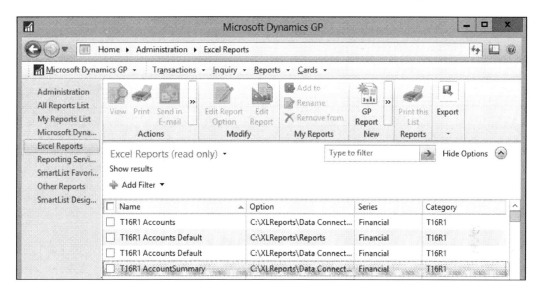

4. Excel will open. Click **Enable** if a security warning opens in Excel.

5. The Excel report will open with filter handles already in place for filtering columns.

6. Right-click on one of the headings and select **Refresh** to force the report to bring in updated information from Dynamics GP.

To start an Excel report directly, follow these steps:

1. Open up Windows Explorer and navigate to the location where the reports were deployed. Drill into the appropriate company and module. In our example, this was `C:\XLReports\Reports\T16R2\Financial`.

2. Double-click on the file named `T16R2AccountSummary Default`.

3. Excel will open. If a security warning displays, select **Options | Enable this content** and click on **OK**:

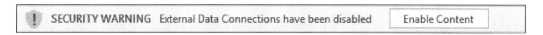

4. The Excel report will open with filter handles already in place for filtering columns.

5. Right-click on one of the headings and select **Refresh** to force the report to bring in updated information from Dynamics GP.

How it works...

Excel reports leverage Microsoft's new Office Data Connection to provide easily accessible, updateable reports. With the older style ODBC connections, users had to have the connection set up on their machine. The portability of the new connectors makes sharing Excel reports based on live data much easier.

Additionally, these reports are much faster than SmartList exports. The data returns almost instantly and is presented with some basic formatting already intact.

For users who want to modify Excel reports or build their own, these reports are still based on Excel at their core. Users can add calculations, move columns, and more, then save the reports with a new name. In most cases, the reports will maintain their connection to Dynamics GP.

There's more...

For users who want to build custom Excel reports, Microsoft offers Excel Report Designer as a part of SmartList Designer. Experienced database administrators will find a lot to like in the new Office Data Connectors and there is an easy way to avoid those security prompts.

Excel Report Designer

As part of SmartList Designer, Microsoft offers an option that allows the user to select fields, order columns, add calculations, and limit records to create a unique Excel report. This is covered in *Chapter 9, SmartList Designer*.

SQL and ODC connections

For experienced administrators, the Excel files can be modified directly by selecting **Data | Connections | Properties from within Excel** and selecting the **Definition** tab. This allows the manipulation of the underlying SQL query, letting administrators add, remove, or reorder fields and in general, manipulate the report in almost any way possible.

Once completed, the changes can be saved to a new Excel file, to the original Excel file, or saved back as part of the ODC file, making the changes available to all reports based on that connector.

This is not for the inexperienced, but knowledgeable database administrators will find tremendous power in the ability to manipulate the underlying SQL code.

Trust and security

When opening Excel reports, Excel will return a Security Warning because there is a live connection back to a database. To prevent these warnings from showing, follow these steps:

1. Select the **File** tab in Excel and pick **Options**.

2. Click on **Trust Center** then **Trust Center Settings**:

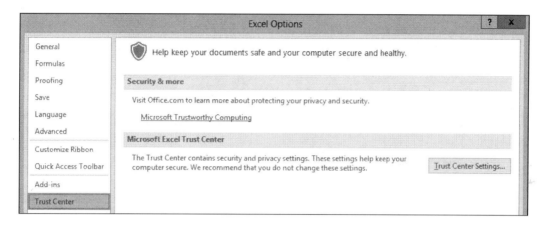

3. Click **Trusted Locations** on the left then **Add New Location** in the center at the bottom.

4. Add the location of the Excel Reports. In our example, this was `C:\XLReports`.

5. Check that the subfolders of this location are also trusted and click **OK**.

6. Click **OK** to accept the changes and return to the **Excel Options** window.

See also

▸ *Reporting on any Dynamics GP data with direct Excel connections*

Delivering the goods with Excel-based dashboards

Hidden in Dynamics GP are a set of pre-built Excel-based dashboards designed to give users an easy start to analyzing GP data. In this recipe, we'll look at how easy it is to use those dashboards.

Getting ready

Prior to using the prebuilt dashboards, refreshable Excel reports should be deployed and working. We cover how to do this in the *Skipping the exports by using pre-built Excel reports* recipe.

How to do it...

Once Excel reports are running, follow these steps:

1. Select **Purchasing** from the Navigation pane. In the top section of the Navigation pane, select **Excel Reports**.

2. Scroll down and double-click the **Purchasing Dashboard** report (it will be preceded by the company identifier. For our sample company it's `T16R2Purchasing Dashboard`)

3. Excel will open displaying **Purchasing Dashboard**:

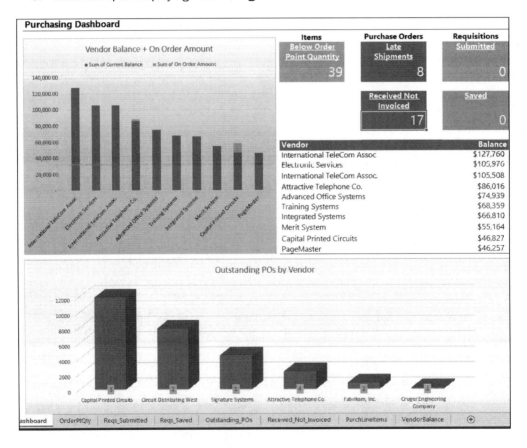

4. From the **Excel** menu, select **Data | Refresh All** to force the report to bring in updated information from Dynamics GP.

How it works...

The data is collected from GP via the different tabs at the bottom of the spreadsheet and consolidated into a dashboard on the **Dashboard** tab.

Like other refreshable Excel reports, dashboards can be opened directly from Excel in the location where refreshable Excel reports are deployed.

There's more...

There are dashboards for other areas of GP. Like Purchasing Dashboard we looked at, they are deployed in their respective areas of GP. GP 2016 includes the following prebuilt dashboards:

- Financial
- Inventory
- Purchasing
- Sales

See also

- *Skipping the exports by using pre-built Excel reports*

Reporting on any Dynamics GP data with direct Excel connections

In an earlier recipe, we looked at deploying and using the Excel reports contained in Dynamics GP. For all of the power of those dynamic reports, one thing is missing, the ability to modify the type of data being returned from within Excel. Excel reports allow filtering. However, if a user only needs a subset of data, using filters can make it difficult to work with only the filtered data. Also, Excel reports bring in all of the available rows, creating a much larger data set to work with and possibly overwhelming Excel.

Fortunately, there is another option. The MS Query tool included with Excel can work with **Open Database Connectivity** (**ODBC**) to connect to live data in Dynamics GP. This process is as fast as Excel reports, allows user-changeable parameters from Excel, and can be refreshed just like Excel reports. However, there are no pre-built reports that use ODBC connections, so users have to build these from scratch.

To demonstrate the power of Excel queries, we'll build a simple account summary report with user-selectable years in this recipe. Our ingredients are Dynamics GP and Microsoft Excel 2013.

How to do it...

To build a direct connection between GP and Excel, follow these steps:

1. Open Microsoft Excel 2016 and select **Data | Get External Data | From Other Sources | From Microsoft Query**. This will start the MS Query Wizard.

2. Select the data source used to log in to Dynamics GP. The default data source is named Dynamics GP 2016*.

3. Click **OK**.

4. Enter sa as the **Login ID** and the sa password. Either sa or another SQL user is required here. A trusted connection can be used if properly set up; encryption between the GP login and SQL Server prevents a regular GP login from being used for this task.

5. Click **Options** and select the TWO database. Click **OK** to start the MS **Query Wizard**.

6. In the **Query Wizard** window, scroll to the table named **GL11110**. Click the plus sign (**+**) to expand the columns available.

7. Find and select the column named **ACTNUMBR_1** and click the right arrow (**>**) to add it to the **Columns in your query:** box:

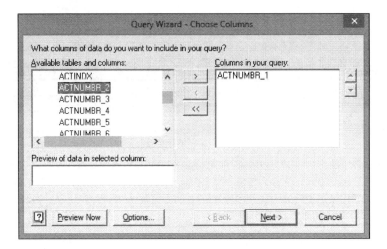

8. Repeat this process for the columns as shown in the following image.

9. The vertical arrow keys on the right can be used to reorder columns if necessary. Click **Next** when finished.

10. In the **Filter Data** window, select **YEAR1**. In the **Only Include rows where:** section pick **equals** and **2017**. Click **Next** to continue:

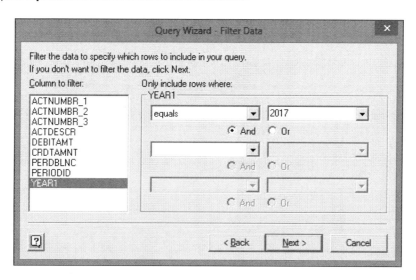

11. Click **Next** to move past the next screen and select **View data or edit query in Microsoft Query**. Click **Finish** to open Microsoft Query and review the details.

12. Once Microsoft Query opens, **Select 2017** next to **Value**. Change it to **[SumYear]** and press *Tab*:

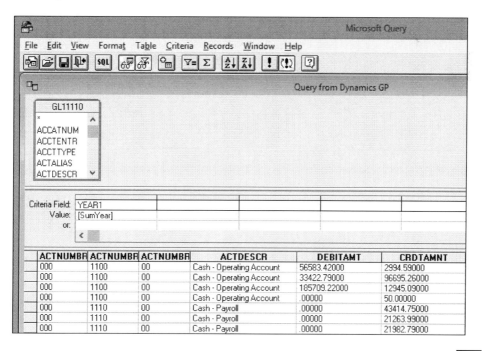

13. Enter `2017` in the box that opens and click **OK**. This changes `2017` from a value to a variable and then inserts `2017` as the initial value for that variable.

14. Select **File | Return data to Microsoft Office Excel**.

15. In the **Import Data** box, check `Existing` worksheet and enter `=A5`, then click **OK**:

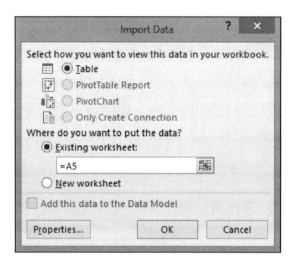

16. The data from Dynamics GP will now show up in Excel:

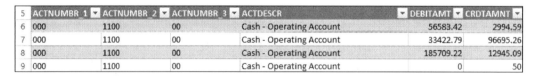

	ACTNUMBR_1	ACTNUMBR_2	ACTNUMBR_3	ACTDESCR	DEBITAMT	CRDTAMNT
5						
6	000	1100	00	Cash - Operating Account	56583.42	2994.59
7	000	1100	00	Cash - Operating Account	33422.79	96695.26
8	000	1100	00	Cash - Operating Account	185709.22	12945.09
9	000	1100	00	Cash - Operating Account	0	50

17. In cell `A1`, type `Year`.

18. In cell `A2`, type `2017`.

19. Click on the **ActNumbr_1** heading from the imported data. Pick **Data | Connections | Properties | Definition** as shown in the image that follows.

20. Click **Export Connection File** and save the file to create a portable Office Data Connection file with the embedded parameter:

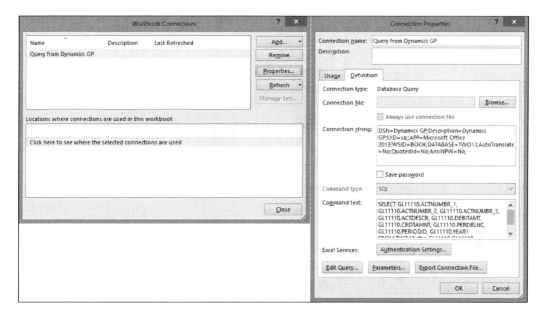

21. Click **Parameters**.

22. Select **SumYear**. Mark **Get Value from the following cell**. Key in **=A2**. Mark the **Refresh automatically when cell value changes** checkbox. Click **OK** and close all of the other open windows:

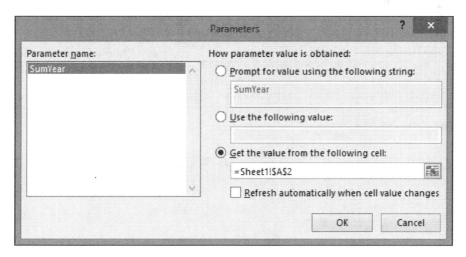

23. Change the cell value in cell A2 to 2016. Press *Tab* and all the values in the sheet will change to reflect the data from 2016:

Year						
2016						
ACTNUMBR_1 ▼	ACTNUMBR_2 ▼	ACTNUMBR_3 ▼	ACTDESCR ▼		DEBITAMT ▼	CRDTAMNT ▼
000	1100	00	Cash - Operating Account		55699.93	0
000	1100	00	Cash - Operating Account		76022.07	5528.13
000	1100	00	Cash - Operating Account		233681.95	140.5
000	1100	00	Cash - Operating Account		5279.5	0

24. Save the Excel file. Reopening the file allows the user to simply change the year, press *Tab*, and get updated values.

How it works...

This recipe provides a live connection from Excel to Dynamics GP and the data returned is determined by selections made in the Excel spreadsheet. In this case, Excel uses an ODBC connection to return data from Dynamics GP, passing a parameter as part of the query to control the information returned. Any field in the query could be used as the parameter field and multiple parameters can be used as well. This provides incredible control for live reporting of Dynamics GP data.

The key differences between this recipe and the Excel reports covered in the *Skipping the exports by using pre-built Excel reports* recipe are the type of connection (ODBC versus Data Connector) and the need to build ODBC-based reports from scratch. GP's Excel-based reports create a portable connection automatically making them easy to share but they don't support user-changeable parameters. Excel reports based on an ODBC connection require the user to have the appropriate ODBC connection set up on their PC for initial creation and then save a portable connection. ODBC-based reports also provide greater control over the data returned. Additionally, since there are no prebuilt reports based on ODBC connections, these reports need to be built from scratch, making them harder to get started with.

There's more...

The biggest difficulty that comes up with this recipe is determining which Dynamics GP tables to use. Also, for experienced database administrators, even more control is available.

Tables

The part that bedevils users is figuring out which table holds the data they need. There are a number of resources available to assist in locating the correct tables:

- A tool in Dynamics GP itself, located at **Tools | Resource Descriptions**.

- MVP Victoria Yudin's blog has a section on GP tables that lists commonly-used tables and fields in each of the core modules.

- An Excel-based table reference available from `DynamicAccounting.net` at `http://msdynamicsgp.blogspot.com/2008/10/lots-of-dynamics-gp-table-resources.html`.

Advanced options

Experienced database administrators will quickly realize that they can use more complex SQL joins, views, and just about anything that they can come up with by using the SQL button in MS Query. There are some limitations though. Excel may refuse to allow parameters if the SQL query is too complex. The best option in that case is to wrap a complex query into a view or stored procedure simplifying it for Excel.

Importing data with Microsoft Word and a Dynamics GP macro

Throughout this chapter, we've looked at a number of ways to send data from Dynamics GP to Microsoft Word and Excel. With this recipe, we'll look at using Word and Excel to bring data into Dynamics GP.

Microsoft offers a number of import tools for Dynamics GP, including Integration Manager, Table Import, and eConnect. In addition, there are third-party tools available, such as **Scribe** (`http://www.scribesoft.com/microsoft-dynamics-gp.asp`) and **SmartConnect** (`http://www.eonesolutions.com/smartconnect/overview/`). However, these tools are not included by default and some firms don't purchase them as part of their solution. Additionally, some areas of the system simply don't have reasonable options to import data. In many cases, the combination of Microsoft Excel, Microsoft Word, and a Dynamics GP Macro can allow importing via the user interface. The basic steps are to create a macro, apply the new data to the macro using Word's mail merge functionality, and then run the macro to import the data. In this recipe we'll take a look at how to do that.

Getting ready

For this example, we'll import segment descriptions for the third segment of the chart of accounts in the sample company. This is a common import requirement and somewhat difficult to do since this is normally updating information, not importing from scratch.

To set up the data to be imported, follow these steps:

1. Open Excel to a new, blank Excel spreadsheet.

2. In cell `A1` enter `Segment3`. In cell `B1` enter `Description`.

3. In cell `A2` enter `'01`. In `B2` enter `Marketing`. Be sure to put an apostrophe in front of `01` to force Excel to treat this as text.

4. Repeat this process with the data included until the spreadsheet looks like this example:

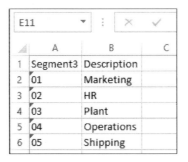

5. Save the sheet to the desktop as `Segment3Import`.

Now that we have our source data, we can import it into Dynamics GP.

How to do it...

To set up and import data via Microsoft Word and a macro, we first create the macro like this:

1. In Dynamics GP, select **Financial** from the Navigation list and pick **Segment** in the **Setup** area:

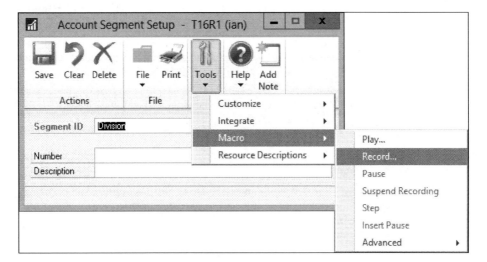

2. Select **Tools | Macro | Record**. Click **Desktop** on the left to save the macro to the desktop. Name the macro `Segment3.mac` and click **OK** to save it.

3. In **Segment ID**, click the lookup button (magnifying glass) and select **Department**. In the **Number field** type `01`. Don't use the lookup button.

4. In the **Description** box enter `Marketing` and click **Save**:

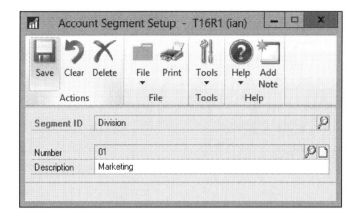

5. Select **Tools | Macro | Stop Record** to end the macro recording.

To use Word's mail merge functionality to add all of the data into the macro, follow these steps:

1. Open Microsoft Word and click **File | Open**. Select **Desktop** on the left.

2. Change **All Word Documents** to **All Files** in the drop-down box next to the **File Name**.

3. Select the `Segment3.mac` file created earlier and press **Open**.

4. In Word, select **Mailings**. Then pick **Select Recipients | Use Existing List**:

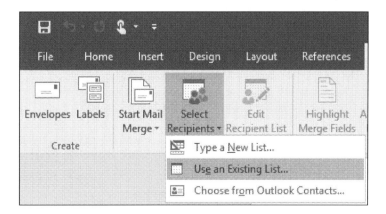

5. Click **Desktop** on the left, select the `Segment3Import` file created in the *Getting ready* section, and click **Open**.

6. Click **OK** to use `Sheet1$`.

7. Find and select `01` with the left mouse button. Do not highlight or delete the single quotes around `01`:

```
ActivateWindow dictionary 'default'  form 'GL_Segment_Maintenance' window
'GL_Segment_Maintenance'
  TypeTo field 'Segment ID' , '01'
```

8. Pick **Insert Merge Field**, then **Segment_3**:

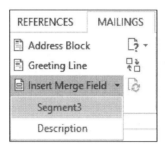

9. This will ultimately replace `01` with the value in **Segment3**.

```
ActivateWindow dictionary 'default'  form 'GL_Segment_Maintenance' window
'GL_Segment_Maintenance'
  TypeTo field 'Segment ID' , '«Segment3»'
```

10. Find and select **Marketing**, but do not highlight or delete the single quotes around `Marketing`:

```
TypeTo field Description , 'Marketing'
MoveTo field 'Save Button'
ClickHit field 'Save Button'
```

11. Pick **Insert Merge Field**, then **Description**. This will ultimately replace `Marketing` with the value in `Description`:

```
TypeTo field Description , '«Description»'
MoveTo field 'Save Button'
ClickHit field 'Save Button'
```

12. Select **Preview Results** to see what the mail merge will send to GP.

13. Pick **Finish & Merge | Edit Individual Documents** then **OK** to have Word merge in all of the values from Excel. A new document opens with the macro code duplicated for each value in the source file.

14. Select the new document and pick **File | Save As | Other Formats**.

15. Select **Desktop** on the left and change the **Save as** type to **Plain Text**. Name the file `Segment3Macro.txt` and click on **Save**. Select **OK** when prompted.

16. Close Microsoft Word.

17. Move to the desktop and right click on `Segment3Macro.txt`. Select **Rename** and change the filename to `Segment3Macro.mac`. Click on **OK** when prompted.

So far, we've created a base macro and populated it with our data. Next, we'll look at running the macro:

1. Back in Dynamics GP, select **Financial** from the Navigation list and pick **Segment** in the **Setup** area.

2. Select **Tools | Macro | Play and pick Desktop** on the left. Click on `Segment3Macro.mac` and click **Open**. The macro will run and populate the description. Click **OK** when the macro finishes:

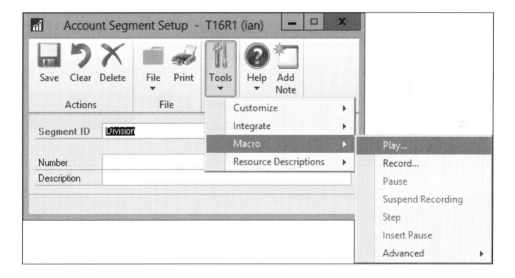

How it works...

Populating Dynamics GP via macros has a long history of use in the product. This process mimics a user's data entry so all of GP's security controls still apply. Additionally, the Dynamics GP business logic is applied as the data is integrated. Macros for import are primarily used when other options are either unavailable or prohibitively expensive in terms of either time or actual costs. Additionally, since the macro simply mimics a user's input, some firms use this process as an accepted way to avoid the paperwork that can be required for updates via SQL.

Though setting up the macro can be a little tedious, imagine how long it would take to correctly enter 200, 2,000, or 20,000 records like this by hand.

There's more...

There are some very important limitations that come with using Microsoft Word and Macros to populate Dynamics GP.

Limitations

Because Macros mimic screen input, screen savers can interfere with macro entry. I've seen employees sit and jiggle the mouse every 5 minutes for hours to prevent a group policy controlled screen saver from blanking their screen. This limitation also applies to Terminal Server and Citrix sessions. Leaving a session, even to just check e-mails, terminates the macro.

If a macro is being run overnight, the User Date Change message will also interrupt the macro and prevent it running. Adding the following to the [General] section of the Dex.ini file will suppress this message:

```
SuppressChangeDateDialog=TRUE
```

Additionally, there is no error control in Macros. If a macro fails because of data or other issues, users have to delete the macro code up to just before the failure, fix the issue, and continue running the macro from the point it failed. One key point to remember is the macro simply fails; it does not roll back any entered data.

Finally, macros only work with consistent processes. If, for example, GP opens a dialog box for one set of circumstances but not for another, a macro won't work because it can't process alternative paths.

Getting fine-grained control of Excel Exports from SmartList

In the previous recipe, we looked at how to export SmartLists to Excel with the push of a button. That method creates a new Excel file each time. In many cases, users need to export the same set of data on a regular basis and build it into a formatted report via Excel. There's a way to accomplish this with SmartList exports. The feature is called Export Solutions and it's the focus of this recipe.

Getting ready

For our recipe, we'll assume that we have an account summary report that we want to format with a title and headers the same way every time. To begin we need to set it up the first time:

1. Select the SmartList icon from the menu bar at the top or select **MicrosoftDynamics GP** menu from the top and click on **SmartList**.

2. Select **Financial | Account Summary** on the left to generate a SmartList.

3. Click the **Excel** button to send the SmartList to Excel.

4. In Excel, select the **File** tab, pick **Options**, pick **Customize Ribbon** and ensure that the **Developer** checkbox is marked in the **Main Tabs** list. Click on **OK**.

5. Click the **Developer** tab and pick **Record Macro**. Accept the default name of `Macro1` and click **OK**.

6. Highlight rows 1-5, right-click, and select **Insert**.

7. Bold the titles in cells `A6` to `F6`.

8. In cell `A1`, enter `Sample Excel Solution`.

9. From the **Developer** tab, pick **Stop Recording**.

10. Highlight and delete all the rows.

11. Save the file in the `C:\SmartLists` with the name `AccountSummary.xlsm`.

How to do it...

To set up an Export Solution, follow these steps:

1. In Dynamics GP, select **Microsoft Dynamics GP** then pick **SmartList**.

2. Select **Financial | Account Summary** in the left pane to generate a SmartList.

3. Click on **Favorites**. Name the favorite `Export Solution` and click **Add | Add Favorite**:

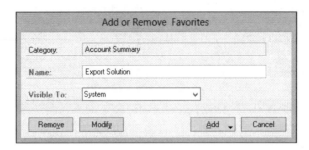

4. Back on the **SmartList** window, pick **SmartList | Export Solutions**. Name the solution `Export Solution`. Set the path to `C:\AccountSummary.xlsm` and the completion macro to `Macro1`:

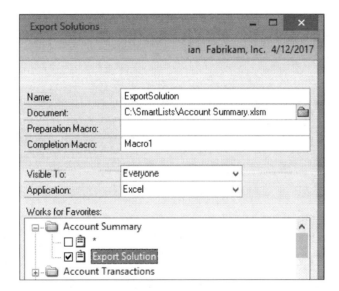

5. Check the box next to the **SmartList Favorite** under **Account Summary** named **Export Solution** and click **Save** then close the window.

6. Back in the **SmartList** window, pick the **Export Solution** favorite under **Account Summary** and click the **Excel** button.

7. Instead of opening Excel, there are now two options. The **Quick Export** option performs a typical Excel export. The **Export Solutions** option will open the Excel file named `AccountSummary.xlsm`, export the data and run the macro named `Macro1`:

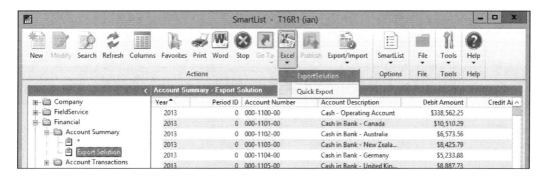

8. Click the **Export Solution** option and watch the file open and the macro execute.

How it works...

The Export Solution feature adds a tremendous amount of power and control to the basic Excel export functionality. The ability to run an Excel macro before and after the export opens up a host of possibilities for reporting. Additionally, once an Export Solution is set up, it's very easy for an average user to run it with just a couple of clicks.

See also

▸ *Building analysis by exporting SmartLists to Microsoft Excel*

Gaining flexibility by printing documents with Microsoft Word

A feature introduced in Dynamics GP 2010 was the ability to print sales and purchasing documents using Microsoft Word templates instead of Report Writer reports; Dynamics GP 2013 adds a number of additional Microsoft Word templates. The use of Microsoft Word to create documents provides greater flexibility in field placement, logo use, and formatting. Users can now print phenomenal-looking documents such as orders, invoices, and purchase orders with Word as the backbone.

For this recipe, we'll look at how to print an invoice using Microsoft Word and the sample company. Then we'll look at some of the setup options for Word templates.

How to do it...

To print an invoice using a Word template in the GP 2013 sample company, follow these steps:

1. Select **Sales** from the Navigation pane on the left.

2. On the **Sales Area** page, click **Sales Transaction Entry** under **Transactions**.

3. Change **Type ID** to **Invoice**.

4. Use the lookup button (magnifying glass) to select invoice **INVS3014** from the sample company:

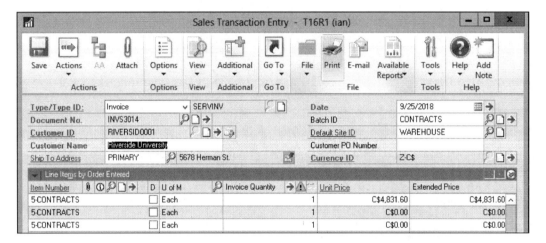

5. Click the **Printer** button on the Action pane.

6. Check the **Invoices** box on the left and click the **Print** button:

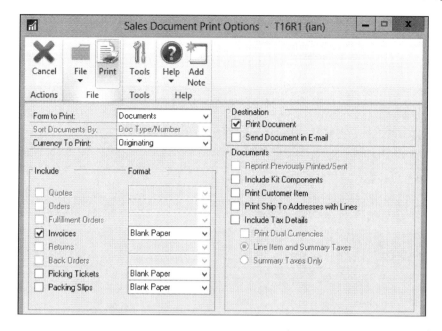

7. Ensure that the **Report Type** in the center is set to **Template** and then check the box next to **Screen**. Click **OK**.

8. Microsoft Word will open and display the invoice for printing.

How it works...

By using Microsoft Word templates, Dynamics GP opens up a world of formatting possibilities for documents. Currently, Word templates can be used for statements, invoices, orders, quotes, packing slips, check remittance, and purchase orders.

There's more...

Dynamics GP 2010 and later versions provide control over what documents use Word templates versus Report Writer documents, and users can create their own templates.

Existing Report Writer documents can be converted to Word templates by using the Word Template Generator. The Word Report Generator should be installed by default.

Which report to use?

Companies upgrading to Dynamics GP 2010 or later may choose to slowly migrate to Word template documents, meaning that they still need the old-style Report Writer documents for a while.

From the main menu, selecting **Reports | Template Configuration** opens the **Template Configuration Manager** window. This window provides control over enabling templates, allowing documents to use Word templates and allowing standard documents when a Word template has been activated. It also holds the images to be sent to Word documents.

All of this is contained in an easy-to-understand window:

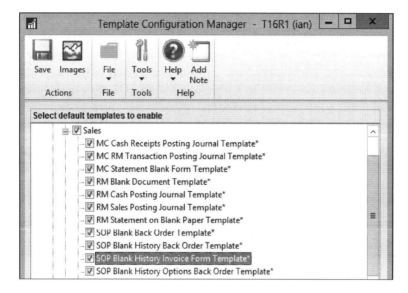

User template creation

Templates can be created by users and specific templates can be assigned to specific companies, vendors, and customers using the **Reports | Template Maintenance** selection from the main menu.

The specifics of creating a new template are beyond the scope of this recipe, but templates can be created from scratch or copied from the default templates included with Dynamics GP 2010 and 2013.

Dynamics GP 2013 includes far more original Word templates than Dynamics GP 2010 did, making the task of creating modified versions far easier.

11
Maintaining Dynamics GP

In this chapter, we will look at some common maintenance items:

- ▸ Speeding up Navigation lists by disabling Business Analyzer
- ▸ Preventing entry to wrong dates by closing periods
- ▸ Improving performance by adjusting AutoComplete settings
- ▸ Cleaning up Accounts Receivable with Paid Transaction Removal
- ▸ Providing correct tax information by updating 1099 information
- ▸ Maintaining updated code by rolling out service packs with Client Updates
- ▸ Improving stability by managing dictionaries
- ▸ Safeguarding data by backing everything up
- ▸ Resolving errors with the Check Links utility
- ▸ Speeding up login by clearing the Menu Master table
- ▸ Validating balances with the Reconcile utility
- ▸ Troubleshooting issues with a DexSQL.log file

Introduction

Basic maintenance is important to keeping Dynamics GP healthy and secure; no complex system runs well without regular maintenance to prevent errors and improve system performance. A significant amount of maintenance isn't normally required for a Dynamics GP implementation, but there are some areas where regular maintenance can provide significant benefits in terms of safety and performance. In this chapter, we will look at recipes designed to help maintain a healthy Dynamics GP system. Most of these recipes will typically be performed by an administrator or power user, since some recipes can have adverse consequences when not properly performed.

Speeding up Navigation lists by disabling Business Analyzer

Reporting Services reports can be of great benefit to users of Dynamics GP by presenting relevant information to them on the home page and also in the Navigation lists. However, loading Business Analyzer in the **Navigation Pane Fact Box** can cause the lists to load slowly, so some customers want to disable **Fact Box**.

Unfortunately, Dynamics GP only allows **Fact Box** to be hidden manually by individual users, and needs to be hidden on each of the Navigation lists separately. Fortunately, Dynamics GP databases are stored in SQL Server and can be updated with a simple **SQL Trigger**, which runs each time a user opens a Navigation list for the first time; this recipe will show you how to add this SQL Trigger.

How to do it...

To hide **Business Analyzer Fact Boxes** in Navigation lists:

1. Open Microsoft SQL Server Management Studio and connect to the SQL Server used for Dynamics GP. Enter a username and password or use Windows authentication to connect.

2. Dynamics GP encrypts the password used with SQL Server so the Dynamics GP username can't be used here. The only exception is the SQL system administrator (sa) user.

3. Click the **New Query** button. Select the **System Database** (usually **DYNAMICS**) from the drop-down box on the top left. Enter the following script in the code area on the right:

```
USE DYNAMICS
GO
CREATE TRIGGER dbo.Update_SY07225_FactBoxVisible ON
   dbo.SY07225 AFTER INSERT
```

```
AS
WITH
   UpdateSY07225 AS (SELECT ListDictID, ListID,
     ViewID, USERID FROM inserted)
UPDATE
SY
SET
   FactBoxVisible = 0
FROM
   SY07225 SY
   INNER JOIN
     UpdateSY07225 USY ON USY.ListDictID = SY.ListDictID
     AND USY.ListID = SY.ListID
     AND USY.ViewID = SY.ViewID
     AND USY.USERID = SY.USERID
GO
```

4. Click **Execute** to run the script. This adds a trigger to the `List View Options` table that sets the `Visible` flag to `false`.

How it works...

Each time a user opens a Navigation list for the first time, an entry is added to the `List View Options` table in the system database. By using a trigger to set `FactBoxVisible` to `false` as the line is inserted, Business Analyzer is not displayed to the user.

If a user wants a particular Navigation list to display the fact box, they can switch it back on through the interface by pressing *Ctrl + F2*.

There's more...

The trigger shown in this recipe only prevents Business Analyzer from being displayed on Navigation lists that a user opens for the first time after the trigger has been added. If a site has been using Dynamics GP for a while, then the table will already be populated with entries. To update all existing entries in **List View Options** to disable **Fact Box**, run the following script in SQL Server Management Studio:

```
Use DYNAMICS
GO
UPDATE SY07225 SET FactBoxVisible = 0
GO
```

If you're using the Dynamics GP 2013 Named System Database functionality, make sure you change the `DYNAMICS` reference in the previously discussed script to your named system database.

See also

▸ The *Personalizing the Home page by selecting the right role* recipe in *Chapter 1, Personalizing Dynamics GP*

▸ The *Further personalizing the Home page by customizing the layout* recipe in *Chapter 1, Personalizing Dynamics GP*

Preventing entry to wrong dates by closing periods

An important step in maintaining any accounting system is controlling access to financial periods. Financial period balances control how financial statements are presented. Once financial statements are complete, they shouldn't change except in very specific, controlled circumstances.

The way to control access to financial periods in Dynamics GP is to close financial periods that are not being used. Dynamics GP provides an easy way to close periods and reopen them for adjustments prior to finalizing financial statements.

In this recipe, we will look at the process to close fiscal periods in Dynamics GP.

How to do it...

To close a fiscal period in Dynamics GP, follow these steps:

1. Select **Administration** from the Navigation pane. Pick **Fiscal Periods** under the **Setup** and **Company** sections on the **Administration** area page.

2. Check the box next to the **Period** and **Module** option to close it. Typically, the **Financial** series, which includes the general ledger, is the last series to be closed:

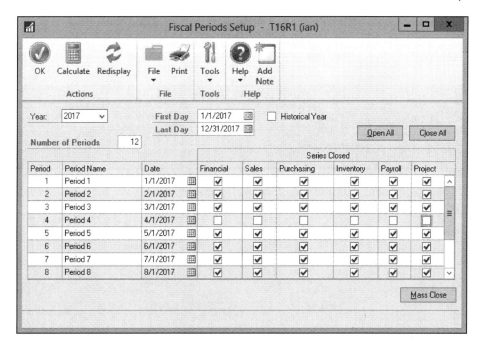

3. Unmarking the checkbox under a series reopens the period for subsequent adjusting entries.

Closing the period is an important monthly maintenance procedure. It is critical to preventing transactions from posting in the wrong period, and it's an important step to ensuring the correctness of the financial statements.

There's more...

By default, the **Fiscal Period** window controls posting transactions to a period for all transactions in a module. Sometimes, though, the module level is too high and companies need the ability to allow certain types of transactions to post while preventing others.

Mass Close

Closing fiscal periods based by series is easy. However, there are times when a company isn't ready to close an entire series, but does need to prevent the posting of certain transaction types. This can be accomplished using the **Mass Close** button on the **Fiscal Periods Setup** window.

For example, if accounts payable needs an extra day to finish cutting checks but the company wants to prevent the entry of new payable vouchers in the period, the **Mass Close** button presents a list of all of the posting transaction types and allows a user to close the period, not for a series, but for one or more transaction types within that series.

To demonstrate closing only a particular transaction type for a period:

1. In the **Fiscal Periods Setup** window click **Mass Close**.

2. Set the **Series** to **Purchasing**.

3. Set the **Period From** and **Period To** to **3**.

4. Scroll to **Payables Trx Entry** and check the box next to it:

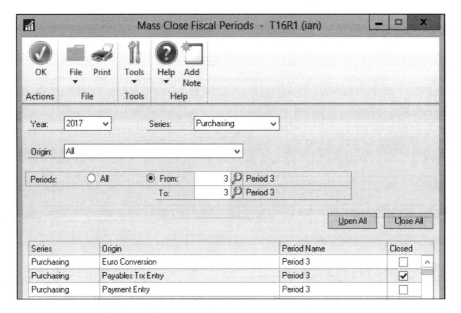

5. Click **Save** to close the period for that transaction type.

6. Notice that the entire series is checked as closed. There is no visual cue that only part of this module has been closed.

Improving performance by adjusting AutoComplete settings

Dynamics GP provides auto complete functionality that remembers previous entries and displays them to users during subsequent data entry. Users can pick the appropriate item without having to type the entire text. This is a great feature, but the entries are stored per user and per field. That means that each time the system saves a vendor number that has been keyed, it's saved as one entry for that user. By default, Dynamics GP is set up to hold 10,000 entries, per user, for each field.

As you can imagine, over a long period of time and in organizations with heavy entry volume, the number of entries can build up, slowing down AutoComplete performance significantly. Additionally, the number of choices presented to users can become unwieldy. For this recipe, we will look at a two-part solution to this problem. First, we will set up a maintenance routine to clean out any entries not used over the last 60 days and then we will reduce the number of results being saved per field to a more manageable 1,000.

How to do it...

To get control over AutoComplete entries, follow these steps:

1. Select **Home** from the Navigation pane. Pick **User Preferences** in the shortcut bar.

2. Click the **AutoComplete** button.

3. Set **Remove Unused Entries After** to 60 days. Click **OK** to finish.

4. Change the **Max. Number of Entries to Store per Field** setting to 1,000:

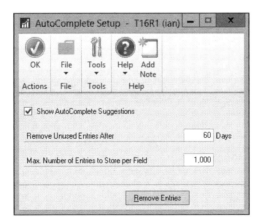

5. The new settings will take effect once the user logs out and back in.

How it works...

Companies can help prevent system slowdown by controlling the volume of entries that Dynamics GP uses for AutoComplete. This setting is a per user setting, so each user needs to make the change for their own login.

There's more...

Administrators can change the AutoComplete setting for all users with an SQL command.

Making the change for all users

Some users obviously make greater use of the AutoComplete feature than others. Consequently, companies may not want to set all users to the same settings. If a firm wants to globally set the number of days to remove unused entries after, and the maximum number of entries to store per field, they can do that by executing this code in SQL Management Studio against the system database (usually DYNAMICS):

```
Update Dynamics..sy01402
Set syUSERDFSTR='TRUE-60-1000'
Where syDefaultType=30
```

The middle line turns AutoComplete on with the True setting, removes unused entries after 60 days and sets the maximum number of entries to store per field to 1000.

See also

▸   The *Cleaning up the mess by fixing AutoComplete errors* recipe in *Chapter 1, Personalizing Dynamics GP*

Cleaning up Accounts Receivable with Paid Transaction Removal

An important maintenance item that is often overlooked is **Accounts Receivable Paid Transaction Removal**. Paid Transaction Removal is the process of either removing paid receivables transactions or moving them to history. Most firms have Dynamics GP set to keep history, so Paid Transaction Removal moves Accounts Receivable transactions to history rather than deleting them. This significantly reduces the number of transactions to be processed by Dynamics GP when running **Accounts Receivable Aging**, and it can provide tremendous speed improvements to the aging process because the aging routine no longer has to work through the pile of completed paid transactions.

Getting ready

To ensure that history is being kept prior to running Paid Transaction Removal, follow these steps:

1. In Dynamics GP, select **Sales** from the Navigation pane. Pick **Receivables** under the **Setup** section of the **Sales** area page.

2. Check **Print Historical Aged Trial Balance** to ensure that transaction history is kept regardless of other customer history options.

3. Click **OK** to save:

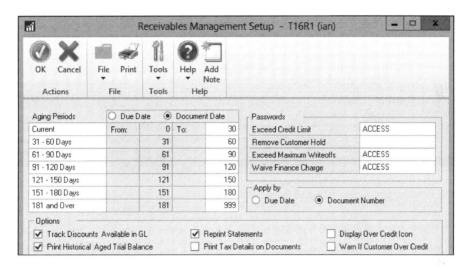

How to do it...

To run Paid Transaction Removal in Dynamics GP, follow these steps:

1. In Dynamics GP, select **Sales** from the Navigation pane. Pick **Paid Transaction Removal** under the **Routines** section on the **Sales** area page.

2. The process can be limited to certain customers and classes, but most firms run the process for all of their customers.

3. In the sample company, change the **Cut Off:** date next to **NSF** to **2/12/2017**:

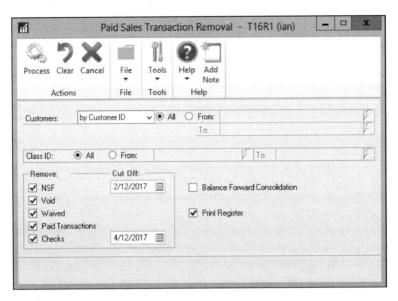

4. This **Cut Off:** date applies to all of the items from NSF down to the next cutoff date. This includes the following:

   ❑ NSF

   ❑ Void

   ❑ Waived

   ❑ Paid Transactions

5. Change the **Cut Off:** date next to **Checks** to **4/12/2017**.

6. Check the **Print Register** box to print the transactions being moved to history.

7. Click **Process**. Choose to print the report to screen and click **Yes** to remove paid transactions.

8. A report will print with the specific transactions moved to history by customer.

How it works...

Regularly running Paid Transaction Removal reduces the workload on Dynamics GP when processing receivables aging. Reports based on open receivables transactions will also run faster. All of these improvements allow receivable employees to spend less time waiting for information and more time collecting open invoices.

There's more...

This process behaves differently for companies tracking receivables using the balance forward method.

Balance forward

For companies using the balance forward balance type, there are only two aging buckets, current and non-current. Most firms do not use the balance forward setting for receivables. For those firms that do use the balance forward method, the **Paid Transaction Removal** window is used to consolidate balances and move current transactions to the non-current bucket.

To consolidate balances for balance forward customers, follow these steps:

1. Check the **Balance Forward Consolidation** box.

2. Uncheck the other boxes and click **Process**:

Providing correct tax information by updating 1099 information

A common problem arises at year end in the United States with vendors that were not properly set up as 1099 vendors. 1099 are required to be sent a 1099 tax form from the company. The types of transactions that can require a 1099 include rent, legal payments, and contract labor among others. The requirement is broad enough that most vendors who are not incorporated (proprietors, partnerships, and so on) may be due a 1099 if they are paid more than $600 in a calendar year.

The specifics of 1099 requirements often mean that vendors are incorrectly set up in Dynamics GP and the amounts required for tax reporting on 1099 forms were not collected for that vendor in Dynamics GP. Dynamics GP 2016 has additional functionality to assist with this: a 1099 utility.

The specifics of figuring out what should be on a vendor's 1099 form are beyond the scope of this recipe. For this recipe, let's look at how to get 1099 information for vendors who weren't initially setup as 1099 vendors.

How to do it...

To correct 1099 amounts for a vendor, follow these steps:

1. Select **Purchasing** from the Navigation pane. Pick **Update 1099 Information** under the **Utilities** section of the **Purchasing** area page.

2. In the **Update** field, choose **Vendor, 1099 Transactions** or **Vendor and 1099 Transactions** and press *Tab*. The following options will tell you about your choices:

    ❑ Choosing **Vendor** will update the selected vendors to 1099 vendors and adjust their 1099 setup based on the selections

    ❑ The **1099 Transactions** option will update transactions for selected vendors, marking them as 1099 transactions and recalculating the vendor's 1099 totals. Vendors should already be marked as 1099 vendors prior to using this option.

    ❑ Selecting **Vendors and 1099 Transactions** will mark the vendors as 1099 vendors and recalculate the vendor's 1099 totals.

3. For our example, select **Vendors and 1099 Transactions**.

4. In the **From** box, set **Tax Type** to **Not a 1099 Vendor**. This will clear the **1099 Box Number** field.

5. In the **To** box, set **Tax Type** to **Miscellaneous** and **1099 Box Number** to **7 Non employee Compensation**. This will change any of the selected vendors from a non-1099 vendor to a 1099 vendor making non-employee (contractor) payments. This is a very common scenario.

6. Enter a range. For our example, select vendor IDs that begin with the letter A. Other range options are available, including the following:

    ❑ **Vendor ID**

    ❑ **Vendor Name**

    ❑ **Vendor Class**

    ❑ **Type**

    ❑ **Voucher Number**

    ❑ **Document Date**

7. Click the **Print** button to preview changes and transactions that will be updated.

8. Click **Process** to update vendors and 1099 transactions:

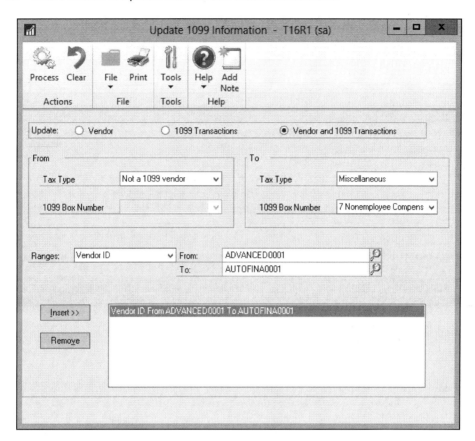

How it works...

Maintaining 1099 vendors and amounts is something that many companies do a poor job with. This maintenance recipe will at least correct things for year-end and provide correct 1099 amounts for tax filing. Ultimately though, better vendor setup is the answer to reducing this maintenance requirement.

There's more...

A better option to correcting 1099 amounts at yearend is to get vendor setup right in the first place.

1099 vendor setup

The preferred alternative to correcting 1099 amounts is to improve vendor setup. Often the problem is that vendor setup is rushed and insufficient information is provided. A vendor's requirement for a 1099 comes to light later, after invoices have already been processed.

The key is to get control of the vendor process by placing all new vendors on hold until the vendor record contains specific information like the vendor's tax ID number, whether or not this is a 1099 vendor, and if so, the type of 1099 expenses to be incurred. Most of the required information can be gathered by obtaining a completed W-9 form from the vendor. Vendors are happy to provide the necessary documentation if they know up front that their invoice won't be paid without it. Communicating and enforcing this policy is a step to better 1099 reporting.

Even with proper vendor setup discipline, it is possible for someone to erroneously remove the 1099 amount from a payables voucher, but the number of vendors that need to be corrected will be dramatically reduced and this maintenance recipe becomes a simple year-end process, not an onerous one.

Maintaining updated code by rolling down service packs with Client Updates

Applying service packs to Dynamics GP is an important part of maintaining the system. Service Packs provide bug fixes, close potential security holes, and improve system performance.

Service packs should be applied to the company's server first. After that comes the burdensome process of installing service packs on each user's computer since users won't be able to log in after the service pack has been applied to the server. A better alternative is to use the Client Updates functionality for service packs in Dynamics GP.

That's right, Dynamics GP provides a mechanism to make the service packs available on the server. When a user without the appropriate service pack logs in, Dynamics GP notifies the user, downloads the service pack from the server, and installs it on the user's machine, all without the intervention of an administrator. Since rolling down service packs is the focus of this recipe, let's look at how to do it.

 Some service packs, known as Feature Packs, even add new functionality. Service packs should normally be tested on a test server prior to applying them to a production environment. Service packs can negatively affect modified forms, modified reports, customizations, and third party products, so it's important to test them first.

Getting ready

Prior to rolling out service packs to users, follow these steps:

1. Download the service pack from *CustomerSource* (`http://www.microsoft.com/dynamics/customersource.mspx`) and save it to a network location accessible to Dynamics GP users.

2. Apply the service pack to the server and test it to ensure that the system operates as expected.

3. For our example, we'll assume that this is Service Pack 1 and that we've downloaded it to a network location such as `\\myserver\GPServicePacks\MicrosoftDynamicsGP-KBXXXXX-v16-ENU.msp`.

How to do it...

To roll out a service pack to Dynamics GP users, follow these steps:

1. Select **Administration** from the Navigation list. Pick **Client Updates** under the **System** section of the **Administration** area page.

2. In **Update Name**, name the update `Service Pack 1` to separate this from other updates.

3. Check the box marked **Update clients at next use**.

4. Enter the **Update Location** as `\\myserver\DynamicsCentral\Service Packs\MicrosoftDynamicsGP-KBXXXXX-v16-ENU.msp` as shown in the following screenshot :

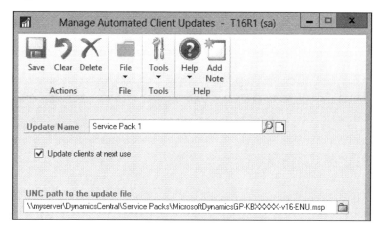

5. Note that this requires the location to be formatted using **Universal Naming Convention** (**UNC**). A typical `c:\mylocation` style path will not work, even though the lookup button allows that.

6. Click **Save** to activate the rollout. Users will get a prompt to start the update the next time they log in.

7. Companies can set up the client update during testing and simply refrain from checking the **Update Clients at Next Use** box. This saves the update until testing is complete. After that it's easy to check the box and start updating clients.

How it works...

Rolling out services packs automatically is a huge time saver in a traditional desktop environment. Administrators need to properly plan and communicate that clients will be updated, since the application of a service pack can be very time consuming. A lot of complaints result when users show up on Monday morning expecting to be productive only to find that they have to wait an hour or more for a service pack to apply.

This feature isn't as important in a Citrix or Terminal server environment. Since only the Citrix or Terminal servers need to be updated in addition to the Dynamics GP server, the Client Update feature doesn't provide big time savings over manual updates.

There's more...

It's also important to avoid the common error of removing a service pack from the server without unchecking the **Update clients at next use** box.

Service pack errors

It's not unusual for someone to delete a service pack installation file from the server without unchecking **Update clients at next use**. When this happens, Dynamics GP displays an error the next time a client computer without the service pack installed tries to log in. In that scenario, either the service needs to be returned to the download location, or the **Update clients at next use** box should be unchecked and the client computer updated manually.

Improving stability by managing dictionaries

Dynamics GP uses dictionary files to hold application code, forms, and reports. Form and report modifications in Dynamics GP don't modify the underlying item; instead, modified forms and reports are modified copies of the original that are stored in the report and forms dictionaries.

They key question facing companies is the placement of the dictionaries, since this can impact the availability of custom forms and reports. Improper placement may mean that users don't get necessary customizations, so dictionary locations need to be set properly with each client installation of Dynamics GP.

We will look at how to set dictionary locations in this recipe.

How to do it...

To change the location of a user's forms and reports dictionary, follow these steps:

1. Select **Administration** from the Navigation pane. Pick **Edit Launch File** under the **Setup** section on the **Administration** area page.

2. Enter the system password if prompted.

3. Click on **Product IDO, Product Name Microsoft Dynamics GP**. This is the main Dynamics GP application. At the bottom of the window are three dictionary locations for **Application, Forms**, and **Reports**:

Dictionary Locations:	
Application	C:\Program Files (x86)\Microsoft Dynamics\GP2\
Forms	C:\Program Files (x86)\Microsoft Dynamics\GP2\
Reports	C:\Program Files (x86)\Microsoft Dynamics\GP2\

4. Changing the location of the application dictionary is not recommended, since this is where the core business logic is stored and moving this file can negatively impact performance.

5. Select the **Forms** field, and scroll to the right to see the full location. This is the location for custom forms. Changing this to a new location will create an empty custom forms file in the new location. If an existing custom forms field is in a different location, either enter the new location or use the file lookup to identify the new location. The same process applies to changing the location of the Reports dictionary.

6. Each installed product outside the core Dynamics GP dictionary has its own application, forms and reports dictionaries.

7. Select the **Fixed Assets** product, and notice that the dictionaries have names specific to the Fixed Asset module ID.

8. Click **OK** to save any changes.

How it works...

Dictionary control is an important piece of maintaining Dynamics GP. As new users are added and more instances are installed, it's important to ensure that the dictionaries are pointed to the right place. Without this, companies end up with an incoherent mess of customized windows and reports.

The two most common placements are locally on each user's machine and centrally on a file share. Local placement was preferred for a long time, since this resulted in significantly fewer incidents of dictionary corruption. Typically, a master copy of the forms and reports dictionaries was maintained and copied to user machines via a network login script.

Over time, the problem of corrupt dictionaries was significantly reduced as improvements in Dynamics GP and network reliability made dictionary corruption extremely rare. This made centrally managing dictionaries much more feasible.

There are pros and cons to each approach. Locally managing dictionaries provides a type of backup. In the event of damage to a dictionary file, the file can be replaced by another user's copy. Conversely, locally managing dictionaries lets users have different customizations from their peers since each user's files can be unique. Finally, locally managing dictionaries permits forms and reports to be customized while Dynamics GP is in use.

Local placement of dictionaries does cause additional IT overhead in creating and managing login scripts to update dictionaries with changes. Also, if users leave Dynamics GP logged in over several days, dictionary updates won't propagate to their machines during that time period. Finally, users could customize forms and reports locally only to have them overwritten the next day when central dictionaries are rolled down via a login script.

Central management of dictionaries provides a consistent experience for users, since everyone gets the same set of customizations in their dictionaries. Backup can be centrally managed as well. Customizations can't be made directly while other users are in the system, but forms and reports customizations can be exported locally, modified, and then applied to a central dictionary.

There's more...

For administrators there is another option for setting dictionary locations outside the interface.

The Dynamics.set file

Installed dictionaries and their locations are held in the `Dynamics.set` file. The preceding recipe shows how to set dictionary locations via the interface. This process changes the `Dynamics.set` file. The same changes could be made in the file with Notepad instead of via the interface. The `Dynamics.set` file could also be copied to a user's computer (assuming that they have the same modules and dictionary locations). This process is faster and easier than changing each user via the interface.

Safeguarding data by backing everything up

Data backup may be the single most important maintenance item related to Dynamics GP. Backing up data is crucial to ensuring the long-term integrity of the system. Dynamics GP provides a basic backup process designed to protect data.

The built in Dynamics GP backup routine is not intended to be a one size fits all backup process. For example, it doesn't provide a mechanism for transaction log backups via the interface. Most companies prefer to use SQL tools to manage their backup process. Ultimately, each company should determine a recovery plan and then work with IT professionals to create an appropriate backup process.

However, the Dynamics GP backup process is an acceptable option, especially in preference to no backup at all. The focus of this recipe is on setting up a backup process using the Dynamics GP backup routine.

With Dynamics GP, there are two built-in options. Backups can be saved to a local drive, location or they can be saved to Microsoft Azure in the cloud.

How to do it...

To setup a Dynamics GP backup routine, follow these steps:

1. Log into Dynamics GP with the sa user.

2. Select **Microsoft Dynamics GP** at the top. Pick **Maintenance | Backup from the Microsoft Dynamics GP** menu. Enter the system password if prompted.

3. Select the company to backup. For our example, select **Fabrikam, Inc.**

4. Choose **Use local storage** and set a backup file location. The backup location needs to exist or be created using the file lookup button to the right of the field:

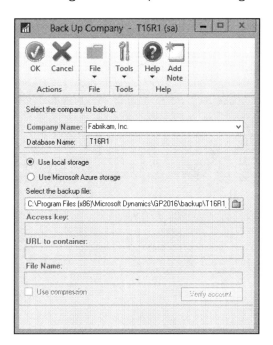

5. Click **OK** to start the backup.

6. Repeat this process for other company databases and the system database.

To use the Azure storage options instead, you must be using SQL Server 2012 Service Pack 1 Cumulative Update 2 or later. Also, a storage account and container need to be created in the Microsoft Azure storage location prior to backing up. To use Azure storage for backups, follow these steps:

1. Log into Dynamics GP with the sa user.

2. Select **Microsoft Dynamics GP** at the top. Pick **Maintenance | Backup from the Microsoft Dynamics GP** menu. Enter the system password if prompted.

3. Select the company to backup. For our example, select **Fabrikam, Inc.**

4. Choose **Use Microsoft Azure Storage** for the next three items:

   ❑ Enter **Storage Account Name** for Azure

   ❑ Enter the Azure storage access key

   ❑ Enter the URL to the Azure storage container

5. Optionally adjust the file name.

6. Optionally check the **Use Compression** button to compress the file.

7. Select **Verify Account** to ensure that the Azure credentials are appropriate.

8. Click **OK** to start the backup.

How it works...

Backing up data is the single most important maintenance function. Companies may need to go beyond the built-in backup routine to intra-day transaction log backups for true point in time recovery. The built-in routine does provide at least a daily backup option for protection.

There's more...

Additional specifics on setting up Azure storage for backup can be found at http://azrcrv. co.uk/3hF0G1

Other files need to be backed up in addition to the databases.

Additional backups

Backing up the company and system databases provides the ability to restore a firm's information; financial statement layouts and generated reports from **Management Reporter** are also stored within a database on an SQL server and should be backed up. But it's also important to back up the infrastructure around that information as well. Dictionary files hold customized forms and reports that can be extremely time consuming to restore. This also applies to integration definitions in the IMD file that stores integrations. Key items to back up include the following:

- Any files with a DIC extension
- Any files with a VBA extension
- Any files with an IMD file from Integration Manager
- Exports of VBA Code, Custom Forms, and Custom Reports as an additional backup. These are created with the **Export** button found using the **Microsoft Dynamics GP** menu, then **Tools | Customization Maintenance**.

Resolving errors with the Check Links utility

Check Links and Reconcile are the two most commonly used utilities in Dynamics GP. Despite their common usage, their roles and outcomes are regularly misunderstood. We will look at Check Links in this recipe and move on to Reconcile for our next dish.

Check Links is a utility designed to review links between related tables for data consistency. For example, if there is a detail record, there should be a header record. The Check Links utility is able to compare header and details records and potentially rebuild damaged or missing data. When transaction data is unrecoverable, running Check Links will remove the damaged records, possibly requiring re-entry.

In many cases, if a header record is damaged, much of it can be repaired from the information in detail records. When possible, running the Check Links utility will rebuild header records. If a record is unrepairable, the Check Links utility can and will delete data, so it is a good idea to run a backup prior to running Check Links.

 Depending on the number of transactions being checked, Check Links can take a long time to run. Since the reports generated by running Check Links are not reprintable, it's a good idea to send them to a file as well as the screen. The reports can be very large, so blindly sending them to a printer is usually not a good idea.

With that background, let's cook up some Check Links.

How to do it...

To run Check Links for Sales Order Processing transactions, follow these steps:

1. Ensure that a current backup of the company database has been created.

2. Select the **Microsoft Dynamics GP** menu and from there pick **Maintenance | Check Links**.

3. In the **Series** field, select **Sales**.

4. Select **Sales Distribution** and click **Insert** to add this item.

5. Repeat this process with **Sales History** and **Sales Work** and click **OK**:

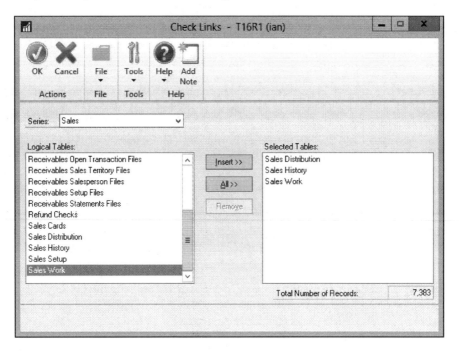

6. Select **Screen and File** in the **Report Destination** window. Enter a location for the file and format it as a text file.

7. Click **OK** to run Check Links.

8. A report will print to the screen with the results, including any additions or deletions made by the utility.

How it works...

The Check Links utility works throughout Dynamics GP to validate data and connections between tables. There is still plenty of debate about whether Check Links should be run regularly to maintain the health of the system, or if it is only needed when an issue has been identified. There are good arguments on both sides. As a practical matter, I've always preferred to run Check Links only when necessary.

Since System and Company setup tables don't have dependent links in the same way that transaction tables do, Check Links typically won't solve issues with those tables. The Reconcile utility checks for data consistency among unlinked but still associated tables. Consequently, Reconcile should be used with System and Company tables in place of Check Links.

See also

▸   *Validating balances with the Reconcile utility*

Speeding up login by clearing the Menu Master table

The **Menu Master** table in Dynamics GP holds details of all the menu options to which users have access. Over time this table can accrue rogue entries that can slow down the login process, or even cause errors to be displayed.

Clearing Menu Master is a fairly simple process and is often scheduled in during an upgrade, or run on an ad hoc basis if it has become corrupt and is producing error messages when a user starts GP or switches companies. This recipe will show how to clear down Menu Master, which causes it to be rebuilt for each user as they next log in.

How to do it...

To clear Menu Master, follow these steps:

1.   Make a backup of Dynamics GP.

2. Select the **Microsoft Dynamics GP** menu, and from there, pick **Maintenance |
   Clear Data**:

3. Click **Display** on the menu and then select **Physical**:

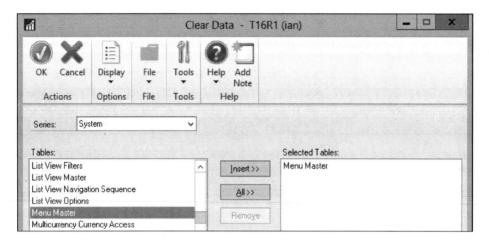

4. Select **Menu Master** and click **Insert** to add this item.

5. Click **OK** to run clear data.

6. A report will be produced showing any errors that occurred.

With Menu Master cleared, the table will be repopulated with valid entries as users next log
into Dynamics GP. This has the benefit of removing both corrupt entries causing problems and
also invalid entries that need to be processed even though they are not used, which improves
the login speed.

Chapter 11

Validating balances with the Reconcile utility

Next to Check Links, the Reconcile utility is the most commonly used utility in Dynamics GP. The job of the Reconcile utility is to replace or remove erroneous data that is related but isn't necessarily linked. For example, to improve reporting speed, Dynamics GP stores the summary totals of each account in a table. Unlike Check Links, these tables aren't related to each other, they simply hold the same information in different formats, one in detail and one in summary.

The summary total of an account should equal the sum of all of the detail transactions for an account. If it doesn't, the Reconcile utility will recalculate the totals from the detail and replace the summary total.

Like Check Links, the Reconcile utility can remove data and should be run after a backup. Additionally, any reports that are available to be printed should be printed to the screen and to a file. There is no option to reprint these reports. In this recipe, we'll look at the most common use for Reconcile, ensuring that financial summary data matches the detail.

How to do it...

To reconcile financial totals, follow these steps:

1. Make a backup of Dynamics GP.

2. Select **Financial** from the Navigation pane. Pick **Reconcile** under **Utilities**.

3. Check **Year**, select **Open** and pick **2017** in the drop-down box:

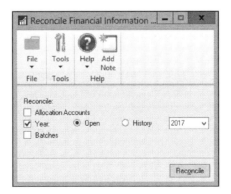

4. Unlike other Reconcile processes, no report prints when reconciling the year. Using the Reconcile utility on other parts of the system will result in a report showing changes.

313

How it works...

The Reconcile utility is designed to help ensure data integrity in Dynamics GP by correcting mismatched data and updating totals for summaries, batches, and headers. It is a powerful utility, and shouldn't be used without a good backup. Like Check Links, there is disagreement in the Dynamics GP community over whether or not Reconcile should be run regularly. As with Check Links, my slight preference is to run it only when there is suspicion of a problem.

See also

▶ *Resolving errors with the Check Links utility*

Troubleshooting issues with a DexSQL.log file

When trying to troubleshoot issues, a common request from Microsoft support and from Partners is to run a `DexSQL.log` file. A `DexSQL.log` is a file that logs commands made from Dynamics GP to the database to help understand performance issues. After creation, this file is sent to the company's partner or to Microsoft for assistance in troubleshooting.

When creating a DexSQL.log file, the key is to capture only the amount of data related to the problem. In this recipe, we will look at creating a `DexSQL.log` file to provide more information to Microsoft support.

For our example, we will assume that the problem relates to creating a financial batch, so that is the process that will get captured in the `DexSQL.log` file.

How to do it...

To create a `DexSQL.log` file, follow these steps:

1. Ensure that Microsoft Dynamics GP is closed.
2. Open the Notepad utility in Windows.
3. Select **File | Open** in Notepad and navigate to the location where the `Dex.ini` file for Dynamics GP is installed. By default, this is `C:\Program Files\Microsoft Dynamics\GP2016\Data\Dex.ini`.
4. Once the `Dex.ini` file is opened in Notepad, find these two lines in the file:

   ```
   SQLLogSQLStmt=FALSE
   SQLLogODBCMessages=FALSE
   ```

5. Change both lines to a value of TRUE and save the file. This turns on logging in Dynamics GP:

    ❑   The first line, SQLLogSSQLStmt=TRUE, logs all SQL statements that are sent to the server by the application.

    ❑   The second line, SQLLogODBCMessages=TRUE, logs all ODBC messages returned to the application by ODBC:

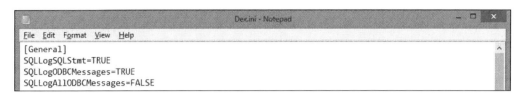

    ❑   Either line or both lines can be set to TRUE. Typically, Microsoft support asks that both lines be set to TRUE.

6. Start Dynamics GP and log in. This creates a file named DexSQL.log in the same location as the Dex.ini file:

    ❑   Results will be logged to the DexSQL.log file regardless of which lines are set to TRUE.

    ❑   Any ODBC messages are prefixed by [Microsoft].

7. Select **Financial** from the Navigation pane on the left. Select **Batches** under **Transactions**.

The DexSQL log now holds all the information related to logging in and everything done so far in this GP session. The log now needs to be cleared prior to recording the actual problem scenario:

1. To clear the DexSQL log file, find the DexSQL.log file in the same directory as the Dex.ini file. Using File Manager, select and delete the file. Once activity starts in Dynamics GP, a new file is created.

2. Return to Dynamics GP. In the open **Batch** window, type TEST BATCH in the **Batch ID** field. Set the **Origin** field to **General Entry** and save the batch. Now the DexSQL.log file needs to be renamed to avoid adding unrelated data.

3. Return to the DexSQL.log file in File Manager. Right-click the DexSQL.log file and rename it DexSQL-Batch.log.

4. Once the DexSQL.log file has been renamed, it's important to close Dynamics GP and turn off logging. If this doesn't happen, Dynamics GP can significantly slow down and the DexSQL.log file can grow to consume all of a computer's hard drive space.

5. To turn off logging, close Dynamics GP, and reopen the `Dex.ini` file.

6. Find these lines in the `Dex.ini` file and change `TRUE` to `FALSE`:

   ```
   SQLLogSQLStmt=TRUE
   SQLLogODBCMessages=TRUE
   ```

7. Save the `Dex.ini` file and delete the leftover `DexSQL.log` file that was created when closing Dynamics GP.

8. What is left is the `DexSQL-Batch.log` file that holds specifics from right before and after the problem area. This file can be opened using Notepad to see what information is being sent to Microsoft or the company's Dynamics GP partner.

How it works...

Creating a `DexSQL.log` file is an important maintenance process for companies to understand. Microsoft and Microsoft Partners often ask for this information when troubleshooting errors. Being able to generate a `DexSQL` log to facilitate problem resolution is important for maintaining a healthy Dynamics GP system.

12

Extending Dynamics GP Professional Services Tools Library

This chapter will take a look at some of the tools available in the Professional Services Tools Library, and show how they can be used amend data or improve company setup and maintenance. This chapter will cover the following topics:

- Replicate settings and data to a new company with Company Copy
- Duplicate data between companies using Master Triggers
- Merge records with Combiner
- Change data using Modifier
- Using Customer Name Modifier
- Set a minimum PO/receipt number
- Preventing date errors with Doc Date Verify

Introduction

Over the years, the Microsoft Professional Services Team has produced a variety of tools to meet requirements for modifying data from both customers and partners. These tools were combined into the Professional Services Tools Library and were available at a cost; as of March 2012 they became available to all for free. In this chapter, we'll take a look at how to install and configure PSTL as well as using some of the tools that can improve company setup and data maintenance.

One point to remember is that not all ISV solutions support, or are supported by, the Professional Services Tools Library, so caution may need to be taken if third-party add-ins are being used.

Replicate settings and data to a new company with Company Copy

Creating a new company can be a chore if there are a lot of modules and settings that need to be copied over to the new company, but PSTL provides a tool, Company Copy, that makes this process much easier.

Getting ready...

This tool requires the user to be logged in as a user with SQL Server administrator privileges (typically this will be the `sa` user) and should be the only user logged in.

A good backup of the destination company should be made before running the tool, as the copy is not reversible because it deletes tables from the destination company before creating new ones.

If there is a substantial amount of data (such as a lot of vendor records if Payables is being copied), the copy can take a while to run, so should be done outside of peak hours.

A second company database needs to exist to have the settings copied into.

How to do it...

To use **Company Copy**, follow these steps:

1. In PSTL, select **Company Copy** from **Misc. Tools**.
2. Click **Next**:

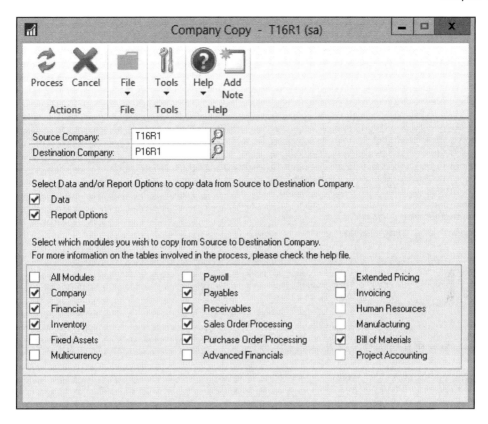

3. Enter or select **Source Company**.

4. Enter or select **Destination Company**.

5. Choose whether to copy across data or report options by marking the relevant checkbox:

   ❑ If **Data** is marked, then **Financial** will auto-mark.

   ❑ If **Report Options** is marked, then **Company** will auto-mark.

6. Mark the checkbox next to the module for which data should be copied to **Destination Company**. Some modules have prerequisites that will auto-mark (such as **Inventory** when **Extended Pricing** is marked).

7. Click **Process** to perform the copy.

When copying data, the **Destination Company** tables will be replaced, so this function should only be used for newly-created companies.

How it works...

Company Copy deletes tables from the **Destination Company** table and replaces them with exact copies of the **Setup and Master** tables in **Source Company**. For example, if **Payables** is copied, the following tables will be copied:

PM00100	PM Class Master File	PM00101	Vendor class accounts
PM00200	PM Vendor Master File	PM00203	Vendor accounts
PM00300	PM Address Master	PM40100	PM setup file
PM40102	Payables Document Types	PM40103	Payables distribution type

See also...

> *Duplicate data between companies using Master Companies*

> *Merge records with Combiner*

> *Change data using Modifier*

> *Set a minimum PO/receipt number*

> *Prevent date errors with Doc Date Verify*

Duplicate data between companies using Master Triggers

After a new company has been created and settings replicated to it using Company Copy, it can have Master records created and updated automatically from another company using Master Triggers.

These Master Triggers are available for the General Ledger, Payables Management, and Receivables Management. In this recipe, we'll take a look at using Master Triggers to create a new vendor into the Fabrikam (Pacific), Inc. database automatically when we create the vendor in Fabrikam, Inc.

How to do it...

To enable Master Triggers for Payables Management, follow these steps:

1. Log into the Dynamics GP company, which will be the Master database from which the information will be entered and replicated.

2. Click on the **Professional Services Tools Library** shortcut.

3. Select **PM Master Triggers** from **Purchasing Tools**.

4. Click **Next**.

5. Select the destination database ID in **Replicate To DB** (in this example, **P16R1**):

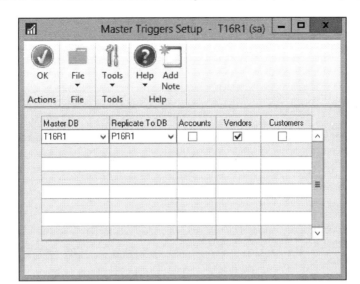

6. March the **Vendors** checkbox.

7. Click **OK**.

Now that **Vendors Master Trigger** has been enabled, any vendor record created or updated in Master DB company will be copied across to the Replicate To DB company.

How it works...

To use Master Trigger to replicate a new vendor, follow these steps:

1. Select **Purchasing** from the Navigation pane. Pick **Vendor** under the **Cards** section on the **Purchasing** area page.

2. Enter the new vendor information.

3. Click **Save**.

4. Click the **Microsoft Dynamics GP** menu, then navigate to **User | Company**.

5. Select the company configured in the Master Triggers.

6. Click **OK**.

7. Select **Purchasing** from the Navigation pane. Pick Vendor under the **Cards** section on the **Purchasing** area page.

8. Enter **Vendor ID** created in step 2, and the new vendor created in the Master company will be displayed:

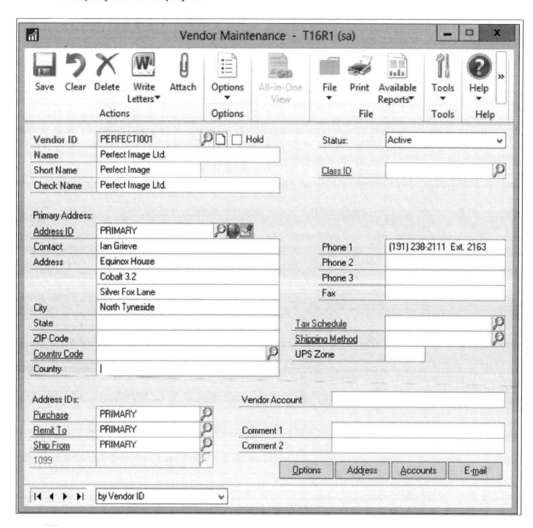

There's more...

Master Triggers are also available for General Ledger for replicating the Chart of Accounts and Receivables Management, where they will replicate customers.

Merge records with Combiner

PSTL includes several Combiner functions that can merge records together; for example, if a duplicate site record has been created in error, or if two sites are merged into one, Inventory Site Combiner can be used to combine these records into one without losing any history.

How to do it...

To combine 01-NW Northwest Regional into 01-N North Regional using Customer Combiner, follow these steps:

1. Open PSTL and select **Inventory Site Combiner** from **Inventory Tools**.

2. Click **Next**:

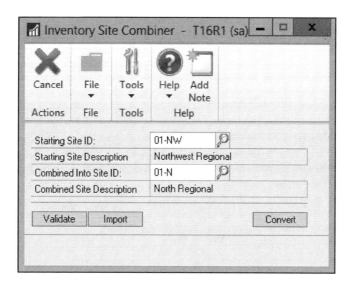

3. In the **Starting Site ID** field, enter 01-NW.

4. In the **Combined IntoSite ID** field, enter 01-N.

5. Click **Convert**.

Inventory Site Combiner removes Site IDs and recalculates the summary records to include both sites' records so Northwest Regional will be merged into North Regional with no loss of information, leaving the combined transaction information in the system under the North Regional site ID.

There's more...

As well as being able to combine customer numbers individually, this can also be done en masse by importing from a spreadsheet. To do this, follow these steps:

1. Set up a spreadsheet with two columns, the first containing **Starting Site ID** and the second containing **Combined IntoSite ID**.

2. Save the spreadsheet as a tab delimited text file.

3. Open PSTL and select **Inventory Site Combiner** from **Inventory Tools**.

4. Click **Next**.

5. Click **Validate**, and then browse to and select the Tab delimited text file.

6. When prompted, select a destination for the **TA Invalid Sites** report.

7. If there are errors, address them in the file and revalidate, or click **Import**, browse to the file, and click **OK** to process the import.

Each row of the spreadsheet will be processed and the customers combined; any errors will be reported at the end.

Other Combiner functions

Combiner functions also exist for General Ledger Accounts and Inventory Items, providing both the ability to combine records individually or en masse using imports from spreadsheets.

See also...

▶ *Replicate settings and data to a new company with Company Copy*

▶ *Duplicate data between companies using Master Companies*

▶ *Change data using Modifier*

▶ *Using Customer Name Modifier*

▶ *Set a minimum PO/receipt number*

▶ *Prevent date errors with Doc Date Verify*

Change data using Modifier

Modifer functions exist in PSTL to allow record IDs to be amended. One such use might be if a non-standard ItemNumber was created or if ItemNumber Combiner has been used to combine two item records that now have a new name and the item number reflects the description. For example, if Attr. 5352-Red was combined with Attr. 5352-Wht, the merged Item Number may change its description to Attr. 5352-Wht/Red and for ease of use the Item Number in Dynamics GP may need to be changed.

How to do it...

To change and item number from an existing ID to a new one, follow these steps:

1. Make a backup of the SQL Server database.

2. Open PSTL and select **Item Number Modifier** from **Inventory Tools**.

3. Click **Next**:

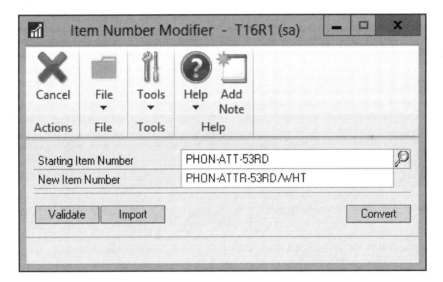

4. In the **Starting Item Number**, enter PHON-ATT-53RD.

5. In the **NewItem Number**, enter PHON-ATTR-53RD/WHT.

6. Click **Convert**.

7. Click **Continue** on the warning prompt regarding having a backup of the SQL Server database.

There's more...

As with the Combiner function discussed in an earlier recipe, there is more than the single record merge available.

Import from spreadsheet

As with the Item Number Combiner, the Item Number Modifier is capable of using a Tab delimited file to modify Item Numbers in bulk.

Other Modifier functions

Combiner functions also exist for General Ledger Accounts, Checkbooks and Fiscal periods, Sales Salepersons and Territories, Inventory Sites and Items Descriptions, and Fixed Assets, providing both the ability to combine records individually or en masse using imports from a spreadsheet.

Using Customer Name Modifier

Dynamics GP stores the Customer Name on transactions when they're created, and amending the name through the Cards window does not update the transactions.

How to do it...

However, the Customer Name stored on transactions can be modified using the **Customer Name Modifier** tool. To update the customer name field at the transaction level, follow these steps:

1. Open PSTL and select **Customer Name Modifier** from **Sales Tools**.

2. Click **Next**:

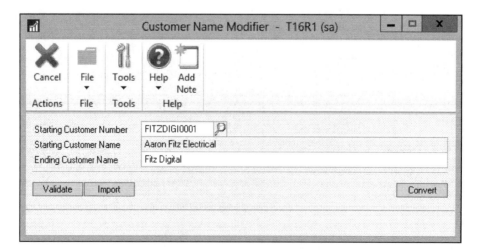

3. In the **Starting Customer Number** field, enter `FITZDIGI0001`.

4. In the **Ending Customer Name** field, enter `Fitz Digital`.

5. Click **Convert**.

If there are a number of customers to be renamed, this can be done using the **Validate/Import** functions.

Import from spreadsheet

Customer Name Modifier is capable of using a Tab delimited file to modify Customer Numbers in bulk.

Other Name Modifiers

Vendor Name Modifier provides the ability to rename Vendor records individually or en masse using imports from a spreadsheet.

Set a minimum PO/receipt number

It is not unknown for Dynamics GP to set a next PO or receipt number to an unexpectedly low number when a transaction has been deleted from the system. PSTL provides a tool which can be used to prevent this happening by using the Minimum PO/Receipt # tool.

Getting ready

This tool differs from the ones already covered in this chapter in that it requires PSTL to be installed on each machine in which the PO/receipt number is to be checked. Activating the tool only needs to be done on one machine.

To switch on **Minimum PO/Receipt #**, follow these steps:

1. Open PSTL and mark the **Minimum PO/Receipt #** checkbox from **Purchasing Tools**:

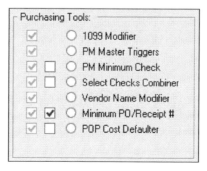

2. Close PSTL.

How to do it...

To set a minimum PO/receipt number or prevent defaulting to a previous number, follow these steps:

1. Select **Purchasing** from the Navigation pane. Pick **Purchase Order Processing** under the **Setup** section on the **Financial** area page.

2. Click the **Additional** menu and then click **Minimum PO Numbers**:

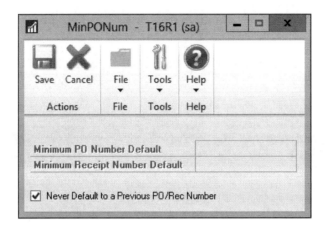

3. Enter the **Minimum PO Number Default** and **Minimum Receipt Number Default** options if you want to set minimum numbers that could be used as defaults.

4. If, instead, you'd prefer that no number previous to the next number should be defaulted in, mark the **Never Default to a Previous PO/REC Number** checkbox.

How it works...

The Minimum PO/Receipt # tool will prevent the **Purchase Order** or **Receivings Transaction Entry** window from defaulting back to a previous number. If a minimum number has been defined, then the length of the minimum number needs to be the same as the PO number defined in **Purchase Order Processing Setup**, or it will be ignored.

See also...

▸ *Replicate settings and data to a new company with Company Copy*

▸ *Duplicate data between companies using Master Companies*

▸ *Merge records with Combiner*

▸ *Change data using Modifier*

▸ *Preventing date errors with Doc Date Verify*

Preventing date errors with Doc Date Verify

Microsoft previously provided a small add-on for Dynamics GP called **Doc Date Verify**, but this has now been added to PSTL. Doc Date Verify prevents users from entering dates in subledgers for fiscal periods that have not been set up, or where the Fiscal Period is closed.

Without Doc Date Verify, it is possible to accidentally date a payables transaction with the year 2103 instead of 2013. Since payables document dates are often different from general ledger posting dates, the transaction could post just fine but would never be selected for payment because of the odd year. It's also hard to fix, because other parts of Dynamics GP do validate against the fiscal period and prevent users from voiding some of these incorrectly-dated transactions. Doc Date Verify rectifies this by preventing the entry of dates that don't exist in fiscal periods that have been set up.

Doc Date Verify works in core financial and distribution modules to validate date entry. In this recipe, let's look at how it works.

Getting ready

Doc Date Verify differs from most other PSTL tools in that PSTL needs to be configured on each client PC on which the **Doc Date Verify** tool exists to check dates. To enable **Doc Date Verify**, follow these steps:

1. Open PSTL and mark the checkbox next to **Doc Date Verify** from **Misc. Tools**:

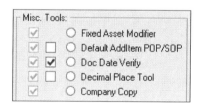

2. Close PSTL.

With the **Doc Date Verify** checkbox marked, no transactions can be entered for either a closed period or one that has not been set up.

How to do it...

To see how Doc Date Verify protects dates in Dynamics GP, follow these steps:

1. After Doc Date Verify has been installed, select **Purchasing** from the Navigation pane. Pick **Transaction Entry** under the **Transactions** section on the **Purchasing** area page.

2. In the **Doc. Date** field enter 4/12/2103.

3. Dynamics GP responds with a message that **A fiscal period for this date has not been set up**. Users must change the date to continue with the transaction.

How it works...

Doc Date Verify provides some peace of mind for core financial and distribution transactions. Other modules, such as the Contract portion of Field Service, actually need to put dates out beyond the existing fiscal periods because of the nature of the transaction. For financial and distribution modules, Doc Date Verify does not work with Quotes and Orders since it is reasonable that those transaction types could affect fiscal periods not yet set up.

See also...

- ▸ *Replicate settings and data to a new company with Company Copy*
- ▸ *Duplicate data between companies using Master Triggers*
- ▸ *Merge records with Combiner*
- ▸ *Change data using Modifier*
- ▸ *Set a minimum PO/receipt number*

13
Modern Business Intelligence for Dynamics GP

In this chapter we will look at some new, modern business intelligence features in Dynamics GP through the following recipes:

- ▸ Activating OData for better external analysis
- ▸ Securing OData to control access
- ▸ Connecting OData to Excel for Business Intelligence
- ▸ Connecting GP to Power BI with O Data
- ▸ Adding Power BI to the home page in Dynamics GP

Introduction

Dynamics GP already has a lot of business intelligence options, some of which have been covered in this book. Excel, SQL Server Reporting Services, and Business Analyzer can all deliver dashboards and key performance indicators, but all of these options have limitations. None of them are particularly good at mobile delivery, selection of data can be complicated, and security, particularly for external access, can be difficult. Dynamics GP 2016 adds some modern business intelligence elements to provide more options for users. These include OData connections, which provide simpler discovery of data elements and easier security maintenance, and connections to Power BI, Microsoft's new, flagship, business intelligence offering.

Activating OData for better external analysis

OData stands for **Open Data Protocol**. It is an open protocol that allows the creation and consumption of data. In particular, OData allows web clients to publish and edit resources, identified using URLs and defined in a data model. With respect to Dynamics GP, it facilitates easy, secure access to GP data for any number of needs, including reporting and analytics.

There are some pretty significant installation and setup requirements for OData before it's ready to use, but the end result is worth it, so we'll cover that here.

Getting ready

OData is installed separately from the GP installation media. Ian has already done a terrific job of explaining how to install OData for Dynamics GP at `http://azrcrv.co.uk/EL80CN`.

Also, there was an early update to fix issues with OData connections. Make sure to visit CustomerSource to obtain the latest updates. The initial update can be found at `http://azrcrv.co.uk/IyRK5V`.

When you install the OData service, the user account you specify to run the service may not automatically be granted permissions to the GP SQL data. You will want to go in and grant that user access to `DYNGRP` on the GP databases. It is also recommended to make the user a member of the `rpt_all` user role in the system (typically called `DYNAMICS`) database specifically.

How to do it...

To setup OData, follow these steps:

1. Select **Administration | Setup | System | OData | Configure OData Service**.
2. Enter the URL used to access the OData service. The place to find this is in the `Microsoft.Dynamics.OData.Host.EXE.config` file. All files related to the installation are located in `%Program Files\Microsoft Dynamics\OData Service`. The OData host config file is located there. This file holds all of the setup information specified during the installation. You can use this file to determine what the OData Service URL is by finding the following key:

```
<add key="ODataServiceHostAndPort"
  value=https://Servername:port/GPOData/>
```

3. The URL follows `Value =` in the key and does not include anything after the port. In my example, the URL is `https://MDPCPA.cloudapp.net:443/`:

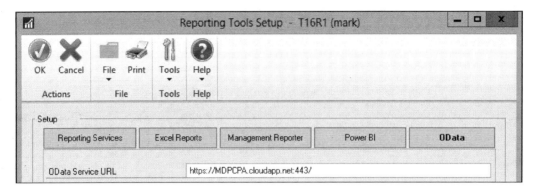

4. Select **Administration | Setup | System | OData | Data Sources**.

5. The **Data Sources** window is used to specify what data is available to connect to. In the **Data Sources** window select a **Product**. Typically, this is Microsoft Dynamics GP, but it could be another product, such as Fixed Assets or Project Accounting. For now, select **Microsoft Dynamics GP**.

6. Select the **Company**. For this example, use TWO, the sample company (our system has the sample database named T16R1).

7. Select **Object Type**; the choices are **Views**, **Stored Procedures**, **Tables**, and **All**. For beginner users, views are going to be the friendliest choice so for now, pick **Views**.

8. Check the box next to **Individual Views**. For our purposes check the boxes next to the following items:

    ❑ **AccountSummary**

    ❑ **AccountTransactions**

    ❑ **Accounts**

    ❑ **Bank Transactions**

9. As of the initial release of GP 2016, its not recommended to hit **Mark All** or to make every view, table, and stored procedure available. Since this is an initial release of the OData functionality, there can be timeouts with large amounts of data.

10. Click **OK** to complete the selection:

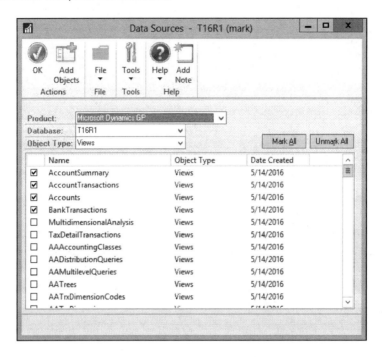

11. Select **Administration | Setup | System | OData | Publish OData**.

12. Review the data to be published, adjusting the **Data Source**, **Company**, and **Object Type** as necessary. Ensure that items to publish are checked. The service name and URL can be manually changed if required.

13. Click **OK** to publish the data:

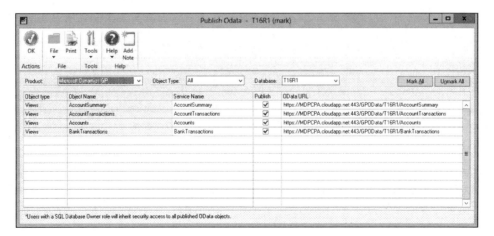

How it works...

When an OData request is initiated to one of the websites, the user logs in with their active directory login and, once authorized, data is returned to the application making the request. This provides a secure, easy-to-use way to access Dynamics GP data for analysis via other tools.

There's more...

There are a couple of other important things to note:

▸ The OData service only works in single tenant environments in this release

▸ The installation only supports a 64-bit server

▸ The setup requires the desktop version of GP, not the web client

OData is a brand new feature and it can be a little fragile. Returning large amounts of data can cause timeouts. It's recommended to limit the data that is published and not reflexively publish every available option.

See also

▸ *Secure OData to control access*

▸ *Connecting OData to Excel for Business Intelligence*

▸ *Connecting GP to Power BI with OData*

Secure OData to control access

Since OData provides access to information in GP, it's important to ensure that this access is secure. Dynamics GP uses active directory connected to GP users and SSL to provide secure access to data. OData specific roles and tasks are used to ensure that users can only access data they have authorization for.

Getting ready

For companies that have upgraded to Dynamics GP 2016 from a previous version, the new security roles and tasks are missing. There is a SQL script that needs to be run to add the new roles and tasks. The script is available at `http://azrcrv.co.uk/1bVUnr`

New installations of GP 2016 will include these roles and tasks as part of the installation. Only upgraded versions require running the script.

How to do it...

To set up security for OData, follow these steps:

1. Select **Administration** from the Navigation pane. Pick **User** under the **Setup and System** sections on the **Administration** area page.

2. Look up or enter a user.

3. Click the **Directory Account** tab.

4. Look up or enter the corresponding active directory user to connect an Active Directory user to a GP user.

5. Click **Save** to save the user association:

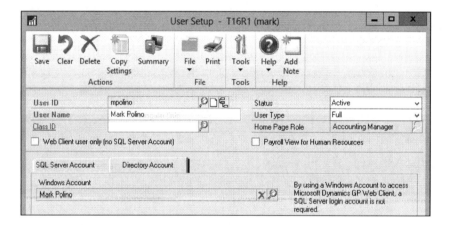

6. Select **Administration** from the Navigation pane. Pick **User Security** under the **Setup and System** sections on the **Administration** area page.

7. Look up the user to give access to in the **User** field.

8. Select a company in the **Company** field.

9. Scroll down and select a role that begins with OD. All of the OData roles start with the letters OD:

There's more...

The OData roles and the tasks included in those roles are documented in the OData Feature Documentation available as part of the `Microsoft Dynamics GP 2016 Detailed Feature Documentation` package. A link to the documentation is available at `http://azrcrv.co.uk/ehP9M5`.

Users with the SQL Database Owner role will inherit security access to all published OData objects, even if they aren't given explicit security.

SQL objects

The **Security Task Setup** window will have a new type added by the script in the *Getting ready* section of this recipe for SQL objects. This allows a user to build additional security tasks that allow access to views and/or stored procedures:

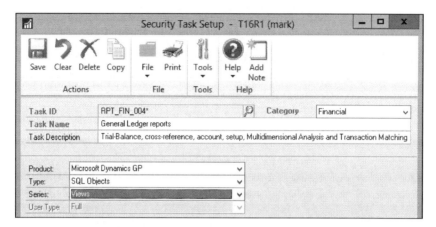

Connecting OData to Excel for Business Intelligence

Any number of applications can consume OData, but because of its ubiquitous presence, Excel is a common option. In this recipe, we will look at how to bring OData into Microsoft Excel for additional analysis.

Getting ready

Before we begin, ensure that OData has been set up and security has been set for the user that will log in. You can review the other OData recipes to validate the setup.

How to do it...

To bring OData information into Excel, follow these steps:

1. Open a new workbook in Microsoft Excel.

2. Select **Data | From Other Sources | From OData Feed**.

   Enter or copy and paste an OData URL and click **OK**. The simplest place to find one is in Dynamics GP in **Administration | Setup | System | OData | Publish OData**. In our example, I'm using `https://MDPCPA.cloudapp.net:443/GPOData/T16R1/Accounts` to return the chart of accounts.

3. If you are using the credentials you are already logged in with, select **Use my Current Credentials**. If you need to enter your credentials, for example, you are accessing the data from your home computer, select **Use Alternate Credentials** and enter your login information:

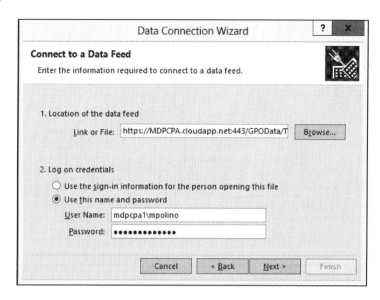

4. Click **Next**.

5. Check the box next to **Accounts** and click **Finish**.

6. Excel may open a box asking where to place the data. Select **Table** and click **OK**. Optionally select **Pivot Table** or **Pivot Chart** to analyze the data that way.

7. Data will be returned to Excel:

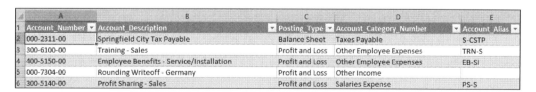

How it works...

Excel uses the OData connection to identify the data location and make the connection. Windows authentication is used to connect and verify with Dynamics GP that the user is permitted to access the data. Once the connection is successful, the full range of Excel functionality is available.

Connecting GP to Power BI with OData

Microsoft is making significant investments in its Power BI analytics suite. The free tier of Power BI can be used to connect and analyze information from Dynamics GP via OData. The full range of Power BI functionality is well beyond the scope of this book, but in this recipe we'll see how to make a connection.

Getting ready

Prior to connecting GP to Power BI, a Power BI account needs to be set up. Power BI offers a free tier that can be used for this connection. A Microsoft account is required, but it doesn't have to be a business or an Office 365 account. A personal account also works.

Currently, the option to connect via OData is only available to set up using Power BI Desktop, not Power BI on the web. Power BI Desktop can be downloaded and installed from `PowerBI.Microsoft.com`. Once visualizations have been built using Power BI Desktop, they can be uploaded to Power BI on the Web. Data can be viewed and updated using Power BI on the Web, but currently, the OData connections can't be built there.

How to do it...

To connect GP to Power BI via OData, follow these steps:

1. Launch Power BI Desktop.

2. Select **Get Data | OData Feed**.

3. Enter or paste in the URL for the specific OData feed. This is available in Dynamics GP in **Administration | Setup | System | OData | Publish OData**. In our example I'm using `https://MDPCPA.cloudapp.net:443/GPOData/T16R1/Accounts`.

4. If you are already logged in with the appropriate credentials, select **Use my Current Credentials**. If you need to enter your credentials, for example, you are accessing the data from your home computer, select **Use Alternate Credentials** and enter your login information:

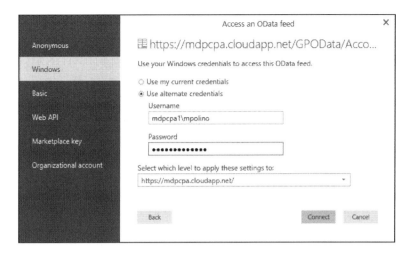

5. Click **Connect**.

6. Click **Load**:

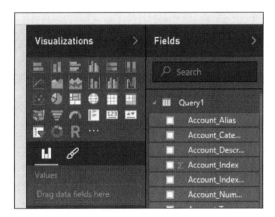

7. The fields are now available in Power BI to build visualizations.

How it works...

Power BI uses the OData connection to connect to securely connect to GP and provide data for analysis. Power BI is more efficient with fewer columns. Limiting the number of columns makes processing larger amounts of data more efficient.

There's more...

Microsoft has promised content packs for Dynamics GP to make connections to GP data even simpler, but as of now, these are still in development.

Adding Power BI to the home page in Dynamics GP

Dynamics GP 2016 provides additional connections to Power BI allowing Power BI visualizations to be presented inside of Dynamics GP. These visualizations can contain Dynamics GP data, but they don't have to. Any Power BI data can be presented in GP. In this recipe, we'll look at making the connection to Power BI and presenting it in GP.

Getting ready

Prior to connecting GP to Power BI there are some prerequisites:

- The user setting this up should have access to Power BI and at least one report must have been created and available

- The user should be able to log in to the Power BI site and view a report

- Currently this only works for the GP Desktop Client

There is also some initial setup. To set up the connection between Power BI and Excel, follow these steps:

1. Select **Administration | Tools | Setup | System | Reporting Tools Setup | Power BI**.

2. In Power BI site URL, enter the URL from your dashboard. It typically looks like this: `https://app.powerbi.com/groups/me/dashboards`. Once connected, this URL provides a list of available dashboards, each with their own visualizations:

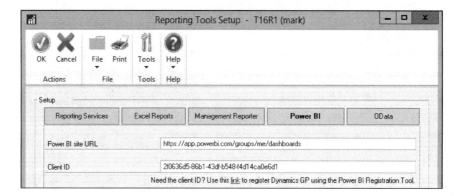

3. Enter the client ID. To get the client ID, follow these steps:

    1. In a web browser, navigate to `https://powerbi.microsoft.com/en-us/documentation/powerbi-developer-register-a-client-app/` (`http://azrcrv.co.uk/n8Kgf`).

    2. Click **Sign In with Your Existing Account** and log in with your Power BI credentials:

        ❑ In **App Name** enter `Dynamics GP`

        ❑ In **App Type** enter `Native App`

        ❑ In **Redirect URL** enter `https://login.live.com/oauth20_desktop.srf`

    3. In the Step 2 section, check the boxes by all of the APIs.

    4. Click **Register App**.

    5. Power BI will provide the client ID.

    6. Copy the client ID and paste it into the **Client ID** field.

4. Click **OK** and GP will validate the information.

How to do it...

To add Power BI to the home page, follow these steps:

1. On the GP home page, select **Customize this Page**.

2. Check the box next to **Power BI** and click the expansion button (blue arrow):

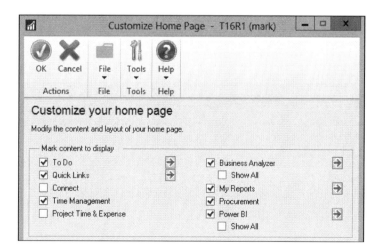

3. Expand the **Dashboard** section.

4. Expand one of the dashboards.

5. Select a visualization and click **Insert** to move it from the left to the right:

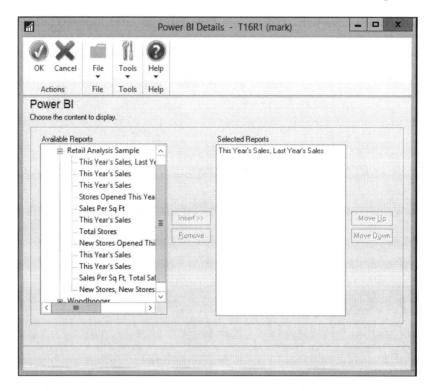

6. Click **OK** twice to add the visualization to the home page. Power BI will refresh automatically:

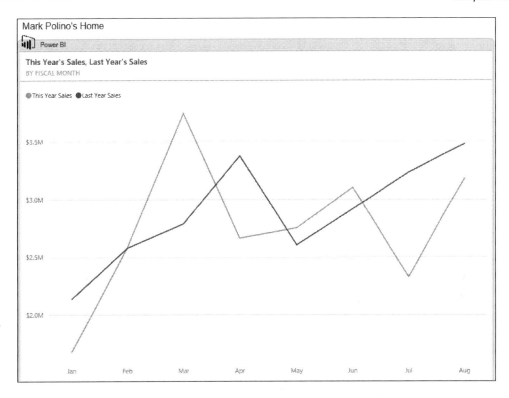

How it works...

Once the initial connection is made, adding Power BI visualizations to the home page in Dynamics GP is easy. These will typically be based on information in Dynamics GP, but they could be Power BI visualizations from another system, making Power BI an important tool for cross-system reporting.

Index

Symbols

1099 information
updating, for providing correct tax
information 300, 301
vendor setup 302

A

account
accessing, with Favorites in lookups 17-19
Account alias
about 26
setting up 26
used, for speeding account entry 26, 27
account rollups
used, for controlling reporting 38-41
Account Segment warnings
reactivating 171-173
account selection errors
preventing, with Segment names 197-199
Accounts Receivable
balance forward balance type, using 299
cleaning, up with Paid Transaction
Removal 296-298
Accounts Receivable Aging 296
**Accounts Receivable Paid Transaction
Removal 296**
ad hoc workflow
about 42
creating 42, 43
working 44
Advanced Lookups
used, for speeding lookups 46-48
All-In-One View
used, for obtaining complete view 109, 110

Allow Account Entry
used, for reducing out of balance
problems 190-192
analyses
building, by exporting SmartList to Microsoft
Excel 258, 259
Asset Details
used, for tracking asset's financial
information 145-148
Auto Complete errors
Auto Complete entries count, reducing 23
Auto Complete, resetting 23
fixing, by cleaning up mess 21, 22
unused entries, removing 22
AutoComplete settings
adjusting, for improving
performance 295, 296
modifying, for all users 296
Azure storage
reference link 308

B

balances
validating, with Reconcile utility 313, 314
batch
setting up, with best practices 187, 188
Batch Date
management, by preventing posting
errors 186-190
posting, considerations 189
beginning and ending date options
used, for controlling reporting 57-59
Budget Import Exception reporting
using 93

purchase requisition
about 123
entering 123-125
purchasing accounts
splitting, for improvement of financial
reporting clarity 44, 45

Q

Quick Links
used, for speeding access to data 9, 10

R

Reconcile to GL functionality
reference link 158
The Closer from Reporting Central option 158
used, for speeding up month-end
processing 155-158
year, balancing 158
Reconcile utility
used, for validating balances 313, 314
records
documents, attaching to 129-131
merging, with Combiner functions 323, 324
merging, with Customer Combiner and
Modifier 104-106
recurring batches
setting up, for clearance after
posting 183, 184
refreshable Excel report
creating, from SmartList object 253-256
remaining statements
printing, for statement delivery
simplification 84-86
reminders
about 57
used, for remembering important
events 55, 56
Remit-To Address
modifying, on posted Payables
Transaction 144, 145
report
controlling, with account rollups 38-41
improvement, by sending SmartList to
Microsoft Word 261, 262

reporting dates
beginning and ending Fiscal year and
calendar year 60
controlling, with beginning and ending
periods 57-59
Fiscal period, versus month 59
reports dictionary
location, changing 305
results, SmartList
Field Comparison checkbox 219
limiting, with Search feature 217-219
Match Case checkbox 219
Search type 219
Wildcard search 220
Reverse Tax functionality
reference link 181
used, for tackling self-assessed
taxes 177-181

S

Sales Order Ship To Address
modifying 106-108
Search feature
used, for limiting results of
SmartList 217-219
security access
copying, from existing user 54, 55
segment names
used, for preventing account selection
errors 197-199
self-assessed taxes
tackling, with Reverse Tax
functionality 177-181
serial numbers
tracking, on drop ship POs 110-112
service packs
errors 304
reference links 303
rolling down, with Client Update for updated
code maintenance 302-304
SmartConnect
reference link 277
SmartList
creating 239-243
creating, from SQL View 245-247
default columns, configuring 244

Made in the USA
Middletown, DE
25 January 2018